**CONTESTED
GROUND**

A VOLUME IN THE SERIES
Culture and Politics in the Cold War and Beyond
EDITED BY
Edwin A. Martini and Scott Ladermen

CONTESTED GROUND

THE TUNNEL AND THE STRUGGLE
OVER TELEVISION NEWS IN
COLD WAR AMERICA

MIKE CONWAY

University of Massachusetts Press
Amherst & Boston

Copyright © 2019 by University of Massachusetts Press
All rights reserved
Printed in the United States of America

ISBN 978-1-62534-451-9 (paper); 450-2 (hardcover)

Designed by Sally Nichols
Set in Adobe Minion Pro

Cover design by Dr. Danielle Kilgo
Cover photos: (foreground) *Luigi Spina crawls through the tunnel as the diggers get close to finishing the project in September 1962*, from *The Tunnel* documentary. NBCUniversal Archives; (background) *Berlin Wall*, courtesy of the author.

Library of Congress Cataloging-in-Publication Data

Names: Conway, Mike, 1961– author.
Title: Contested ground : The tunnel and the struggle over television news in Cold War America / Mike Conway.
Description: Amherst : University of Massachusetts Press, 2019. | Includes bibliographical references and index. | Summary: "In 1962, an innovative documentary on a Berlin Wall tunnel escape brought condemnation from both sides of the Iron Curtain during one of the most volatile periods of the Cold War. *The Tunnel*, produced by NBC's Reuven Frank, clocked in at ninety minutes and prompted a range of strong reactions. While the television industry ultimately awarded the program three Emmys, the U.S. Department of State pressured NBC to cancel the program, and print journalists criticized the network for what they considered to be a blatant disregard of journalistic ethics. It was not just *The Tunnel*'s subject matter that sparked controversy, but the medium itself. The surprisingly fast ascendance of television news as the country's top choice for information threatened the self-defined supremacy of print journalism and the de facto cooperation of government officials and reporters on Cold War issues. In *Contested Ground*, Mike Conway argues that the production and reception of television news and documentaries during this period reveals a major upheaval in American news communications"— Provided by publisher.
Identifiers: LCCN 2019019886 | ISBN 9781625344502 (hardcover) | ISBN 9781625344519 (paperback) | ISBN 9781613766958 (ebook) | ISBN 9781613766941 (ebook)
Subjects: LCSH: Berlin Wall, Berlin, Germany, 1961–1989. | Escapes—Germany—Berlin—History—20th century. | Escapes—Germany (East) —History. | Tunnel (Television program) | Documentary television programs—United States—History—20th century. | Television broadcasting of news—Political aspects—United States. | National Broadcasting Company—History—20th century.
Classification: LCC DD900 .C66 2019 | DDC 070.1/95097309045—dc23
LC record available at https://lccn.loc.gov/2019019886

British Library Cataloguing-in-Publication Data
A catalog record for this book is available from the British Library.

Contents

Preface   vii

Introduction   1

CHAPTER ONE
Captured on Film
A Daring Escape from a Divided Berlin   11

CHAPTER TWO
Parallel Paths
Television, the Cold War, and Reuven Frank   44

CHAPTER THREE
The Transmission of Experience   81

CHAPTER FOUR
Journalist vs. Filmmaker
The Tunnel and the Elusive Definition of Documentary Films   118

CHAPTER FIVE
Adventurous Laymen
Print vs. Broadcast in Journalism Boundary Work   157

CHAPTER SIX
"The Necessary Restraints of National Security"   197

Epilogue   223

Notes   235
Index   263

Gallery follows page 156.

Preface

The Tunnel is a journalism documentary produced by NBC's Reuven Frank that tells the story of an elaborate five-month escape project under the Berlin Wall, broadcast on American network television during one of the most volatile periods of the Cold War.

The above sentence appears to be fairly straightforward. This project is an attempt to show why it is also complicated, contested, and controversial, revealing the competing visions for American journalism and television in the early 1960s, during a critical juncture in American media history. The sentence contains the keys to understanding why an NBC documentary and its producer earned both high praise and intense criticism for months in 1962, with most of the strongest reactions occurring before the program even ran.

The pivotal words to unlock the weight of the project and the volatility of reaction include *journalism, documentary, television, story,* and *Cold War.* The meanings and implications of each of these words had, and still have, strong constituencies that protect their history and acquired knowledge, forcing *The Tunnel* project through their specific prism of acceptability and opinions. The story of the passionate West Berlin students who risked their lives to help their friends trapped in East Berlin is so compelling that it has been retold numerous times through different media during the subsequent half-century. The producer's insistence on the importance of employing techniques from fiction writing to tell a true story ran him afoul of print journalists who found the story approach unsettling. *The Tunnel* as journalism brought NBC in front of the press's court of opinion, dominated by print practitioners, who focused on decisions the network made to secure the project and even questioned the medium's competence to handle sensitive Cold War issues.

Television as a medium not only came under attack by print journalists, but also by elites in American society who shunned the format as it diffused to become the most popular mass communication platform in the United States. The producer's vision on how to combine visuals with sound and words was even beyond the grasp of many who worked in television news, most of whom learned their craft in print or radio.

As a documentary, *The Tunnel* joined more than a half-century history of a specific type of nonfiction film and the generations of documentarians and scholars that have followed. Even though the producer employed many of the same techniques popular in celebrated American documentaries of the early 1960s, the broadcast is rarely acknowledged for reasons both within and beyond his control.

The Cold War hangs over and permeates everything. *The Tunnel* is itself a look at a herculean effort to help East Germans escape oppressive communism to begin a new life in the West. Cold War ideology affected all aspects of this project and reaction, from the telling of the story on television, the reaction of the United States and foreign governments, to journalists who often worked in tandem with the government to control what topics should be covered and what should be kept from the public.

Finally, the producer. Reuven Frank was one of the most influential people in the early development of television news in the United States. He was a mid-twentieth-century visionary with regard to how to utilize the sight and sound medium to convey important issues and events to the largest simultaneous audience in history. *The Tunnel* was one of Frank's most cherished accomplishments in a career filled with significant achievements. The project helped solidify his views on television as a communication source, views that influenced not just documentaries, but nightly newscasts and weekly public affairs programs. The documentary proved to be a major influence on a groundbreaking memo Frank wrote during the following months, positioning a specific form of television news as a key journalistic platform.

Origin

The original impetus for this project began more than fifteen years ago when I conducted oral history interviews with Reuven Frank a few years before he died. It was obvious to me that Frank had a vision for what television news could be at a time when most journalists were still focused on words, either on paper or through the airwaves. I had embraced the idea of video storytelling during my television news career, so his ideas on the effective use of television to convey an experience resonated strongly with me.

My first plan was to focus mostly on Frank's most popular production, the *Huntley-Brinkley Report*. A few years of searching brought me to the sad realization that most of those newscasts no longer exist, especially in the first years after the 1956 launch. Next, I considered more of an overview of Frank's career, with *The Tunnel* as one chapter. As I researched and wrote about *The Tunnel* production and reception, I found myself frustrated that the usual academic research areas were inadequate in explaining Frank's production approach and the wildly diverse reactions. Thankfully, fellow media historian Michael Stamm witnessed one of my tortured conference presentations in which I tried to explain the different boundaries of journalism, television, documentaries, and Cold War ideology at play in *The Tunnel* story. He recognized that all the areas were important and should be investigated in-depth. Concentrating on *The Tunnel* and recognizing the obvious connections with Frank's later television news memo revealed the critical juncture in American journalism history as television becomes popular with the American public.

Acknowledgments

I would like to thank University of Massachusetts Press, including Matt Becker, Clark Dougan, Sally Nichols, Rachael DeShano, Courtney Andree, and copy editor Eric Schramm for their support and guidance on this project, as well as the anonymous reviewers who helped make this a stronger book.

The journalism program at Indiana University has encouraged my media history research for many years. I've had the privilege of working with some amazing research assistants over the years, some of whom are now tenured professors themselves, a testament to their ability as well as the speed of my research. Thank you to Kevin Grieves (who also co-authored the first version of Chapter 6 and translated all of the German documents), Lindita Camaj, Nate Floyd, Rashad Mammadov (who found and translated Soviet news articles), and Cox Scholar Alexandra B. Hitchcock, among others. IU colleagues and other scholars have been generous with their encouragement and support, including David Nord, Radhika Parameswaran, Gerry

Lanosga, Bonnie Brownlee, Mark Deuze, Nick Cullather, Lou Malcolm, Ira Chinoy, Tom Mascaro, Maddie Liseblad, and Don Heider.

I would gladly serve as Indiana chapter president of the Bambi Tascarella fan club, because she is such a helpful, wonderful person, and she knows everything about NBC. One of her NBC partners, the late Marilyn Schultz, was also a mentor at the University of Texas at Austin, and they both made sure I was present at the *Huntley-Brinkley* fiftieth anniversary event in 2006, an experience that focused my attention on Reuven Frank's work.

Those of us who study twentieth-century broadcast history are painfully aware that "everything" isn't on the internet. We would not be successful without the amazing work of librarians and archivists around the world, who not only collect and preserve important primary sources, but also help us make use of the material, even when it adds to their already overloaded schedule. Sources and encouragement for this project came from Tufts University Digital Collections and Archives (Susanne Belovari, Pam Hopkins, Helen Stec), the Briscoe Center for American History at the University of Texas at Austin, the Mass Media and Culture Archive at the University of Maryland (Michael Henry, Jim Baxter), Broadcast Education Association (Heather Birks), the Television Academy Foundation Interviews (Jenni Matz), the Eyes of a Generation (Bobby Ellerbee), Columbia University Rare Book and Manuscript Library (Susan Hamson), the Paley Center for Media, the Wisconsin Historical Society, the Library of Congress (Zoran Sinobad, Cary O'Dell, Bryan Cornell), and the National Archives.

The late James Baughman and Hazel Dicken-Garcia were early encouragers of my history work and the American Journalism Historians Association (AJHA) has been a welcoming and supportive group since my graduate school days. Jim Wrocklage helped shoot my early oral history interviews, while Scott Myrick and Allen Major helped me with all my audio-visual material over the years.

This book is dedicated to Larry Hatteberg, one of American television's greatest storytellers. For more than a half-century, Hatteberg told the stories of the people who live in his home state of Kansas, through his work at KAKE-TV in Wichita. He also influenced generations of video storytellers, including myself, who came to Kansas to learn from the master.

**CONTESTED
GROUND**

Introduction

ON ONE LEVEL, this is a book about a documentary and a staff memo, as well as the person responsible for both. The documentary was nearly never broadcast at all, as governments and groups on both sides of the Berlin Wall tried to kill it. The memo revealed the rationale and inspiration for the most popular source of American journalism in the early 1960s, and its ideas continue to have influence well into the twenty-first century. While one was a motion picture film and the other thirty-two pages of the printed word, they are deeply intertwined.

NBC's Reuven Frank produced *The Tunnel* in 1962 and wrote the memo to his NBC television news staff the following year. Frank was one of the most influential people in the early development of television news in the United States. At the time of the documentary and memo, Frank also produced (after having created) the *Huntley-Brinkley Report,* NBC's nightly newscast, which in seven years had grown to attract the largest simultaneous news audience in history. *The Tunnel* was one of Frank's most cherished accomplishments in a career filled with significant achievements. The documentary helped crystallize his views on television as a communication source, which he chronicled in the staff memo, views that influenced not just documentaries but nightly newscasts and weekly public affairs programs.

Overall, this book is about a critical juncture in American journalism and media history, as people turned to a new format to learn about their world in the mid-twentieth century, just as the Cold War entered one of its most dangerous periods. The surprisingly fast ascendance of television news as the country's top choice for information signaled the public's acceptance, while the response from print journalism, other media professionals, and government leaders was decidedly less enthusiastic. The galvanized reception reveals a major upheaval in American news communication as all groups involved, from sources to competitors, reacted to the shifting media power dynamics.

Contested Ground

This book is also about borders and boundaries. *The Tunnel* is a gripping account of a harrowing five-month project to dig a tunnel under the Berlin Wall to sneak East Germans across the border to the West. *The Tunnel*, and television news in general, threatened many media and practice boundaries. The US and West German governments felt the documentary crossed the boundary from being informative to being a threat to international security. The popularity of Frank's *Huntley-Brinkley Report*, and all of television news, disrupted the information and economic model of media in the mid-twentieth century, causing the print journalism community as well as other media industries to protect their professional boundaries from the growing power of television.

The innovative production of and polarized reception to *The Tunnel*, as well as the most popular network television newscast, is best understood by a historical analysis into the making of the documentary, the writing of the memo, and the strong reaction to that broadcast and the medium. Using a variety of historical research methods and sources, including personal and company archives, historical broadcasts, production notes, internal memos, oral history interviews, declassified government documents, and newspaper and trade publications, this project converges the usually separate research areas of journalism history, broadcast history, Cold War history, and documentary film studies to analyze the production and reception of *The Tunnel* and Reuven Frank's television news memo. This documentary, and television news, became contested ground as Frank negotiated the disparity of accepted practices and ethics in print journalism, television news, documentaries, the relationship between journalists and government in the Cold War, and the powerful yet fragile position of the American television networks in the 1960s.

Critical Juncture

In addition to the importance of the program and the rise of television as a mass medium, the era in which it was created is crucial to understanding a dramatic shift in American media and journalism's relationship with the government in the mid-twentieth century. Taken together, the world situation and the upheaval in communication platforms created a critical juncture in American media and journalism history.

In the decades after World War II, television news disrupted journalism by moving past newspapers, magazines, and radio in importance to the American public. Television became a platform for moving-picture nonfiction, helping speed the demise of the theater newsreel. The medium also offered a new outlet for documentary films, providing a much larger audience than any projects from earlier in the century.

By 1962, more than nine out of ten American households had at least one television. NBC broadcast *The Tunnel* less than a year before network newscasts expanded from fifteen to thirty minutes as well as before the dramatic four days in 1963 when most of the country was riveted to a television set after the assassination of President John F. Kennedy. The first Roper Poll showing television news as more popular and trustworthy than newspapers in the United States was released the same year, but in the journalism community, the printed word was still revered as the primary and most professional communication method.[1]

The concept of critical juncture has been most widely used in the area of political science, including international relations and comparative politics. While scholars have taken a range of narrow to more broadly conceived approaches in identifying a critical juncture, a general definition involves a period of time when an institution, nation-state, economy, or some other defined group is in flux, allowing for a wider range of voices and choices on future direction than is available in more stable periods. Giovanni Capoccia and R. Daniel Keleman refer to these situations as "moments of fluidity."[2]

The early 1960s gave way to a critical juncture in American journalism and media history because of television's ascension as the most popular mass medium in the country at the same time as some of the Cold War's more dangerous moments, with journalism as the main conduit passing along information to the public.

The groups involved in producing or responding to television news, including *The Tunnel*, had the opportunity to react in a variety of ways to this new medium. The public could have ignored television news in favor of existing formats. Print journalists could have embraced television news as a fresh new way to reach the public with important issues, especially for those people who favored the mix of visuals and audio over the printed word and for those who could not afford a newspaper or magazine subscription. Documentary filmmakers could have adopted the journalism mantra of objectivity when producing their films. Government officials could have allowed journalists, without pressure, to present all sides of international issues, even from the Soviet perspective, trusting the public to recognize the superiority of American democracy and capitalism.

None of the above scenarios played out in any meaningful way. They are mentioned only to highlight the fluid nature of this critical juncture and the other possible directions that could have been taken.

Cold War and Television

In the Cold War timeline, *The Tunnel* aired eight years after the height of the Red Scare spearheaded by Senator Joseph McCarthy. By 1962, the Cold War was more than a dozen years old and the fear of communism in the United States had settled into a daily existence while many members of the media remembered the people who lost their jobs after being accused of communist sympathies during the McCarthy era. *The Tunnel* was produced six years before the 1968 Democratic National Convention in Chicago, when politicians began to overtly question the motives of journalists as television cameras chronicled police violence against Vietnam War protestors. Finally, *The Tunnel* was broadcast seven years before President Richard Nixon and Vice President Spiro Agnew began their attacks on what they considered the liberal network television news media.

The Tunnel involves two of the key events in Cold War history: the building of the Berlin Wall and, coincidentally, the Cuban Missile Crisis. The program was conceived and produced in an era of unspoken cooperation between national journalists and government officials to keep Americans safe from communist aggression, with the government source usually holding the upper hand. *The Tunnel* is a rare case when the journalists did not need the government's cooperation to produce such a program, but government leaders still expected the journalists to support US foreign policy directives.

Contested Ground is not about the peak of the Red Scare in the 1950s when Wisconsin senator Joseph McCarthy became one of the most powerful men in America through his constant charges of communists infiltrating American government and media. It is not about journalists or entertainers forced to testify at emotional and dramatic congressional hearings or CBS journalist Edward R. Murrow taking on McCarthy on his *See It Now* program. *The Tunnel* and its reception expand our understanding of the relationship between television and the Cold War by moving beyond those popular Cold War media touchstones.

The filming of and fight over *The Tunnel* happened two years after the televised Kennedy-Nixon debates and one year before television's marathon coverage of President Kennedy's assassination and funeral. By moving beyond these oft-described events, I hope to provide, as historian Thomas Doherty wrote, a Cold War and television "portrait more textured and multicolored than the monochrome shades fogging the popular imagination."³

Omnipresent Haze

The Cold War hangs over this book, obviously given the subject matter of *The Tunnel*, but also because the emergence of television news occurred after World War II, as the United States' enemies shifted from Germany and Japan back to that from before World War II: communism, specifically in the form of the Soviet Union and China. In the midst of media transitions, the American government and politicians were relentless with their messages of threats both far away, from the communist countries, and right here, the fear of subversives walking among us, slowly eroding the fabric of democracy without our diligent watch.

Cold War ideology was as constant and omnipresent in mainstream American journalism in the 1950s and 1960s as the cigarette smoke that permeated newsrooms, studios, restaurants, and bars where those journalists spent their time working and talking about work. The odor and haze were part of the scene, and the act of smoking was part of the job.

Mostly due to addiction and partly for style, Murrow was always accompanied by a waft of smoke rising next to him on camera, like a ghostly co-host, from a sometimes visible and sometimes off-camera cigarette. In a more overt example, an advertising agency made sure Camel ashtrays were visible on the NBC *Camel News Caravan* news desk, sometimes with a burning cigarette in view.

That stench fouled one's clothes and seeped into the pores of one's skin. But you didn't notice the overpowering smell and then think about the unpleasant effect of that atmosphere until you removed your shirt at the end of the day and took a deep inhale. Maybe you wouldn't notice its absence until decades later, when smoking had disappeared from newsrooms and, eventually, most public places. Then, when you would walk into a place that still allowed smoking, you might be overcome by the foul stench and wonder why you put up with it for all those years. The basic premise of Cold War ideology, much like smoky offices, was accepted in newsrooms across the country, just as it was accepted by most of the public, who relied on the journalists to help them understand how the world worked.

In hindsight, it is tempting to single out journalists as dupes of the government or of following simplistic Cold War themes. In reality, the two superpowers *did* pose a serious threat to each other and those nuclear weapons were, and are, real. Most journalists, like most Americans, worried about atomic bombs and communism. A 1961 Gallup Poll showed that more than eight of ten Americans would rather fight a nuclear war than live under communism. Journalists were well aware of how the people felt.[4]

Those journalists were also dependent for interviews and information about our government policies on the very government sources who were pushing the Cold War ideology. Those journalists cashed their paychecks from individuals and companies that often supported the government views on the evils of communism, or at least did not want to upset the very politicians or government officials who could influence the profit margins of those newspapers or broadcast networks and stations through new restrictions or regulations.

Boundary Work

While Reuven Frank produced *The Tunnel* in 1962 and wrote the television memo in 1963, the motivations, decisions, and reactions to the broadcast and medium are the result of histories dating back at least to the start of the twentieth century. "Histories" is plural because all the groups involved, either in the production or reaction to the documentary and the rise of television news, had a separate path to 1962, with some events and people remembered and others forgotten. Each group could draw upon its own history to place *The Tunnel* and television news within or outside acceptable practice.

The concept of *boundary work* is employed throughout this project to help explain why Frank and his NBC crew produced *The Tunnel* in a specific way and why the program sparked such divergent and passionate responses.

Reactions to television as an information source also benefit from this approach. Sociologist Thomas Gieryn first developed the idea of boundary work to describe efforts of the scientific community in the nineteenth century to gain the trust of the public as experts in areas that had previously been the domain of religious leaders. Groups use boundary work tactics to both burnish their reputation and also to protect their niche by demonizing people or other groups that attempt to encroach on their perceived expertise. Boundary work does not presuppose the group is a true profession or even that the members actually fulfill the role they propose that they play. Boundary work is aspirational. Boundary work is what the group says it does, not necessarily what it actually does.[5]

Gieryn proposed that boundary work is best studied in periods when a group is either trying to expand its authority into new areas or protect its boundaries from outsiders attempting to encroach into its expertise, which aligns with the idea of a critical juncture. When either expanding or protecting boundaries, groups will attempt to damage the reputation of others with similar goals, often "with labels such as 'pseudo,' 'deviant,' or 'amateur.'"[6]

In boundary work, a group's history is a key component of how that collection of people defines itself. Past events and issues are held up as instances of either exemplary work or deviant behavior that must not be repeated. Over time, a group can reconsider a previous event and present it in a new light. Understanding a group's history and, more specifically, how that group employs its history to protect or expand its boundaries becomes illuminating when exploring the various responses to *The Tunnel* and television news.

From just the journalism aspect of *The Tunnel* broadcast and reaction, boundary work is a fluid process since the First Amendment precludes tests or formal accreditation to determine who is or is not a journalist. For media scholar Jane Singer, twentieth-century American print journalism used ethics as a way to marginalize new media encroachers. When threatened with radio and television, print journalists "drew on eloquent evocation of ethical standards and a declaration that the 'traditional' journalist would uphold them against challenges from poseurs."[7]

Boundary work is especially helpful for understanding the various journalism and media groups involved in *The Tunnel* and television news. The early 1960s was a period of changing boundaries in the fields of journalism, television, broadcast news, and documentaries, and in Cold War ideologies. Legacy media, especially the printed word, were trying to protect their boundaries while television was becoming more powerful because of audience acceptance. Radio as an important news source in this period found its impact disappearing under the darkening shadow of television.

Boundary work helps with an understanding of not just the different groups, but how they interacted with each other. *The Tunnel* and the television news memo sparked the boundary work and histories of journalism, television, television news, visual storytelling, documentary film, and Cold War ideology. Each of these groups, as well as the US government, had a history that it drew upon to justify its reaction to the project. If a group felt *The Tunnel* did not reflect its traditions or was encroaching on its expertise, it may have ignored it or lashed out and demonized the project. Throughout the first half of the twentieth century, these group histories may have run parallel, converged, or diverged, depending on the issue and the group involved.

Reuven Frank had worked as a newspaper journalist, in television news, as a documentarian, and as a visual storyteller. Frank pulled together specific practices from each career and created his own boundaries that he defended against criticism. His professional journalism career began just as the Cold War unfolded, and his move to television happened at the start of the Korean War. Many of his biggest television projects involved Cold War issues and themes.

Since boundary work involves aspirational practices, the protection of boundaries can involve both a public and private response. For public consumption, the group espouses its values or marginalizes an interloper. Behind the scenes, different negotiations take place that the groups know would not fit with their public persona. Through the use of company and personal archives, as well as declassified government documents, both the public and private arguments and bargaining are considered, especially in the dispute between television news and the State Department.

Academic Research Boundaries

The 1962 NBC broadcast and reaction might be explored more coherently by limiting the scope: *The Tunnel* as journalism. *The Tunnel* as television news. *The Tunnel* as narrative visual storytelling. *The Tunnel* as Reuven Frank's vision for effective use of a mass medium. *The Tunnel* as a documentary film. *The Tunnel* as a help or hindrance to America's Cold War efforts. *The Tunnel* as an interesting historical story. Some of these areas have been explored, and any of these approaches would be insightful and would dovetail more smoothly within existing research areas.

While a narrower path might be clearer, the negotiations, decisions, responses, and outcomes would be devoid of some of the key influences at the time. Frank was not just a television newsman. He was not just a documentary producer. He was not just a journalist. He was not just someone trying to understand the threats of the Cold War. He was all of these things at the same time.

Reuven Frank also did not work alone. The bulk of the filming and logistics for *The Tunnel* was handled by Germans or Americans living in Berlin and employed by NBC. They had their own views on the Berlin Wall and the Cold War. Frank also had to appease his bosses at NBC. In this case, NBC even had to win over critics from foreign governments.

Another key element of this approach is to acknowledge the historical events and approaches that shape the production and reception of *The Tunnel* and the television news memo. While the documentary and memo date from 1962–1963, the influences take us back to earlier in the twentieth century. Each of the media groups producing or responding to Frank's work are drawing upon their history to engage in the boundary work of acceptable practices.

In order to best understand the complexities of this critical juncture in American media history, this approach cuts across traditional academic historical research boundaries, including journalism, media, television, documentary film, and the Cold War, areas that have been surprisingly separate. The point, and hopefully the execution, is not to make this era of media history more confusing. Instead, the purpose in moving beyond traditional research area boundaries is to provide a more representational look at the influences, complications, and pressures at play for the journalists and other media professionals.

A guiding principle in this research is a firm belief that if we understood more about the complexities of the shifting communication landscape in the mid-twentieth century, we would be better prepared to handle the challenges and opportunities in the twenty-first century digital transformation. Even though television news has been the most popular form of journalism in the United States since the early 1960s, the format has been significantly underrepresented in academic research, especially in the areas of journalism and media history. The dearth of serious research has allowed personal stories, memoirs, anecdotes, and specific events to represent all of television news history, usually omitting or smoothing over the chaotic, risk-taking, early years when the eventual path had not yet become clear. Linking the mid-twentieth-century media and political disruptions to the challenges faced by journalists in the first decades of the twenty-first century can provide insights, or at least comfort, that previous generations had to wrestle with their own set of obstacles and uncertainties. "One of the great pleasures of studying media history," wrote historian Lisa Gitelman, "is the way it cuts against the exceptionalism of the present."[8]

Because of the variety of and, at times, contradictory responses to the documentary and memo, the structure of the book might be better compared to a website than to a traditional chronology. In keeping with Frank's insistence on storytelling, the first chapter tells the story of how Germany's major city became divided, leading to the harrowing, dramatic, and controversial dig under the Berlin Wall, chronicled in *The Tunnel* documentary production and reception.

The subsequent chapters concentrate on the different historical influences on the production and reception of *The Tunnel* and television news: government pressure, journalism, documentary films, television, Cold War ideology, and producer Reuven Frank himself. In the parlance of digital media, you might consider the first chapter as the main webpage, with the following chapters acting as hyperlinks in *The Tunnel* story, taking you deeper into the areas that reveal a more complete story.

CHAPTER ONE

Captured on Film

A Daring Escape from a Divided Berlin

A MAN OF LESSER confidence might have been a bit anxious sitting in that dark West Berlin room in 1962. There, he would finally see the first images of a documentary project that already involved questionable ethical decisions and a dose of company and government deception. The American documentary producer sitting in that chair was accustomed to having full control of his projects: from the research and the filming to the writing, scoring, and editing. In this case, for reasons that will become obvious, he had to trust his West German crew that the money and risks would be worth it.

For the rest of the afternoon and evening and well past midnight, the man watched hours of silent film shot over the previous four months. After a little bit of sleep, he got up and spent much of the next day reviewing more film. After the marathon screening, he was so taken with the images that had been projected on the screen for the past two days that he scrapped his original ideas for the documentary. He knew he finally had a project that would fulfill his evolving ideas on the power of visual communication, especially on television.

He even called his boss back in New York and asked for ninety minutes of primetime on American network television, which commanded the largest simultaneous audience in the world at the time. His confidence was so strong that when he made that request, the documentary still did not have an ending. The critical, dangerous, and potentially life-threatening conclusion, which involved the most important global issue, was playing out nearby. No one in the room yet knew if the documentary subject would project triumph or tragedy.

While the producer was confident that he had a plan for an important and powerful documentary, he could not foresee how his production decisions, both before and after that Berlin screening, would launch him and his project into the middle of the Cold War struggle between the two post–World War II superpowers. During the next three months, the man and his project would be subjected to criticism and condemnation on both sides of the Iron Curtain: from government officials in the United States and West Germany, from some of the key people involved in the documentary, and from the journalism community itself. Communists said he worked as an agent for his government while the US State Department tried to shut down the project, saying it was not in the country's best interests. He would be accused of turning dangerous altruistic work into crass commercialism. Fellow journalists called him an amateur dabbling in topics beyond his competence, potentially triggering a nuclear war.

Most of these attacks would be made before more than a handful of people had seen a single frame of the documentary film.

Dividing a City

Reuven Frank was not thrilled about heading to Berlin in August 1961. Mostly he was trying to justify the cost of flying a film crew to Europe for a separate project. Frank, age forty, a National Broadcasting Company television news producer, and newscaster David Brinkley, forty-one years old, were on their way to Vienna to work on the third installment of their popular *Our Man* project, featuring Brinkley as global tour guide with his unique perspective and delivery. Their most recent production, titled *Our Man in Hong Kong*, had run earlier in the year.[1]

The NBC news bureau in West Berlin had been reporting on the tensions in the divided city since the end of World War II for radio and television. Roughly 19,000 East Germans had left home for the West every month since 1950. The NBC West German crew had noticed even more anxiety in the summer of 1961, with 30,000 crossing the border in July and even higher numbers in early August. Frank knew the West Berlin bureau could use some help, and it would not hurt to have his popular newscaster seen covering a major world event.[2]

Brinkley and Chet Huntley were the newscasters on NBC's nightly *Huntley-Brinkley Report,* the most popular and honored American nightly television network newscast. Frank created the newscast in 1956 and had continued as executive producer. In addition to appearing on the nightly newscast, both Huntley and Brinkley had their own weekly public affairs programs and also pursued other longer-form projects. Frank split his time between the nightly *Huntley-Brinkley Report* and the longer projects. By 1961, Frank was one of the most seasoned television producers of newscasts, documentaries, and election night programs, with over a decade of experience on the visual medium.

At breakfast the next morning, Frank was trying to think of a fresh angle that Brinkley could cover concerning the influx of East Germans in West Berlin. Frank, who did not speak German, realized everyone around him was excited and sharing newspapers. While he was sleeping, the East Germans had shut down the border between West and East Berlin. By chance, Reuven Frank and David Brinkley were witnessing the birth of the Berlin Wall on Sunday, August 13, 1961.[3]

They postponed their Vienna plans so Brinkley could cover the story for the first few days after the border closed. Eventually, they were ready to turn the story back over to the staff in the NBC West Berlin bureau. Frank was already anticipating stories they should be covering as the East Germans turned the temporary barbed wire fences into a more permanent wall. Western reporters and film crews normally could not work in East Germany without a government escort, so journalists would need to be looking for evidence of the West Berlin reaction to the wall. Frank had worked with Gary Stindt of the NBC Berlin bureau for years, especially on Cold War projects. He told Stindt, correspondent Piers Anderton, and the NBC camera crew consisting of German brothers Peter and Klaus Dehmel to be on the lookout for any signs of what was happening in East Germany since people could no longer leave for the West. He wanted stories on whatever "was building up inside." Since Frank was the executive producer of the *Huntley-Brinkley Report* and other NBC news programs, he had the budget to cover whatever the crew could find.[4]

Frank's news career had paralleled the rise of the Cold War and the increased tensions involving the Berlin border. The major events that had culminated in the separation of Germany's most important city had been part of his first fifteen years as a journalist, so he knew the impact of the past decade in understanding this historical moment. He also understood he was working in a medium that now had the power and audience to tell the important story.

While the closing of the Berlin border came as a surprise to many in the West in 1961, the United States and the Soviet Union had been arguing and posturing about the fate of the German city since before the end of World War II. The maneuvers and decisions that led to the divided city began when the United States and the Soviet Union were allies, and the events that happened since that time help illuminate the strong feelings on both sides of the Berlin Wall.

Cold War Flashpoint

Soviet premier Nikita Khrushchev referred to Berlin as "the testicles of the West." If he wanted to get the United States' attention, he would apply pressure at Berlin. The prewar capital of Germany became one of the key geographic locations in the Cold War because of decisions made during World War II, when the Soviet Union was still part of the alliance to defeat Germany.[5]

As the Allies began to get the upper hand on Germany in World War II, the United States, Great Britain, and the Soviet Union began planning for postwar Europe. On the question of Germany, the Allied nations wanted to make sure the country could not easily rebuild any kind of military presence, so as to avoid a repeat of the century's two world wars. They had agreed that for the short term, the military of the Soviet Union, Great Britain, the United States, and eventually France would each occupy a section of Germany, allowing time for a more permanent solution.[6]

The fate of Berlin became a problem of geography. Each Allied nation realized the importance of the capital, but the city was not situated in a part of the country that could easily be connected to different zones. As a compromise, Berlin itself was also split into sectors, with the city deep within the Soviet zone of the country. Under the agreement, each occupying country had free access between the sectors, especially to and from Berlin within the Soviet sector.

The geographic isolation of Berlin became a serious issue as relations between the Soviet Union and the other Allies deteriorated after the war. The Soviets allowed the communist leaders in their occupation zone to set up a separate country, the German Democratic Republic (GDR), also known as

East Germany. The British, French, and American sectors were combined into the Federal Republic of Germany (FRG), or West Germany. The Allies, especially the United States, would not recognize East Germany as a true nation, which later led to some of the most intense moments along the Berlin Wall.

Berlin Airlift

The Soviets first took advantage of Berlin's location within East Germany in 1948 because of a dispute over monetary policies. The Soviets quietly shut down all vehicle and train travel to and from West Berlin in June 1948. The idea was to slowly starve the people in West Berlin until the Allies agreed to give up their occupation zones in the city, allowing East Germany control of all of Berlin.

The Allies' choices included ceding West Berlin to the Soviets, trying to force through the barriers at the East German borders, or flying in supplies over Soviet airspace. The Soviets gambled that the Allies would not want a direct confrontation at a border crossing and that the logistics of keeping the Berlin sector going through the air would be too complicated.

The Allies, led by US General Lucius Clay, chose to avoid the direct confrontation and instead set up an airlift operation. It became clear the Soviets did not want to start a war over the situation, so the planes were allowed to use Soviet airspace, although Soviet war planes did harass the planes as they crossed East Germany. For the first few months, supplies were limited because the airports in West Berlin, Tempelhof and Gatow, were too small. The Allies built Tegel Airfield during the blockade, and by Easter 1949 supply planes were landing in West Berlin at roughly one every minute. The Soviets backed down and reopened vehicle and train traffic into West Berlin starting in May 1949.[7]

While the Soviet Union may have used the border closing to test the will of the Allies, the Berlin Airlift also signaled a change in the mood of West Germans as they realized they were not going to be sacrificed in the larger machinations of the Cold War. While the Berlin Airlift was seen as an early victory for the Allies in the Cold War, the precarious geographical position of Berlin would become a key to American and Soviet foreign policy for the next four decades.

Cold War Settles In

In the global Cold War, the Berlin Airlift was quickly forgotten when the Soviet Union tested its first nuclear weapon in August 1949, much sooner than the Allies expected. The two-nation dynamic of the Cold War was now set; both the United States and the Soviet Union possessing weapons that could obliterate major portions of the world. Western nations created the North Atlantic Treaty Organization (NATO) while the Soviet Union and its Eastern Bloc nations combined into the Warsaw Pact.

When Chairman Mao Zedong's army prevailed in the China Civil War to create the People's Republic of China in 1949, communism was seen as an even bigger world threat to the West. US foreign policy coalesced around the idea of containment, to keep communism from making more inroads around the world. When the communist North Koreans invaded South Korea in June 1950, the United Nations immediately came to the defense of South Korea, with almost 90 percent of the military coming from the United States. US General Douglas MacArthur was in charge of UN forces and eventually pushed North Koreans back over the border and beyond, triggering China to get involved in the conflict. The fighting continued for another three years until the two sides agreed to an armistice, setting up a demilitarized zone between North and South Korea.

World War II hero Dwight Eisenhower replaced Harry Truman as US president in 1953, the same year Joseph Stalin died. Nikita Khrushchev eventually succeeded Stalin, while both countries built up their nuclear arsenal and made provisions on how to possibly survive a nuclear attack. The threat of communism from abroad and internally became the major political issue in the United States, especially during the height of Senator Joseph McCarthy's power.

While American leaders confidently told their people that democracy was winning over communism, a 180-pound object shaped like a beach ball caused Americans to dramatically question that assertion. In 1957, the Soviet Union launched Sputnik, the first space satellite to orbit the earth. American radio and television broadcasts featured the "beep, beep" sound of the orbiting satellite. Sputnik started a space race that the Soviet Union was clearly winning into the mid-1960s, while American scientists and military leaders argued over jurisdiction. Sputnik also raised questions about America's commitment to science and technology, as well as its military preparedness. In an early 1958 poll, more than two-thirds of Americans thought the Russians were winning the Cold War, and almost three out of ten thought the chance of war would increase that year. A key issue during the 1960 presidential election was whether or not there was a "missile gap" between the two nations that favored the Soviet Union.[8]

Germany's Future

In the mid-1950s, West Germany had emerged as a strong economic power, which strengthened its hand in negotiations, both with the Soviet Union and its NATO allies. By contrast, East Germany was struggling economically, even dependent on trade deals with West Germany. Because of the stark economic, as well as political, differences, East Germans were flooding across the borders to West Germany, especially in the divided city of Berlin.

Khrushchev began pushing the United States and its allies for a Berlin peace treaty, allowing the East Germans to gain control of the entire city. This solution would halt the migration of people from East Germany, at least at the borders in the city.

Part of the pressure on the Soviet Union came from East Germany's leader. Walter Ulbricht was determined to annex West Berlin at any cost, and he was not above allowing provocations to happen that might spark a military takeover of that part of the city. Khrushchev both supported and cautioned Ulbricht, thankful for his loyalty but worried the East Germans would initiate an incident that could lead to military action.

In 1958, Khrushchev felt it was time to push the United States for a decision on Berlin. He hoped to convince Eisenhower that by giving up West Berlin, the Cold War could be over. The Soviet premier even visited Vice President Richard Nixon in the United States with the hope that Eisenhower would later visit the Soviet Union. While Khrushchev expected a summit in the tradition of World War II's Yalta or Potsdam, the American position remained that the two countries were enemies, not equals.

New Administration

The Soviet Union watched the 1960 American presidential election with great interest. The Republican Party's candidate, Vice President Nixon, had built his career on a strong anticommunist stance. The Democratic Party's nominee, Senator John F. Kennedy, was more of a mystery in the Soviet Union, but Khrushchev hoped that if Kennedy won, there might be more room for negotiation.

After his victory, Kennedy excited Americans in his first year when he made the pledge of pushing the Americans past the Soviets in the space race and putting a man on the moon within the decade. While the speech gave hope, the first Cold War action of his administration belied that confidence. Kennedy had inherited a plan from the Eisenhower administration to storm Cuba and take out socialist leader Fidel Castro. Kennedy chose to go forward with the April invasion, which resulted in a dismal failure and painted the Americans as inept aggressors.

Khrushchev saw Kennedy's Bay of Pigs debacle as evidence of a weak leader who did not have the courage to cancel the plan or to fully support it. The Soviets were also worried that if Kennedy was weak, he might not be able to stand up to the military and business hardliners in the United States. The two leaders had entirely different intentions when they met for first time, in Vienna in June 1961, resulting in a contentious discussion. Kennedy was expecting a fairly routine session while Khrushchev wanted an end to a divided Berlin. During their meeting, Khrushchev turned on the American president, vaguely threatening retaliation if the Americans did not get serious about negotiating over Berlin. The Vienna meetings left Kennedy shaken, feeling Khrushchev had ambushed him.

After the Vienna conference, Kennedy gave a live televised address in which he promised the United States would not let the Soviet Union or East Germany take over West Berlin. East German leader Ulbricht held a press conference and specifically invited reporters from the West. In the midst of the session, he assured the journalists there were no plans to build a wall on the Berlin border between East and West. The reporters found his comment puzzling because no one had asked him about such a plan.

Ulbricht had long wanted to at least shut down the border in Berlin, with the ultimate hope of gaining control of the whole city. In early August 1961, Khrushchev finally agreed to allow Ulbricht to take that action. The Soviet premier knew he needed to stop the emigration of East Germans, which was draining the communist nation of its people and resources. Khrushchev also saw the move as a way, short of military action, to show Americans the Soviets were not going to accept the current arrangement.

Sensing Ulbricht's ultimate goal of getting control of West Berlin, even by force, Khrushchev made it clear he did not want the closing of the border to lead to military conflict. He told the East German leader that the project must not infringe on even a part of West Berlin territory. Much like the blockade in 1948, the Soviet Union was ready to test again what the Allies would accept and what would cause a military reaction in Berlin. Khrushchev already had intelligence that NATO leaders were not inclined to go to war over a Berlin border closing.

The closing of the border in Berlin happened very quickly, which is one reason it was such a surprise to the West. Khrushchev did not give Ulbricht permission until Saturday, August 5. By the time Ulbricht put Erich Honecker in charge of the secret project, the East Germans had less than a week before the plan to shut the border at midnight on Sunday morning, August 13, 1961.[9]

Shutting the Border

The closing of the border between West and East Berlin gave the Cold War a very strong, stark, visual symbol. The different ideologies of democracy and capitalism versus communism, which had dominated Western political thought since the end of World War II, had often been hard to present visually in newsreels and television news, with the exception of war or other military maneuvers. Now, television news could easily picture the sharp differences between the two superpowers.

When Reuven Frank, David Brinkley, and the NBC Berlin camera crew ventured to the Berlin border on that Sunday morning, they witnessed many more images than they could fit in a television news report: East German military putting up concrete posts with barbed wire across streets that had been quiet and accessible just hours earlier; tanks lurking in the background; separated families tearfully yelling to each other across the border; East Germans, realizing their path to a different life might now be blocked, trying to sneak over or around the barriers, sometimes successfully, and other times thwarted by the East German police force, the Vopos (short for Volkspolizei).

All this visual drama was on display just yards away from the Western side of the new barrier. Since the concrete wall would not be built until later, people (and cameras) could look right across the barriers to see what was happening on the Eastern side.

Frank, Brinkley, and the NBC crew, as well as many other journalists, gravitated to a part of Berlin that offered a unique vantage point: Bernauer

Strasse. This street in the working-class Wedding district of Berlin was situated right on the border. In fact, for a few blocks, the border ran along the edges of the buildings. In this section, in the first days, people could jump out of East Berlin windows onto the sidewalk in West Berlin along Bernauer Strasse. West German police and citizens stretched out sheets and blankets so East Germans could jump from the higher floors without getting hurt.[10]

Once the border was secure with barbed wire and other barricades, the East Germans began working on ways to thwart the most obvious efforts to sneak across the border. They moved people out of the apartment buildings along Bernauer Strasse and bricked up the windows. They added concrete barriers to keep vehicles from crashing across to West Berlin. Once it became clear the Allies were not going to contest the border closing, the East Germans started to build the more permanent Berlin Wall, the visual representation of the Cold War for the next three decades.

Through it all, television and newspaper photographers had images to share with the world. West Berliners often protested on their side of the wall, sometime forcing West Berlin police to keep them away from the wall itself to curb any violence. People could lift their children up above the barriers so relatives on the other side could see them.

Cold War Compromise

While the Berlin Wall signified an extremely aggressive and oppressive action, especially for the people of West Berlin and West Germany, both the Soviet and American leaders recognized it as a compromise, even if that conclusion was not offered for public consumption. For Khrushchev, allowing Ulbricht and the East Germans to build the wall revealed the West was not willing to go to war over the border, so he could back off a more aggressive approach of allowing the East Germans to take over West Berlin. President Kennedy had a more delicate communication approach to master. He needed West Germans to feel as if they had not been forgotten, but he did not want to taunt the Soviets into gaining the confidence to go after West Berlin.

The American caution caused anger among West Germans. The day the border was closed, the senior State Department official in Berlin, Allan Lightner, wanted to issue a statement to show Americans were not abandoning their allies. The State Department in Washington nixed that plan and instead offered a tepid response from Secretary of State Dean Rusk. West Germans were perplexed by the weak response to the border closing, especially since President Kennedy had given such a tough talk on the matter back in July.

West Berlin mayor Willy Brandt, who had designs on the West German chancellorship held by Konrad Adenauer, sent an angry list of talking points and demands to Kennedy, a communication that was leaked to the press. Lightner sent a note to the State Department saying a stronger response to the border closing was necessary to keep people from fleeing West Berlin because of the destruction of "that perishable commodity called hope."[11]

Kennedy sent Vice President Lyndon Johnson to Berlin to talk to government leaders and show the German people the Americans still cared about West Berlin. As part of the public relations trip, he also sent General Lucius Clay, the hero of the Berlin Airlift. Clay would stay in West Berlin as a personal representative of the president.

Kennedy administration hopes that the excitement and anger over the wall would die down and that American journalists would move on to other stories proved to be wishful thinking. There were two main reasons the Berlin Wall continued as a top story for the next year and beyond. First, the physical presence of the wall and the cat-and-mouse games to help people get out of East Germany offered a consistent stream of stories to cover. Reporters and photographers could focus on protests on the Western side. They could cover valiant, and sometimes fatal, attempts to swim across rivers or canals to West Berlin. They could cover the brave souls who snuck through the sewer systems until the East Germans shut down that option. These were often strikingly visual stories, happening just as television news was challenging newspapers as the most popular journalistic format in the United States. Reuven Frank understood the importance of the images in television news, and the Berlin Wall provided the dramatic pictures.

The other reason the wall continued as a big story in the United States involved Americans and others in West Germany informally known as the Berlin Mafia. This group involved both government officials and journalists who lived and worked in Berlin, or other parts of West Germany, and sympathized with the local situation. In military and anthropological parlance, they had "gone native." The US government officials pushed for a stronger response to the wall through back channels. They did not discourage West Germans from speaking their minds. Journalists in West Berlin also wondered why the Americans or NATO did not have a stronger response to the wall, so they kept up the pressure through news coverage.[12]

For the American television networks, both NBC and CBS had full-time bureaus in West Germany. NBC's head of European film operations, Gary Stindt, was born in Berlin before emigrating to the United States and serving in World War II as a film photographer. He set up NBC's Berlin bureau in 1948. The NBC film crew, brothers Peter and Klaus Dehmel, were German. Correspondent Piers Anderton was an American, hired by NBC as the correspondent for the Berlin bureau. CBS's correspondent in West Germany, American Daniel Schorr, had been hired by Edward R. Murrow and opened CBS's first Moscow bureau in 1955, landing a rare television interview two years later with Khrushchev for *Face the Nation*.

Schorr scored another interview with a prominent communist a few months after the Berlin border closed when he sat down with East German leader Walter Ulbricht. When Schorr pressed Ulbricht on Stalin's legacy, the East German leader got up and stormed out of the room while the camera was rolling, ending the interview. CBS highlighted that scene in a special *CBS Reports* on East Germany broadcast in January 1962.[13]

Reporters who were sympathetic to the Berlin cause did not need to manufacture any stories to keep the issue at the top of the news agenda; the US government's Berlin Mafia provided enough opportunities through their own actions. While sending General Clay to Berlin may have been a smart move to placate West Berliners, Clay did not hide his wish for a stronger response to the wall. Clay even had American troops attacking and tearing down a replica of the Berlin Wall located within West Berlin, a practice that did not escape the attention of East German and Soviet leaders.[14]

Wall Confrontations

Clay decided to test the Soviet resolve through an incident that brought the Soviet Union and the United States physically closer to war than at any other time in the Cold War, just two months after the border closed. Part of the four-power treaty on Berlin after World War II involved allowing military and government officials from all four nations access to all the occupation zones. In Berlin, the East Germans, not the Soviets, manned the border crossing. The United States did not recognize the existence of that country. In a gesture of protest, American government leaders would not show their credentials when they stopped at the border on their way to East Berlin. The

British, by contrast, did not mind waving their ID cards at the East German guards when crossing the border.

On Sunday evening, October 22, 1961, Allan Lightner and his wife stopped at the Checkpoint Charlie border crossing at Friedrich Strasse on their way to an opera performance in East Berlin. This time, when Lightner refused to show his ID, the East Germans would not let him through. Lightner said he would only show his ID to a Russian soldier, since East Berlin was in the Soviet occupation zone. No Russian appeared. Close to two hours later, still waiting, American troops showed up at the border. On foot, a group of soldiers with fixed bayonets flanked Lightner's car and walked beside the car into East Berlin. Meanwhile, General Clay was moving tanks up toward the border.

The American couple missed the opera, but Allan Lightner was not done with his performance. After driving a few blocks in East Berlin, he took his wife back across the border. Then he repeated the drill. Soldiers once again escorted Lightner's car across the border while East German guards watched. He drove around for a few minutes before returning to West Berlin. The Soviets responded that the border dispute was merely a miscommunication with the East German border guards. Coincidence or not, the Soviet Union carried out two nuclear weapon tests that week.

Three days later, Clay tested the border again. This time, Clay gave the East German guards a one-hour deadline to have a Soviet guard appear to receive credentials or the Americans would come across in force. A half-hour later, American tanks appeared near the border. When no Russians appeared, the Americans once again escorted the car into East Berlin for a quick visit and return. The American tanks were moved back. The Americans continued this border crossing exercise through the day, with large crowds surrounding the border to see what would happen.

Overnight, more than thirty Soviet tanks appeared near the border at Checkpoint Charlie. Ten American tanks returned to the border on October 27. The Soviet Union ordered ten tanks to move up and face the American tanks right at the border, guns pointed at each other. There is some speculation that Khrushchev had erroneous intelligence that Clay planned to storm the wall. Instead, the Americans once again crossed the border with military help.

Unbeknownst to Clay, Attorney General Robert Kennedy had started backchannel negotiations with a top Soviet in Washington as a way to potentially diffuse these types of situations. While it is not known what was said in these discussions, at some point Khrushchev ordered his tanks to retreat to a side street, supposedly to allow the Americans to also retreat without appearing to back down. The tactic was successful. The American tanks left the border and that stalemate was over.[15]

Underground Escapes

During the months after the border closing, the East Germans not only built a ten-to-twenty-foot wall, but they also tore down buildings and cleared the land immediately adjacent to the East side of the wall. Vopos, in newly constructed guard towers, had orders to shoot anyone seen running toward the wall. These "death strips" dramatically cut down the number of people who tried to escape around or over the wall. With each move the East Germans made, people who were trying to escape had to adapt. For several months, the best way to get people to West Berlin was with forged passports. A collection of students from Berlin's Free University, led by Detlef Girrmann, helped close to five thousand people get out of East Germany through false documents in 1961. The "Girrmann Group" tried various escape methods, but the passports worked best until East Germans figured out the process in early 1962.

According to East German secret police records, in the period after the border closed until the end of 1961, more than three thousand people were captured trying to escape the country: close to three-quarters of these tried to get over or around the wall, 19 percent attempted to leave by rail or car, 4 percent via the north coast through the Baltic Sea, and 3 percent by swimming across canals and rivers along the border.[16]

Escaping under the Wall

Tunneling under the wall began as soon as the border closed, but it did not become a popular approach until the East Germans closed off the easier escape methods. The first tunnels were short and only open long enough for a specific group of people to escape. Tunnels were dangerous because there was always a chance at a collapse, especially if they were quick projects. Tunnels also involved having people on the East side, known as runners, who could round up people quickly and get them to the location where the tunnel would open up in East Berlin. With all the spies and informants on both sides of the wall, the longer the project took, the better chance that the Vopos would be waiting as the diggers came up in East Berlin. In other cases, the East German police would notice a flurry of people heading to a specific location and intercept the people just as they were ready to climb down into the ground.

By 1962, tunneling had become both a passion and a business along the Berlin Wall. Many of the projects involved students from West Berlin universities because they had college friends who were now stuck in East Germany. Tunneling also became a business opportunity as people would plan and dig a tunnel for a specific price. The West Berlin police and intelligence agencies found themselves in an awkward position when it came to border escapes. They wanted to help efforts to get people out of East Germany, but they could not be officially involved in any projects that crossed into East Germany, because that would be seen as an act of aggression under the four-power treaty. Instead, West Berlin would lend help to escape projects with seed money and encouragement but would have to disavow direct knowledge. West German intelligence also kept track of escape projects and warned groups if they suspected the East Germans might be aware.

Unfortunately for television journalists and newsreel photographers, the secrecy involved in tunnels meant they would not know about them until after either the people escaped or when the East German police arrested those involved, which was hard to present visually after the fact. The NBC Berlin bureau remembered Reuven Frank's encouragement to look for evidence of what was building up inside East Germany. The staff let it be known in escape efforts that the network was interested in filming a tunnel while it was being dug, and not just after it was completed.

The Tunnel

Reuven Frank thought that it was a bit odd that Berlin correspondent Piers Anderton backed him into a corner at Anderton's wedding reception in New York in June 1962 and demanded they have a meeting later in Frank's office. Anderton did not want anyone else at his reception to hear his news. The NBC Berlin bureau had found a tunnel project and had an opportunity to film it while the diggers went under the wall. Since Frank had given them permission to pursue any such projects when the border closed in August 1961, the NBC Berlin bureau had already started to work on the arrangement.[17]

It may be fitting that a documentary that was later lauded as comparable to a fiction film got its start, in a way, because of Hollywood. By the start of 1962, stories about tunnels under the Berlin Wall became fairly frequent in American media. Some tunnels were successful; others were discovered by East Germans and shut down. In one instance, people used spoons to dig to freedom. In January 1962, a specific tunnel escape caught the eye of a veteran movie director. This project became known as "Tunnel 28" for the number of people who made it to West Berlin, at that time a record for a tunnel escape under the Berlin Wall.[18]

Movie director Robert Siodmak, known for his *film noir* style, took note of the "Tunnel 28" escape. Siodmak was born in Dresden and made movies in Germany until he came under attack by the Nazis both for his Jewish heritage and his movie topics. Siodmak fled to Paris and then to the United States, where Universal Studios hired him as a director during the war. He returned to Europe in the 1950s. Siodmak then convinced another Hollywood studio, Metro-Goldwyn-Mayer (MGM), to let him make a fictional account of "Tunnel 28." MGM thought it could cash in on all the stories about tunnels by filming the movie in West Berlin. They filmed some scenes at the real border, but also constructed a wall replica in West Berlin, which became a tourist attraction in the city.[19]

Meanwhile, a group of students from Berlin's Technical University were working on an ambitious real tunnel project in the spring of 1962. Engineering student Domenico Sesta and his childhood friend Luigi Spina, both from Italy, came up with the idea. They wanted to have a German involved in the project, so they turned to classmate Wolf Schroedter. Since the border had closed in August 1961, the students started that school year without their classmates stuck in East Berlin. With Sesta's engineering background, the students were determined to take the time and build a lasting tunnel to help their friends escape to West Berlin. They spent days scouting locations in Berlin for a tunnel project. They needed a building on the West Berlin side of the wall where they could dig in the basement without notice. Most Berlin Wall tunnels began on the West side and then, at the last minute, the diggers would burst through on the East Berlin side, preferably in a basement, hidden from the Vopos patrolling the border. Abandoned or partially used buildings were not too difficult to find on both sides of the wall because of World War II bombing damage that had never been addressed. In East Berlin, diggers could also look for buildings that had been evacuated because of their close proximity to the wall.[20]

The students made a bold decision to dig their tunnel in a popular location in Berlin, partly because they hoped the East Germans would be less likely to think someone would be so brash as to attempt an escape project in such an obvious location. They started digging on May 9, 1962, in a basement in West Berlin. They first had to dig down fifteen feet, to get below the sewer pipes and streetcar lines, and to create enough distance so their digging and equipment could not be heard above on the street. Even with their elaborate plans, they soon realized they needed more people and more money for supplies.

The students knew that a Hollywood production company was working on a tunnel movie in West Berlin, so they thought they might be able to get funding that way. They approached the MGM crew and offered to let them film scenes of a real tunnel dig in exchange for supply money. The production company said no, but someone involved in the meeting knew that NBC was looking for a tunnel project.[21]

This was exactly what NBC wanted: a serious tunnel project unknown at least to other American journalists. NBC wanted exclusivity and the students needed money for supplies. They began negotiating a price. This is when Piers Anderton knew he had to get NBC in New York involved in the process. One of the realities of living in West Berlin was knowing that any phone call to outside the city could be monitored by both the Americans and maybe the East Germans. Anderton would not talk about the tunnel project by telephone, telegraph, or mail, so he waited until he headed to New York for his wedding.

Initially, the diggers wanted $50,000. Eventually NBC and the students settled on $7,500, with $5,000 more when the project was complete. Frank knew the payment would be seen as controversial, so he told very few people about the arrangement. The true amount was never disclosed during the months the project came under attack. His boss, NBC News president William McAndrew, was aware of the arrangement and the money, but the two men kept it from NBC lawyers or budget administrators. They moved the money into a separate account where the Berlin bureau could access it to pay the diggers.[22]

Because of the communication issues, the Berlin crew would only discuss the project with Reuven Frank in person. Frank did not risk a trip to Germany because his arrival would immediately be known among the tight-knit group of competitive Western journalists. Instead, they would meet in other European cities and discuss the tunnel project only in loud bars and restaurants where there was less chance of anyone overhearing their conversations. On purpose, Frank knew little about the diggers or the tunnel. He did not even know the location until the day he arrived in Berlin when the project was almost complete.

With the NBC money, the students expanded the project. They brought on more people and started a twenty-four-hour rotation of digging. NBC had agreed it would only film in the tunnel when Spina, Sesta, or Schroedter were working, or anyone else who agreed to be identified on camera. As the project expanded to more than twenty diggers, most of those involved did not know about the NBC agreement, and very few of the diggers ever saw Klaus and Peter Dehmel when they would periodically visit to film the progress.[23]

Fatal Summer

Even with both Khrushchev and Kennedy hoping the Berlin Wall issue would fade from news coverage, events kept happening along the wall to keep journalists busy. Khrushchev warned East German leader Ulbricht that he did not want any confrontations along the wall that were not necessary. East Germans were not to shoot women or children, or anyone who made it into West Berlin territory. Ulbricht, on the other hand, may not have minded if a minor conflict along the wall led to military action, which could bring West Berlin under East German control.

Just two weeks after the students started their tunnel, a fatal encounter on the border topped the headlines. An East German teenager, Walter Tews, jumped into the Spandau Ship Canal in an attempt to swim across to West Berlin. East German police shouted at him to stop; when he kept swimming, they opened fire with automatic weapons. Tews was hit but was still able to make it to the other side, where he was trapped in an alcove along the canal wall. West Berlin police attempted to pull him to safety, but the East Germans kept shooting, prompting West Berlin police to fire back. Tews survived, but during the gunfire East German Private Peter Goring was killed. Goring became a symbol of Western aggression in East Germany, with the news stories calling it an ambush, neglecting to mention Tews, or that the East Germans had fired their weapons first.[24]

Less than a month later, a skirmish at the East Berlin side of a tunnel ended with another East German martyr. Not far from Checkpoint Charlie, on June 18, 1962, Private Reinhold Huhn and other Vopos confronted a group of people walking into a building near the wall. One of the people pulled a gun and shot at Huhn as the group escaped through a tunnel in the building, while Vopos returned fire. Huhn later died from gunshot wounds and became another symbol of the Cold War, with streets, schools, and other buildings later bearing his name. Western media insisted that Huhn was killed by his own men during the shootout.[25]

Throughout the summer, as the NBC film crew periodically visited the tunnel dig, under strict secrecy efforts, the project progressed beyond the wall and into East Berlin. Each new story of violence along the wall, or a project betrayed by an informant, caused concern for the diggers, especially since the effort now involved so many people, any of whom could turn out to be an informant.

The tunnel project itself was a backbreaking process with diggers forced to sit down in the small tunnel, hunched over their shovels and stabbing forward in the dark and then contorting their bodies to get the shovelful of dirt behind them. The dirt was loaded into small carts on rails that were taken to the Western side. The project stalled for a few weeks when a water main broke and flooded the tunnel. The diggers had to delicately tell West Berlin utility officials about the broken pipe without letting them know about the tunnel.[26]

On June 21, Secretary of State Dean Rusk spent two hours in West Berlin during a tour of European cities. More than ten thousand people came out to greet Rusk, who visited the wall along with West Berlin mayor Willy Brandt. Rusk called the wall an "affront to human dignity" and promised it would not last. During part of his tour of the area, Secretary of State Rusk stood roughly fifteen feet above where the students were digging under the wall.[27]

Anniversary

Throughout the summer, Frank would periodically check with Berlin to find out when the tunnel would be completed. As producer of the planned documentary, he wanted to be there just as people began escaping from East Berlin. He did not want to arrive earlier than necessary to avoid tipping off other Western journalists in Berlin. Meanwhile, reporters began working on plans for covering the one-year anniversary of the wall, which would occur on August 13, 1962. They expected major protests along the wall because many West Germans were still unhappy the Americans had allowed the barrier to become part of life in the city.

Roughly three months after the start of the NBC tunnel project, CBS found its own tunnel. Correspondent Daniel Schorr planned to run a documentary on the anniversary of the border closing, so he needed a project that would be completed by early August. In late July, Schorr met with a group of diggers who were almost finished with their tunnel and were looking for money and publicity. CBS paid the diggers roughly $1,250 and had one chance to film in the tunnel before dozens of people were scheduled to escape under the wall.[28]

Even though CBS may have had exclusive access inside the tunnel, the project was not a secret. An hour or so before the scheduled escape, reporters and film photographers, including Piers Anderton and the NBC film crew, showed up on the Western side of the wall with a view of the East Berlin escape location.

Unfortunately, the plan was also not a secret to the East German police. West German secret police spotted a "heavy concentration of uniformed personnel"[29] gathered around the tunnel entrance in East Berlin and warned their sources, diverting a truck with thirty-seven would-be escapees. Observers on the West side of the wall watched the Vopos arresting two people with the possibility of more than a dozen in custody.

One news crew was noticeably absent that evening among the reporters and film photographers: CBS. Daniel Schorr and his main photographer were not waiting at the Western terminus of the escape route. There was talk that the US government was somehow involved in warning CBS about the compromised project. Schorr would not have a tunnel escape documentary for the anniversary of the closing of the border on August 13, 1962.

NBC also did not have a tunnel escape documentary ready for the anniversary. Reuven Frank was still waiting for the signal from Anderton and Stindt that the tunnel project was close to completion. The Technical University students had now been digging for more than three months with no target date for completion. They lost three weeks of digging waiting for the water main break to be fixed.

The project took on another leader when Hasso Herschel joined the group. Herschel spent years in an East German labor camp before escaping to West Berlin and was determined to get his family out of East Germany. The group added on two more diggers who had been working on another tunnel project that was discovered by the East Germans. These two men were greeted with suspicion and the leaders would not trust them with any sensitive information, even though they already knew the tunnel route.[30]

With each passing month and more people involved in the dig, the project leaders increasingly worried about the chance of discovery. Less ambitious tunnel projects with fewer people had been compromised. Precautions intensified. Diggers were getting anxious. The project leaders made the bold decision to change the East Berlin terminus of the tunnel to save time and to avoid the possibility the East Germans knew the original plan. They decided to come up in a basement on Schonholzer Strasse, one street closer to the wall than the original plan. Only a few people were told about the change in location.

The anniversary of the border closing brought the expected protests and calls for a stronger American reaction. Five days later, a tragic death at the wall became one of the most emotional moments in the entire history of the East-West conflict. On August 17, 1962, Peter Fechter, age eighteen, and a friend tried a risky escape within view of the Checkpoint Charlie border crossing. The two men took off running across the death strip and scaled the first barbed wire barrier. East German police began shooting at them. The first man was able to avoid the bullets and scale the eight-foot wall to safety. But as Fechter reached the wall, he was shot in the hip and hit the ground. He was alive but could not move. As crowds on the West side ran to the wall, Fechter was moaning for help. The East Germans made no move to rescue him and the West Berlin police were not allowed to scale the wall. Crowds on the West side could see him squirming on the ground next to the wall as Fechter's cries grew fainter. People begged the American military at Checkpoint Charlie to help since they had the right to cross the border. According to at least one report, an American soldier told bystanders that it wasn't his problem. This supposed interaction became a sore point for West Germans for years.

East German police finally came and took Fechter's now motionless body away, shooting angry glances at the people yelling from the other side of the wall. Fechter's death sparked the most violent protests since the wall was built. Day after day, angry people arrived at the wall and harassed Soviet soldiers who came across the border daily to guard a Russian memorial in West Berlin. The protests threatened to turn into another international crisis, fueled by what Berlin Wall historian Frederick Taylor called a combination of "East German brutality, Russian Pride, and West Berlin anger." The United States did not take any action after Fechter's death, hoping the situation would diffuse, which eventually happened. East Germans decided they should make a stronger effort to help wounded escapers in the future to avoid the bad publicity.[31]

Tunnel Escape

A few weeks after Fechter's death at the wall, Reuven Frank received word that the tunnel was almost finished. Frank and NBC film editor Gerald Polikoff flew to West Berlin, arriving on Thursday, September 13. Gary Stindt and Piers Anderton met the two men at Tegel airport and told them the escape was set to begin the following evening. As they were heading to the NBC office, Stindt and Anderton drove by the tunnel location, still unknown to Frank. The diggers had chosen one of the most popular spots along the wall: Bernauer Strasse, the street where the border ran right along the building line.

They were digging in a building behind a gas station. The building was partially destroyed during World War II, but the upper floors were being used as, of all things, a swizzle stick factory. The diggers had basement access where they could come and go without detection. Reuven Frank realized that he and David Brinkley had stood very close to that location on Bernauer Strasse the day the border was closed in 1961.

After driving by the tunnel site and hearing the latest updates from Stindt and Anderton, Frank and Polikoff settled in for the marathon viewing of all the film the NBC Berlin crew had shot for the documentary project.

They watched images from the previous year with people jumping out of buildings along Bernauer Strasse. They watched film of the Berlin sewer system, another early escape route. They watched tragic deaths along the wall, including the Peter Fechter incident the previous month. What struck Frank as the hours went by that evening was the digging: the unbelievable work that went into planning and executing that tunnel over the past five months. He watched scenes of the diggers bent over in the three-foot by three-foot tunnel, thrusting their shovel forward into the darkness.

One reason the tunnel took so long is the students planned an escape route that would last. They built a rail line so carts could easily move the excavated dirt to the Western side. They even installed a telephone for quick communication with the forward location of the digging. Water pumps were added to dry out the tunnel during the water main breaks and major rains. Peter and Klaus Dehmel had filmed all these parts of the project.

Another reason the tunnel took so long was the length. The underground route stretched roughly 140 yards. Even with digging shifts that covered twenty-four hours a day, diggers had to remove a lot of dirt to cover that kind of ground. One serious problem rarely discussed in tunnel work: Where do you put the dirt? It was hard enough to find a basement on the Western side with enough privacy for undetected digging. They also needed room to store the dirt where it would not be found. In this case, they were able to build wooden partitions in basement rooms and pile up the soil there.

Frank and Polikoff experienced all these scenes as they watched the film that Thursday evening past midnight and then again on Friday morning. But they did not just see the process; they watched images of why these students were putting in so much time to complete the tunnel. Domenico Sesta had been able to sneak a film camera over to East Berlin to visit the home of Peter Schmidt. Schmidt was a college friend of Spina and Sesta, but the wall meant he could no longer cross the border and go to school. Schmidt lived in East Berlin with his mother, his wife, and their eighteen-month-old daughter, Annett. In addition to the Schmidt family, Sesta had secretly filmed the train ride through East Berlin and even a location where the people might meet before the escape.

By Friday afternoon, Frank knew he had the elements of a compelling documentary. He may have had some of the same thoughts as movie director Robert Siodmak as he worked on the fictionalized version of the "Tunnel 28" escape. The amount of work and risk these people endured showed how important it was to help family and friends escape communist oppression. That is why Frank had the confidence to call his boss in New York and ask for a ninety-minute primetime timeslot for the documentary before anyone had escaped.

NBC had a film camera set up in an apartment with a view of the building on Schonholzer Strasse in East Berlin where the people would enter to access the tunnel. Peter and Klaus Dehmel positioned themselves in the basement off Bernauer Strasse in West Berlin to film the first people to crawl up the ladder from the tunnel.

And they waited.

The expected evening escape dragged into the early morning hours, and the film crews had not returned. The plan called for Domenico Sesta's fiancée and other couriers to head to East Berlin and round up the people who were supposed to escape. Unfortunately, most of the other couriers either decided not to take the risk or missed their rendezvous, so one person had to try and reach most of the people waiting for the signal. The organizers also decided to keep two suspicious diggers in the tunnel on the Western side and not let them leave to avoid the new East Berlin location from being shared with East German police.

Frank was not in communication with the rescue scene, so as the evening wore on, he did not know if it was delayed, compromised, or successful. The crew became so restless around 11:30 p.m. that Frank and a few staff members drove by the location, not slowing down, just to see if there was any evidence of problems. They did not see any activity or police presence on either side, which was a good sign.

Finally, at 2:00 a.m., the film crew burst into the NBC office with great news. The tunnel escape had been a success. More than two dozen people had been able to crawl for roughly twelve minutes from East to West Berlin. Halfway through the muddy tunnel, they looked up to see a sign letting them know they were safely across the border into West Berlin. When they got to the end of the tunnel, they were greeted with a photo of Peter Fechter, cut out of a newspaper and posted on the wall.

After a few hours' sleep, Frank, Polikoff, and the NBC Berlin staff watched the Dehmels' dramatic rescue footage. Frank did not want to risk trying to get twenty hours of film out of West Berlin, so he and Polikoff proceeded to edit the film into a very rough version of the documentary.

Unfortunately for the diggers, there had been another water main break just before the start of the escape on Friday, and the tunnel began to fill with water. After the group escaped on Friday, more escaped on Saturday, for a total of twenty-nine. At that point, the water was so deep in the tunnel that it was considered too risky to use. This caused a rift among the diggers because some wanted to pump out the water to help others in East Berlin. Others felt there was too great a chance the tunnel would be discovered. The West Berlin police knew about the tunnel project and spread the word among the escape community on both sides of the wall that the tunnel was too dangerous to use and needed to be shut down.[32]

After Frank and Polikoff edited down the film to a rough cut of the documentary, they made plans to head back to New York. First, they had to get out of West Berlin, which meant flying through East German airspace with a film canister containing the tunnel and escape footage. They made it from West Berlin to Frankfurt. The two men boarded the plane to New York, and Frank put the tunnel film package under his seat. Before the plane door closed, police came on board and approached Frank and asked him to stand up. The police asked Frank and Polikoff to move because West Berlin mayor Willy Brandt and his staff needed to get on the flight and wanted the NBC seats.

The two men quickly moved, trying to avoid causing suspicion. Frank forgot the film cannister under the seat. He watched helplessly as Mayor Brandt sat down in the seat. The raw cut of NBC's dramatic tunnel documentary flew across the Atlantic Ocean just beneath the mayor of West Berlin. At the end of the flight, Frank nervously approached his original seat after Brandt got off the plane and found the film still sitting where he left it.

NBC's luck continued because news of the dramatic Friday evening escape did not even make the American papers until the following Monday. The first accounts acknowledged the twenty-nine people who escaped the first night and following morning. The escape became known as "Tunnel 29," referencing one more person reaching West Berlin than the "Tunnel 28" project in January that had prompted the Hollywood movie.[33]

Frank continued working on the documentary with Piers Anderton in New York. The Dehmel brothers had not been able to fit a bulky sound camera or audio recorder into the tunnel, so almost all the footage was silent, which was a common approach for documentaries of the period. Instead of natural sound, Frank hired jazz double bass player Eddie Safranski to write the musical score for the project.

Meanwhile, NBC decided to schedule the documentary, titled simply *The Tunnel*, for Friday evening, October 31, at 7:30 p.m., preempting the network's European circus show, *International Showtime* with Don Ameche. The documentary would be up against, among other programs, *Rawhide* on CBS and *The Flintstones* on ABC. The network held off on announcing the program, as Frank worked on the ninety-minute production.[34]

NBC Project under Attack

Unfortunately for the network, NBC waited too long to promote its exclusive program, allowing reporters from other news outlets to set the tone for negative coverage over the next few weeks. Instead of framing the documentary as a daring and historic rescue effort, *Time* magazine first announced NBC's plans in a short article about unsavory methods of getting people from East to West Berlin. NBC's payment to the diggers in exchange for film rights was presented as unethical journalism that tarnished "the difficult and dangerous work of idealistic diggers." The *New York Times* picked up on the *Time* article, emphasizing the idea that the original tunnel organizers had pocketed the leftover NBC money while the rest of the diggers worked for free. NBC was put in the awkward position of refusing to even confirm that it was working on such a project.[35]

NBC waited almost a full week before announcing *The Tunnel* documentary and its scheduled broadcast on Halloween evening. Reuven Frank and Piers Anderton tried to steer the discussion at the press conference announcing the film to the efforts being made to help people flee communism. Instead, reporters questioned the ethics of NBC paying the organizers for exclusive access during the tunnel dig. Frank countered by saying the tunnel was already underway when NBC got involved, so it clearly could not be a considered an NBC project.

The criticisms of NBC's actions intensified a few days later when seventeen of the diggers held a press conference in West Berlin to demand that the network cancel the documentary because the payment tainted the altruistic work they had done. The students claimed the three organizers had never told the rest of the crew about the monetary arrangement and then disappeared after the escape. A spokesman for the group, Eberhard Weyrauch, insisted the diggers were not paid to dig the tunnel, and "our only purpose was to help friends and relatives to get out."[36]

In addition to the diggers, the West Berlin Senat urged NBC to stop the project. Police director Heinrich Albertz said he was worried that a film showing people digging the tunnel and those who escaped could put them and their families in danger and give the East Germans better information about tunnel logistics. NBC's meek response was that the diggers and the West Berlin authorities did not have complete information about the project and the documentary.[37]

The pressure kept mounting on NBC to cancel the documentary. Just two weeks before it was scheduled to run, the State Department and the East German government added their concerns. A State Department spokesman said airing the tunnel footage would be "highly undesirable" and would complicate matters in Berlin. The East German government sent a formal protest to the US government, calling the NBC documentary project "an attack on the state border."[38]

When NBC defended the documentary again, the State Department ratcheted up the rhetoric. Spokesman Lincoln White referred to *The Tunnel* project as "risky, irresponsible," and "undesirable." These characterizations were printed in newspapers across the country. White told reporters that the

State Department had asked both CBS and NBC to stay away from tunnel projects in August and that CBS had complied, but NBC had ignored the government's plea.[39]

If Reuven Frank had been looking for support from the journalism community, he was sorely disappointed. Those that weighed in on the controversy mostly supported the government, especially NBC's network rivals. CBS attempted to turn its tunnel project failure into a public relations success by painting its decision as the sober, correct course of action. CBS president Richard Salant told reporters that his staff had been working on a tunnel project but canceled it after the State Department told them of "certain intelligence information on the U.S. national interest aspect of the Berlin wall tunneling operations." ABC News president James Hagerty, formerly President Eisenhower's press secretary, said NBC was providing communists "valuable propaganda" and "embarrassing the United States and its allies."[40]

The most vicious attack came from *New York Times* television columnist Jack Gould. In a column dedicated to *The Tunnel* controversy, he referred to the NBC News staff as "adventurous laymen" dabbling in a dangerous topic they did not understand. If Reuven Frank's bosses at NBC, and parent company Radio Corporation of America (RCA), were starting to get cold feet about a television program that had stirred up such ill will, world events would quickly push this controversy off center stage.[41]

Cold War Brink

At the start of the week of October 22, 1962, NBC had done enough behind-the-scenes negotiating that it felt it could cut down on the negative reaction to its tunnel project, which was scheduled to run in just a week. The West Berlin Senat withdrew its objections when Frank and NBC made it clear they would not show the faces of any people who did not sign a waiver. If people could not be cut out of the film, their faces would be obscured in the footage. This information also seemed to reduce the concerns of the State Department. While spokesman Lincoln White did not rescind the strong criticism, he made it clear it was ultimately NBC's decision on whether or not the program would run.[42]

On that Monday at 7:00 p.m., the negotiations over *The Tunnel* project stopped. President John F. Kennedy had asked for network time to make a speech to the American public. Fifty million Americans tuned in to watch the president accuse the Soviet Union of building missile bases in Cuba: "The purpose of these bases can be none other than to provide a nuclear strike capability against the Western Hemisphere."[43]

While most Americans learned about the Cuban Missile Crisis during that speech, Kennedy and his staff had figured out the true intentions of the Soviet Union during the previous week. While NBC had been lobbying Secretary of State Dean Rusk and others in the Kennedy administration about the tunnel project, many of those same people were secretly meeting as a group known as the Executive Committee, or Excomm, discussing how to respond to the new Soviet threat. Initially, a tough military response, including invading the country or bombing the bases, seemed to be the most popular course of action.

But as the group met over the next few days, the mood shifted to a less aggressive approach of setting up American ships off the coast of Cuba and keeping Soviet ships from the island. After deciding on a blockade, Kennedy first met with congressional leaders on the Monday afternoon before his live televised address. Even though the threat was in Cuba, Kennedy felt the American response could trigger problems in Berlin. Excomm had even worked on a plan to re-create the Berlin Airlift if the Soviet Union shut down access to the city. Meanwhile, NBC quietly postponed *The Tunnel*, saying that because of the Cuban Missile Crisis, it was not the "appropriate time" to run the documentary. Instead, the network made plans to run a special program on the Cuban missile situation during the October 31, 7:30 p.m. timeslot.[44]

From October 22 to 28, the United States and the Soviet Union came the closest to war than at any time during the Cold War. As historian Robert Caro put it, "These were days of terrible moments." Both Kennedy and Khrushchev talked tough publicly but kept private communications open for a peaceful resolution. US warships moved into position around Cuba and waited for Russian cargo ships on their way to the island. No one knew what would happen if the Soviet Union ignored the blockade.[45]

The darkest day of the crisis was Saturday, October 27. Khrushchev awakened to find out that an American U2 spy plane had been shot down over Cuba, killing the pilot. Cuban leader Fidel Castro felt an American invasion was inevitable, so he had told his pilots to shoot down any American planes. Members of Excomm began working on a military strike or invasion to take place on Monday. The group asked Robert F. Kennedy to set up a short-term Cuban government to put in place after the invasion.

Before the U2 plane incident, the two sides were working on an agreement by which the United States would agree not to invade Cuba and the Soviet Union would remove the missiles. Khrushchev realized the Americans were not going to accept the missiles in Cuba, and he did not feel the military advantage was worth going to war. After the death of the American pilot, the Kennedy administration let the Soviet leader know the Excomm group was now ready to take out the missile bases through invasion or bombing, so if he wanted a peaceful resolution, he had better move quickly.[46]

Khrushchev composed a message to Kennedy saying if the United States agreed not to invade Cuba, the Soviet Union would "dismantle the arms which you described as offensive,"[47] and take them out of Cuba. To make sure the offer was not lost in transmission, Radio Moscow also broadcast the message. Khrushchev told his military leaders in Cuba to stop construction and keep the planes on the ground to avoid any confrontations.

By Sunday evening, October 28, the immediate threat of war had passed. While the Soviets and Americans were thankful to have avoided a military battle, Castro was furious with Khrushchev for giving up the missiles without at least getting the Americans to shut down the Guantanamo Bay military base.

With the weekend resolution to the Cuban missile confrontation, Reuven Frank and the NBC News crew produced a ninety-minute documentary on the crisis, *A Clear and Present Danger,* broadcast that Wednesday evening, in the original tunnel project timeslot.

Meanwhile, *The Tunnel* was still on hold. Frank pestered his boss, William McAndrew, for a decision. McAndrew told him to give him some time. Frank could not understand why his project was still considered a controversial program to run. The film shows people successfully escaping communism and East Berlin. The recent Cuban crisis had shown how dangerous the Soviet Union could be. He did not see the project as controversial. Instead, he felt it would be seen as the triumph of democracy over communism.

Reuven Frank was not a patient man. He again visited his boss and this time brought a resignation letter. He told McAndrew that if his employer was so sensitive to government pressure that it could not run a program that celebrated democratic values, he needed to find a job with an organization with more backbone. McAndrew had worked with Frank for a dozen years and knew his personality, so he ignored the letter and told the producer to give him a little time to get the program on the schedule.[48]

While news programs normally did not attract the size of audiences for entertainment programs, NBC did not have as much to lose that season since CBS was the clear leader among the networks in entertainment programming. At the time of *The Tunnel* controversy, CBS had eighteen of the top twenty programs in total viewership, one of the most dominating positions in the short history of American television.[49]

The Tunnel broadcast

Frank put aside his resignation letter. NBC finally rescheduled *The Tunnel* for Monday night, December 10. The network would preempt a new program that had not caught on with the viewers, *Saints and Sinners,* about a fictional New York newspaper-television operation, and the game show *The Price Is Right.* Since documentaries usually did not draw a large audience, *The Tunnel* was scheduled against the top entertainment network's highest-rated night of programming. CBS would be showing the most popular new show of the season, *The Lucy Show,* Lucille Ball's first television series after her divorce from Desi Arnaz, as well as *The Danny Thomas Show* and *The Andy Griffith Show,* all three of which would finish in the top ten in the ratings that season. ABC would be running *The Rifleman* and *Stoney Burke.*[50]

For ninety minutes on that Monday night, *The Tunnel* showed the extensive planning and engineering work involved in digging the 140-yard escape route under the Berlin Wall. The viewers met the students who planned the tunnel and their best friend and his family that they were hoping to rescue from East Berlin. The first hour included all the dangers and setbacks involved in digging the tunnel: flooding, illness, and potential betrayals by people involved in the project. The final thirty minutes included the dramatic escape from the vantage point of the top of the vertical portion of the tunnel in the basement of the building just off Bernauer Strasse in West Berlin. Viewers watched men and women climbing up the wooden ladder to the cellar, with anxious and nervous looks on their faces, their clothes dirty and torn. Children and babies were lifted up out of the darkness to safety. The people cleaned up in water basins placed at the top of the escape tunnel and calmed down anxious children. Eventually, they disappeared into the West Berlin night, ready to begin their new lives on the other side of the wall.

A Critical and Popular Success

The Tunnel proved to be not only a success for NBC News but for the entire network. Just as Reuven Frank had discovered when he watched the Dehmel brothers' footage back in September, the film had all the drama of a good fiction film. Instead of an overview of all the escape methods in Berlin (his original idea), Frank focused on one tunnel, one rescue effort, and the people involved in it. *The Tunnel* received mostly strong reviews in print publications, with many making the comparison to a Hollywood movie or a television drama.

More important for NBC, *The Tunnel* attracted a large audience, especially for a specially scheduled news program. The documentary held its own against the powerhouse CBS lineup that Monday night. More than 13.5 million people tuned into *The Tunnel*, with more than 10 million watching the entire program, compared with just under 15 million average viewers for *The Lucy Show*. When compared with average ratings for weekly series for the 1962–1963 season, *The Tunnel* would have finished in the top thirty of all network television programs.[51]

The National Academy of Television Arts and Sciences honored *The Tunnel* in 1963 with three of the top Emmy Awards for the season. Piers Anderton was recognized for Outstanding Achievement in International Reporting, and Reuven Frank won in the category of Outstanding Documentary or Non-Fiction Special. In the crowning achievement, *The Tunnel* was chosen as The Program of the Year, besting all other entertainment and nonfiction programs that season.[52]

Digging beneath *The Tunnel*

Reuven Frank's dogged defense of *The Tunnel* showed great prescience. The 1962 tunnel project under Bernauer Strasse was, and continues to be, a great story. Tunnel escapes are romantic, daring, and courageous, and they spark people's imaginations. Several Berlin Wall tunnel stories appeared in newspapers in the West in the first years after the border closed. In the fall of 1962 alone, two other motion picture versions of tunnel escapes were offered to the American public in addition to NBC's documentary: CBS's fictional tunnel story, "Tunnel to Freedom," on its *Armstrong Circle Theater* in October, and MGM's fictional version of "Tunnel 28," directed by Robert Siodmak and retitled *Escape from East Berlin*, released to theaters in December.[53]

The story behind the story is just as intriguing: not just digging the tunnel, but also NBC's (and CBS's) efforts to document the process to help Western audiences understand and empathize with those determined to escape and help others get out of communist East Germany. The diggers showed the most courage, but the Dehmel brothers also risked being caught while filming for NBC. Frank showed courage by threatening to quit if his network would not run the program, and, to a degree, NBC showed courage by appearing to stand behind the project until the Cuban Missile Crisis made it easy to at least postpone the broadcast.

Frank also recognized the value of the story behind the story. He wrote an article, "The Making of *The Tunnel*," for *Television Quarterly* the next year. He included a chapter on the project in his broadcast memoir, *Out of Thin Air*. A number of television and theatrical movies about the NBC tunnel, or Berlin Wall tunnels in general, have been made in both Germany and the United States in the past half-century. In just the past few years, a book about the NBC project, *The Tunnels,* has been published, and a top Hollywood director bought the rights to that version.[54]

The Tunnel story on its own, however, leaves too many unanswered questions. Why did the documentary spark such strong negative reactions among other journalists? Why would Western government officials protest a film that celebrates democracy over communism? How did Frank know he had a story that could connect with viewers? To understand the answers to these questions, *The Tunnel* production and reception must be seen as part of a larger story, a critical juncture in American journalism history.

The Tunnel might have been one of Frank's favorite career productions, but his larger legacy in journalism history is in the nightly television newscast format. At the time of *The Tunnel,* he had been working in television news for a dozen years and had developed a strong sense of how to use the medium to tell the news of the day. His *Huntley-Brinkley Report* was the most watched and honored network television newscast as the audience for television news continued to grow exponentially.

The critical and popular success of *The Tunnel* helped cement Frank's ideas on the power of television news just as he was called upon to justify a major expansion of network television news. The resulting memo provided both specific practices and general ideas on why the American public was turning to television news to learn about their community and the world.

The audience embrace of television news caused alarm for people and organizations focused on printed communication. Newspapers and magazines lashed out at the new medium, judging television to be inferior to words on paper. The proper role, and medium, of the journalist was playing out in the midst of the Cold War, in a period when journalists and government officials often believed they were working together to project the West from communism.

The rest of the book explores the histories and roles of various media platforms and groups and their interactions with each other and with the government during the Cold War. *The Tunnel* documentary and the rise of television news are part of a critical juncture in American media history, when the platforms and groups clashed over shifting fortunes. The bonds and fissures between them were exposed and put on display.

First, we take a look at how television emerged from decades of promise and expectations to become the most powerful mass medium in the United States, and the print journalist who took a chance on the new medium and developed into one of the top television producers in just a dozen years.

CHAPTER TWO
Parallel Paths

Television, the Cold War, and Reuven Frank

IN SEPTEMBER 1947, the bulletin board in the *Newark Evening News* newsroom signaled that a new reporter at the paper just might have some promise. Editor Henry Coit tacked up a story from the previous afternoon's paper for all to read, with his added approval: "VERY NICE STUFF!" Fresh out of Columbia University's Graduate School of Journalism, Reuven Frank had landed his first job at the New Jersey afternoon paper. If Coit had not drawn attention to it, few may have noticed a story of fewer than 500 words buried on page 13 with the headline "No Tears for 'Professor.'"[1]

Frank's feature story tapped into growing concerns about a new technology seeping into American culture, especially in the New York City area: television. In Frank's story, television threatened the ambience of the downtown tavern. He quoted unnamed bar owners and musicians on how television was ruining the family and romantic atmosphere of the corner bar. The "Professor" of the headline is a piano player in a downtown Newark bar: "'Television?' said mine host scornfully as he wiped the mahogany bar. 'Nuts, I say! And I say it again.' He said it again. 'Nuts! I would not have that stuff in my bar. It attracts the wrong kind of crowd, transients, temporaries, one-beer nursers.'"[2]

In Frank's story, the corner bar without television is one of the last places where people can sing and harmonize along with the musicians. People can have conversations. Romance can flourish. By contrast, television is distracting, both for the customers and the bartenders. People crowd around the set for sporting events and "if the bartender has a bet, brother, you can die of thirst!"[3]

Coit may have been drawn to the story because of the colorful characters and familiar scenes Frank evokes in the article. He may also have been charmed by the dismissive tone toward television, which had been heralded as the next big thing for decades.

If Frank's corner bar crew disliked television's disruptive nature in September 1947, an event the next month would provide an even sharper image of the future for tavern patrons in the New York City area. The first televised baseball World Series in October 1947 featured two hometown teams, the New York Yankees versus the Brooklyn Dodgers. All three New York City television stations (WABD, WNBT, and WCBS) broadcast the seven-game series won by the Yankees. Appliance stores had a run on new sets just before the event, adding to the roughly 50,000 televisions scattered in bars, home, and apartments in the range of New York City station signals. Nine out of ten televisions in bars and taverns were tuned to the series, compared to about four out of ten in homes and apartments, bringing the Yankees-Dodgers games to close to four million people, the largest television audience up to that point in history.[4]

Television would disrupt much more than just live music and conversation in the neighborhood tavern. Within a decade, television became the most powerful mass medium in the United States, and eventually around the world. In hindsight, Frank could have situated his story in any American newspaper newsroom, given the upheaval television brought to print journalism in the second half of the twentieth century. Fewer than three years after the article, Reuven Frank moved from newspapers into the sight and sound medium. A quarter-century after he wrote his television bar story, the *Newark Evening News* would be gone, along with many other evening papers, victims of the new medium. Meanwhile, Frank had become one of the most powerful and influential figures in American network television news.

Reuven Frank was a reluctant television news pioneer. He had to be convinced to even visit NBC to see what opportunities might be there for him. The dozen years that elapsed between his start at NBC and the work involved in *The Tunnel* coincided with the dramatic growth of television as a mass medium in the United States, as well as the power and importance of television news. When Frank started in 1950, television news was still an afterthought for most broadcast journalists and broadcasting executives. The next dozen years would see the medium and newscast format expand their scope and influence, eclipsing radio, newsreels, magazines, and eventually newspapers. Reuven Frank worked through it all. When he started, there were few television veterans, so people relied on their previous experiences in print journalism, radio, and newsreels to figure out the best ways to combine film, audio, words, and graphics into a journalistic format.

From Hot to Cold War

Television in the United States began gaining a mass audience in the late 1940s around the time Reuven Frank made the jump from newspapers. This coincided with the volatile period after World War II when the United States' main threats shifted from Germany and Japan to the Soviet Union and China. Many of the American journalists who moved from print and radio to television had spent years covering World War II, dealing with outright government censorship and the constant nudging pressure to present the news from a pro-American viewpoint. The Cold War appeared no less a threat than Adolf Hitler, especially when the Soviet Union detonated its first atomic weapon.

Senator Joseph McCarthy and the witch hunt for communists in the late 1940s and early 1950s get most of the historical attention because of his scorched-earth approach to ferreting out people considered domestic threats, especially in government, movies, and broadcasting. Radio and television journalists always faced stronger government intimidation than print journalists because of the Federal Communication Commission's oversight of all broadcast stations. A more specific threat often came from another direction: the advertisers who made the programs possible.

Beyond the extreme cases of people losing their jobs because of rumored communist sympathies lived the Cold War culture that seeped into all parts of American society, including journalism. Communism became the most important world threat, such that without diligence, democracy and the American way of life were in danger, either through annihilation by atomic weapons or by internal subversion. Americans, including government leaders, politicians, and journalists, generally agreed with this basic premise, so journalists did not need to be pressured to present their stories based on this underlying assumption.

From 1950 to 1962, as Cold War issues and events dominated American culture, Reuven Frank worked on daily newscasts, half-hour weekly public affairs programs, documentaries, and one of the early staples of television, presidential election coverage, from the conventions to election night. All those experiences in moving picture journalism during the 1950s positioned Frank as one of the most seasoned television news journalists and one of the most insightful with regard to the strengths and limitations of news on television. The Cold War and the rise of television were intertwined and, for Frank and everyone else, hard to unravel. Many of the stories that he learned to tell through a combination of moving pictures, sounds, and words involved some aspect of the freedom versus communism ideology. As he sat in that room in Berlin in September 1962 watching hours of film on the digging of the tunnel under the Berlin Wall and eventual escape, Reuven Frank *knew* the program would be powerful.

A Career in Journalism

Reuven Frank was born on December 7, 1920, in Montreal, Canada, and grew up in Toronto. His father, Moses Zebi Frank, was also a journalist. Reuven spent three years at the University of Toronto before his family moved to New York City in 1940, where he finished his degree at City College of New York. He also became a US citizen.

Frank's interest in journalism started with his high school newspaper, and he continued working on school papers throughout his education. He later admitted that he skipped many classes in college to work on stories for the paper. He enrolled in the graduate journalism program at Columbia University but had to leave when he was drafted. Frank spent four years in the US Army, working at a prisoner-of-war camp in Huntsville, Texas, and then overseas as part of a hospital unit, eventually promoted to the rank of sergeant.

When he got out of the army in 1946, Frank made two major life decisions. He married Bernice Kaplow in June, a union that lasted the rest of his life. That fall, he returned to Columbia to complete his master's degree. The job market for journalists was tough because new graduates were competing with returning veterans, many with years of wartime journalism experience. In 1947, he found a job with the *Newark Evening News*, starting in its Elizabeth, New Jersey, bureau, where just a few months later he caught his boss's eye with the television article. He spent two years as a reporter for the paper, followed by a promotion to night city editor.[5]

The first inkling Reuven Frank had that his journalism career might take

48　CHAPTER TWO

a different path than the traditional newspaper and magazine route was his interest in photographs. As part of his job as night city editor for the *Newark Evening News*, he helped choose the front-page photographs and write the captions. Frank became fascinated with the images and how they influenced the look of the paper.

Television as a Punch Line

Frank stayed in touch with some of his fellow Columbia journalism graduates, and they would meet occasionally to trade stories and compare careers. One classmate, Gerald Green, had taken a job with the news department at NBC Television.[6] Green's job at NBC became a running joke in the group because television was not considered a legitimate medium for a serious journalist. In the summer of 1950, Green called Frank to tell him of an opening at NBC. Frank started in with the television jokes before Green gave him a challenge. He told Frank he had nothing to lose by just visiting the television network.

Frank had not considered broadcast news, radio or television, as a career option. Like most people in the United States, he had listened to radio news during World War II and appreciated the immediacy and impact of that format. He first saw a television broadcast in 1940 when he visited the New York World's Fair, which had opened in Flushing Meadows the previous year. NBC and its parent company, the Radio Corporation of America (RCA), had a special building promoting television. The television exhibit included a studio for live performances and a series of television screens to see the program on NBC's New York experimental television station, W2XBS. Frank stopped in the building and sat in the dark theater where he could see the live performance as well as the view on the small television screens.

Frank remembered the RCA display as "marvelous," but his impressions later in the decade as a television viewer left him less than impressed. In scenes reminiscent of his article about the saloon piano player lamenting the introduction of television, Frank occasionally shared dinner with a television when he was night city editor for the *Newark Evening News*. "When I went out and took my half-hour break, I'd go into a bar for a sandwich and a beer," remembered Frank. "They always had a baseball game on . . . and I'd try to watch it but I found it very difficult to watch" because of the blurry picture.[7]

His experiences watching news on television were not any better. After work, he sometimes visited friends who owned a television set and he would ask them to turn on the late news. As a faithful radio news listener, what he saw and heard did not compare to the aural medium. He found the writing to be weak and the newscasts "had little or no film, they had some kind of still picture arrangement which usually missed the cue and . . . I didn't get any information from it or any excitement."[8]

Even with his unfavorable impressions, Frank accepted Green's invitation to visit NBC. He admitted he did not mind getting out of the house for one day since he and his wife had a newborn baby, Peter, who tended to cry in the mornings. What he experienced during that first visit helped convince Reuven Frank that he wanted to work in television news.

Lost and Forgotten History

In Reuven Frank's broadcast memoir, *Out of Thin Air,* he positions the start of network television news, and television news in general, in 1948. He chose that year because in May of 1948, AT&T formally opened a commercial coaxial cable system that could link together television stations in more than a dozen cities along the eastern seaboard. Both major political parties, as well as the Progressive Party, chose Philadelphia that summer for their conventions; partly because the city was situated along that coaxial cable network, allowing the conventions to be viewed live by the largest audience in American history.[9]

Compared to other people who moved into television news in the 1950s, Frank is generous by situating the start of real television news two years before his arrival. In most broadcast histories and oral history interviews, television news seems to begin whenever those authors or interviewees arrived. Their move to television may be anywhere from the late 1940s to the mid-1950s, but the stories are fairly consistent: *There was little before I arrived, and we had to make it up as we went along.* From Don Hewitt in 1948 and Walter Cronkite in 1950 to Fred Friendly and Edward R. Murrow in 1951, along with many others, there is little acknowledgment of the years of experimentation involved in presenting news on television before 1950.[10]

Instead, 1940s television news is usually dismissed or marginalized by anecdotal experiences by Frank and other journalists who started in print or radio and then migrated to television in the 1950s. One of the difficulties in moving beyond this myopic timeline is that very little visual evidence survives from the 1940s. Live television programs (almost all early television was live) could not be saved until 1947 when RCA and the BBC began experimental recordings with a process called kinescope, which involved pointing a 16 mm film camera at a special TV monitor. Kinescopes received their first major workouts at the 1948 political conventions when the daytime proceedings would be recorded and edited for night time audiences. Even with the ability to record the programs, kinescopes were expensive and usually limited to programs that were not time-specific and could be run repeatedly.[11]

News programs had a very short shelf life so were only recorded if they were considered prestige programs, including CBS's *See It Now*, or for functional reasons, such as NBC's *Camel News Caravan*. The NBC newscast's sponsor, the R.J. Reynolds tobacco company, was located in an area, Winston-Salem, North Carolina, that only had one station until 1953 and that station did not run the NBC newscast. NBC would record the newscast periodically and send the kinescope to the sponsor. Some of those recordings have survived.[12]

Television was a money-losing venture during the 1940s and early 1950s, and television executives did not see the value in spending the money to archive important events. In one example from September 1951, RCA executive and former FCC chairman Charles Denny wanted to know why the network did not have recordings of specific portions of the Japanese Peace Treaty broadcasts. NBC Television's Davidson Taylor replied that "there has been no procedure set up for making kinescopes of historic events for archive purposes." Even though parent company RCA helped invent the process just three years later, NBC was farming out its network kinescope recording work to a newsreel company, Paramount, which was charging $375 for the first hour and $200 for each additional hour of a special broadcast.[13]

Because of the lack of moving picture archives of most of 1940s television news and public affairs programming, when later television pioneers ignored or trivialized pre-1950s television news, little evidence existed to mount a defense of the earlier work.

Television News Prehistory

By the time Reuven Frank and other print and radio journalists had moved into television in the early 1950s, a quarter of the homes in the United States already had a television set. The medium had been through decades of experimentation, both in technology and in programming formats. Most histories and scholarship involving pre-1950 television focus more on the technology than the programming.[14]

The first television boom happened in the late 1920s and early 1930s in England, the United States, Germany, and other countries, using a mechanical system of spinning discs in both the cameras and television receivers. In the mid-1930s, advancements from inventor Philo Farnsworth, RCA, and others transitioned the medium from a mechanical into an electronic format, resulting in much sharper images. RCA also experimented with "remote pickup" using mobile units, which allowed for live coverage away from the television studio.[15]

In the United States, the government deemed television "experimental," meaning operators could not try to make money on the service, either through running commercials or selling receivers. The lack of revenue along with the devastation of the Great Depression in the United States, and the start of World War II in Europe, slowed or stopped most television experimentation around the world.

Throughout the mechanical and early electronic era, American television operators attempted a variety of programming formats. Since most programming was confined to live studio performances with little money to pay performers, early viewers saw a parade of vaudeville performers willing to try the new medium for the exposure. A few stations experimented with news and public affairs programs. The CBS station in New York City, W2XAB, presented election results for the 1932 presidential race and also simulcast a radio news information program, *Bill Schudt's Going to Press*. Stations in the Los Angeles area filmed local events and presented them on television, much like a theater newsreel.[16]

The British Broadcasting Company had the most extensive television service in this period. The BBC built a special studio and 220-foot iconic television tower at the Alexandra Palace in North London and presented three hours of daily programming at a cost of two million dollars a year. After a few years of this service, only 12,000 people had purchased television sets, a bad omen for US companies that had already spent $13 million on the technology but would be relying on a large audience to lure in advertisers to pay the high cost of television broadcasting.[17]

By the late 1930s, television had become more than a curiosity for several European and Asian countries. Japan, Italy, Poland, Sweden, and the Netherlands were experimenting with technology and making plans for television service, often with help from US and British broadcasting companies. In Moscow, the Soviet Union was constructing a massive Palace of the Soviets government building near the Kremlin that would include television broadcasting and a broadcast tower that would be visible more than sixty miles from the city. In Paris, a television antenna was installed at the top of the Eiffel Tower connected by coaxial cable to a nearby studio. In Germany, television was part of the national postal service. The technology was even used for video telephone calls in certain locations. With the Nazis in power, television became another propaganda tool with promises of a national service.

World War II stopped almost all television operations in Europe and Asia. The BBC television service came to an abrupt halt, in the middle of a cartoon, on September 1, 1939, the day Great Britain declared war on Germany.[18]

US Television Service during the War

In the United States, the government did not nationalize television, but still would not allow it to assume commercial status because of technological uncertainties. RCA had already invested several million dollars in television and would benefit from selling transmitters, broadcast equipment, and television sets if the medium gained an audience. NBC began regular programming in 1939 in conjunction with the New York World's Fair as RCA's way to sell television sets, an aggressive approach to force Congress and the Roosevelt administration to change television from experimental to commercial status.

The Federal Communication Commission finally offered commercial licenses in July 1941, but only if the television stations promised to broadcast fifteen hours of programming a week and upgrade to a new level of technical standards. Just two stations, NBC (WNBT) and CBS (WCBW) in New York City, had the resources to promise the minimum weekly broadcast hours that year. Other stations in Los Angeles, Chicago, Philadelphia, and Schenectady, New York, chose to stay experimental in 1941 to avoid the fifteen-hour broadcast schedule.

The commercial licenses also forced the two stations to follow FCC radio requirements by offering a percentage of news and public affairs programs. NBC chose to simulcast Lowell Thomas's popular radio newscast on television, bringing added value to Thomas's radio sponsor, Sunoco. In 1941, CBS could not meet all FCC technical requirements, so it could not run commercials. Without any advertising expectations, the CBS television staff was kept small and the budget was limited, forcing experimentation in all areas of programming. To fill thirty minutes of air time each day, WCBW chose to start both its afternoon and evening programming blocks with a fifteen-minute newscast, mimicking the time structure popular on radio at the time.

Since radio was the powerful and profitable medium at broadcasting companies like CBS and NBC, television attracted a staff that either could not get hired in radio or had some kind of visual background. The famous CBS radio news staff, including Paul White, Edward R. Murrow, and others, had little to do with CBS television news throughout most of the 1940s.

The CBS television staff in the early 1940s included film and still photographers, documentarians, artists, and graphic designers. As explored in chapter 4, some of the original CBS television staff had strong connections to the documentary film movement in New York City at the time. The CBS television news effort in 1941 only included two full-time staff members, one to write the news and the other to deliver it, so the visualization of the news became a group effort of several members of the overall television department.

Without any reporters, full-time film photographers, or even access to film of current stories, the crew concentrated on different ways to visualize the top stories of the day. The lasting impact of the early to mid-1940s CBS television news effort is the template for the television newscast structure that has survived into the twenty-first century: each story delivered with a different combination of visual and auditory prompts, depending on what was available and best suited for conveying the information of that specific story, presented by a main newscaster. The crew relied on maps, artwork, cartoons, props, live interviews, and film. Staff members also invented early versions of animated graphics.

American television's growth was slow and tentative for most of the 1940s. After the United States entered the war in December 1941, World War II needs siphoned off the resources and engineering staff. Most stations shut down their studios and stopped live productions for a few years and started back with reduced program schedules when the war started to shift in favor of the Allies in 1944.

Business and government leaders had targeted television as one of the new industries that could spur economic growth and avoid another Depression after the war. When the FCC finally decided on a specific technical format in 1947, American television started an amazing diffusion across the country. The 1947 New York World Series was one of the key events to show the potential popularity of the medium because of the advanced state of television in the city and the interest in the crosstown series between the Yankees and Dodgers. Manufacturers turned out 200,000 sets in 1947, and the number of stations jumped from nine to nineteen.

By the time the political conventions arrived in Philadelphia in the summer of 1948, at least 425,000 television sets had been sold in the United States. and manufacturers were turning out 50,000 a month. The AT&T coaxial cable service connected eighteen stations in nine cities, from Boston to Richmond. A separate Midwest network had also been established and the two networks were connected in early 1949.[19]

A Writing Process without Words

Reuven Frank's career epiphany happened in a film screening room in East Harlem. In 1950, NBC television news was located in a building at 106th and Park Avenue,[20] far from the NBC radio operation in Rockefeller Center in midtown Manhattan. NBC moved its newsreel operation to that location in 1948, next to the New York Central railroad tracks, because the building was also home to the *RKO-Pathé News* studios, the company NBC hired to develop its news film. NBC also wanted to keep its television news operations away from Rockefeller Center for safety concerns because of the flammability of film in that era.[21]

During his interview with NBC, Frank met many of the people working on the network and local newscasts and toured the facilities, but what stuck with him was the screening room. More than a half-century later, Reuven Frank still remembered the dark room with the empty theater seats, the three men sitting behind a table, the projector running 35 mm film of people marching in Berlin streets for some forgotten event. He was witnessing a fairly common practice in newsreels and television. The men were watching unedited film and deciding how much to use, in what order the scenes should be edited, and what words should be written to accompany the film for the story. He thought to himself, "What a way to live!"[22]

When pressed on what could be so life-changing about a film screening of some long-forgotten story, Frank had to think for a second: "The manipulation of pictures . . . a writing process without words. The arrangement of ideas. And you know, good pictures are matchless. The 'doing things' that got to me. You start with raw material and you make something of it."[23]

The screening room experience convinced Frank to put aside his previous thoughts on television journalism and quit his job at the *Newark Evening News*. By taking the NBC job, he improved his salary from $90 to $110 a week. He said his parents were "horrified" at his decision to make such a drastic job change with a new baby, but his wife and her parents thought it was a good time to take a chance. Later, Frank asked Arthur Lodge, in charge of the NBC newsreel news desk when he was hired, why Frank rather than all the experienced broadcast journalists working for NBC radio news at Rockefeller Center got the job. Lodge told him simply that "nobody who is any good in radio will come up here because they don't think it'll last."[24]

Television in 1950

By the time Reuven Frank joined NBC in August 1950, television news occupied a contradictory position in the United States. Television itself rocketed into the top ten of American industries as manufacturers built and sold 7.5 million sets that year alone. One hundred and seven stations were broadcasting in sixty-five cities in thirty-four states, within reach of roughly 65 percent of the population. This growth is even more impressive given the fact that the FCC stopped taking new applications for stations in 1948 as it tried to figure out how to best distribute the limited number of television signals around the country. The freeze on new licenses would last until 1952.[25]

Under the competitive license process, the FCC required all stations to broadcast at least some news and public affairs programming, both local and through their network affiliation. In most cases, local television stations allocated minimal resources to these required programs. Building and running a television station, as well as a network, was roughly four to five times as expensive as radio. Most television networks and stations lost money until the mid-1950s. In addition, advertisers focused on entertainment programs with less interest in news and public affairs, mainly because informational programs brought in fewer viewers and potentially more controversy. When stations did find advertisers for their news and public affairs programs, the revenue rarely supported a sufficient staff or equipment for a comprehensive sight and sound newscast. Instead, to keep costs down, many stations only funded an announcer to read wire service stories on camera with occasional local news film and still photographs. The next chapter goes into greater detail on the different formats and economics of news and public affairs programs in this era.[26]

By 1950, the television experience in the United States ranged from saturated to nonexistent. The Los Angeles area already had seven stations, and New York City boasted six television operations, but no licenses had been granted in the Dakotas, Arkansas, South Carolina, Kansas, and several other states. Most stations on the East Coast and in the Midwest were linked by AT&T's coaxial cable network, but stations on the West Coast were not yet part of that live network, with the first east-west link opening in 1951.

When Reuven Frank moved to television, the New York City area already had local affiliates for all four networks (NBC, CBS, ABC, and DuMont) as well as two independent stations, WPIX and WOR, and one station in Newark. All the stations did some level of news and public affairs, with WPIX a pioneer in its focus on local news and relying on a heavy dose of filmed events. The CBS and NBC affiliates, WCBS and WNBT, were closely connected to the networks but also presented local newscasts for the New York City area.[27]

Concerning network news, CBS had continued to refine the television newscast format that it had initiated at the start of commercial television in 1941. By 1948, CBS was running its network newscasts for fifteen minutes five nights a week, settling on Douglas Edwards as its permanent newscaster.

Ironically, NBC's success in luring advertisers to television stifled its momentum in television news through much of the 1940s. Sponsors, through their advertising agencies, purchased the air time, decided on the format, and often produced their own programs. With such power in the hands of the advertising agencies, NBC did not have a strong television program department. Programs and formats would come and go, depending on the interest of the advertisers. During World War II, NBC did hire newsreel veteran Paul Alley to edit military films into a series, *War as It Happens*. After the war, the program was renamed *NBC Television Newsreel*, and Alley built up a small network of staff and freelance film photographers.

In 1948, NBC landed one of the biggest sponsor deals in television when the R.J. Reynolds tobacco company decided to advertise Camel cigarettes through a news program. NBC News and Paul Alley had little to do with the original program. Instead, the advertiser contracted with 20th Century Fox *Movietone News* to produce a daily ten-minute newsreel, *Camel Newsreel Theatre*, to run on NBC. The advertiser requested that NBC radio newscaster John Cameron Swayze voice the newsreel, which ran at 7:50 p.m. each weeknight. A year later, the advertiser scrapped the newsreel format in favor of the television newscast model long used by CBS and other television stations. The sponsor put NBC in charge of the new fifteen-minute program in 1949, renamed *Camel News Caravan* with Swayze as newscaster and incorporating Alley's newsreel camera network, signaling the start of NBC Television News.[28]

Television News and the Korean War

When Reuven Frank started at NBC in August 1950, his first job involved taking the stories and film used the previous night on the *Camel News Caravan* and rewriting the scripts and reediting the film for a noon newscast. During these months, Frank started to learn how to combine the words that the newscaster would say with the moving pictures that would be shown on screen as the newscaster was talking. The ability to let the pictures convey the information and adding the fewest words necessary to complement the visuals became one of Frank's passions.

Frank's early years in television also coincided with one of the major news stories of the 1950s, the Korean War. He began at NBC just after the start of the conflict, and he incrementally discovered the opportunities and challenges of presenting a faraway war on a nightly television newscast. In the early 1950s at the networks, even though television was already becoming more popular than radio, radio news was still the prestige format, with the most experienced people and better resources. NBC television news did not have the budget for a full-time, dedicated Korean War reporter or film crew, so the small New York television staff relied mostly on wire service reports, occasional film from NBC freelance photographers, information from NBC radio reporters, and biweekly newsreel film shot and edited by the government. On the local Washington, DC, station, WTOP, CBS newcomer Walter Cronkite became an audience favorite for his map talks on the nightly newscast, as he pointed out troop movements on a large blackboard within the outlines of North and South Korea borders. In later years, Frank challenged the idea that Vietnam was the first television war, because he was presenting the latest information and film on the NBC nightly newscast throughout the Korean War.[29]

Between government-supplied newsreels and images from NBC camera crews, Reuven Frank had much more film of the war than could be used on the nightly fifteen-minute newscast. A few months into his time at NBC, Frank suggested they might want to put the best film into a special program, a programming strategy rarely employed at NBC at this point. NBC okayed Frank's project, putting him in charge even though he had no documentary experience. He worked nights and weekends on the project for two months.

"Victory in Korea"

The relatively quick transition from the hot war of World War II to the Cold War of the communist threat led to some misguided assumptions for the American public, including journalists—assumptions fueled by political and military leaders. Since the final years of World War II had been such an impressive show of American strength against evil enemies, the Korean War was first seen as an extension of that scenario. World War II reporters, bored with covering national stories the past few years, jumped at the chance to return to a war zone. For those back in the States, including Reuven Frank, the government film, as well as newspaper and wire service accounts gave the impression of a short, successful, war.

After the initial setbacks in the summer of 1950, General Douglas MacArthur made his historic landing at Inchon and drove the troops north, past the Thirty-eighth Parallel, into North Korea. That fall, MacArthur talked confidently of having troops home by Christmas. Frank watched film of American troops heading into Korean villages with cheering crowds, much as he had seen during World War II. He even had a working title for his half-hour special: "Victory in Korea."

As he was finishing up his first big television special in November 1950, the wire services began reporting a different story. The Chinese army joined the war and ambushed the UN forces in North Korea. American troops were forced to retreat back across the border to South Korea. This would not be a quick war, and victory is not a word used to describe America's involvement in that conflict. Not only was his title misguided, but the entire project, meant to be Frank's first television opus, was shelved and forgotten.[30]

Television News and the Cold War

Reuven Frank's assumption about a quick American victory in the Korean War reveals the rapidly changing political climate and the shifting perceptions of American strength and threats. Frank, as a working journalist on a national news program, had access to the best American reporting through wire services, newspapers, and his own network. If he felt the war would be short and successful, there was a serious disconnect between reality and the information coming out of Korea and Washington. Frank, as well as the journalism profession and the American public, would now be rethinking America's security and place in the world.

Television and the Cold War in the United States are forever linked because they gained momentum during the same postwar period, becoming part of American society in "parallel waves"[31] starting in the late 1940s and building throughout the 1950s. In scholarship and other histories, both journalism and television are often offered up as culprits for the excesses of the Cold War period. Journalists are portrayed as providing a mouthpiece for, but not challenging, Senator Joseph McCarthy, while television is the timid yet powerful, shallow but influential, medium that allowed a demagogue to flourish and failed to challenge the government on a simplistic "us versus them" scenario of democracy pitted against communism.

One common theme in explaining McCarthy's rise is that of an openly deceptive public official who exploited the basic tenets of mid-twentieth-century American journalism. US senators are elected national politicians, so journalists had an obligation to report what they said, especially on important issues. The concept of objectivity would not allow that reporter to personally decide if the information was credible or not, so the charges often went unchallenged. When Senator McCarthy stood up at the Lincoln Day dinner for the Ohio County Women's Republican Club in Wheeling, West Virginia, in February 1950 and waved a piece of paper that he said included 205 names of communists in the State Department, the truth of the charge mattered less than that a US senator had said it. McCarthy began a pattern of making inflammatory statements and recklessly accusing people of communist sympathies with reporters dutifully reporting his revelations as news. Given the preference for the latest news and limited budgets, journalism organizations rarely spent the time investigating yesterday's claim for accuracy in favor of today's new revelation.[32]

In his influential 1959 book *The Fourth Branch of the Government*, Douglass Cater put the blame for McCarthy's rise squarely on objectivity: "'Straight' news, the absolute commandment of most mass media journalism, had become a strait jacket to crush the initiative and the independence of the reporter." David Halberstam singled out the Washington insider journalists who "were delighted to be part of his [McCarthy] traveling road show, chronicling each charge and then moving on to the next town, instead of bothering to stay behind to follow up." Some of those reporters may simply have been afraid to take on someone who could get them fired.[33]

Television news was still relatively new and sparsely funded when McCarthy became a household name, so the format is usually lumped with print journalism when explaining McCarthy's rise. Television as a medium is remembered both for fueling his fame and helping bring him down. Even with McCarthy's numerous television appearances between 1950 and his downfall in 1954, or the thousands of news and public affairs programs that dealt with the Red Scare or McCarthyism, most studies on television and McCarthy center on two sets of broadcasts: Edward R. Murrow and Fred Friendly's CBS *See It Now* weekly public affairs program, and the live coverage of the Army-McCarthy hearings in the spring of 1954.

Murrow and Friendly's series of reports and programs on the Red Scare and McCarthy, sprinkled in among the other issues they covered on CBS's *See It Now* in 1953 and 1954, followed the program's attention to the "small stories"[34] that relate to a bigger issue. In October 1953, *See It Now* investigated the case of Air Force Reserve Lieutenant Milo Radulovich, who was asked to resign because of vague charges of communist sympathies, charges he was not allowed to see. The next month, *See It Now* focused on "An Argument in Indianapolis," in which the American Legion helped block the American Civil Liberties Union (ACLU) from using a state building for a meeting.

Finally, in March 1954, *See It Now* went after McCarthy himself, with a special program devoted to McCarthy on film and audio. The *See It Now* team had been collecting McCarthy footage and audio specifically for this type of program, and it was edited to show his recklessness and boorish behavior. Murrow's ending commentary was a scathing indictment of McCarthy, his tactics, and those who had kept silent and let him cause such damage: "We will not be driven by fear into an age of unreason if we dig deep in our history and our doctrine, and remember that we are not descended from fearful men."[35]

Murrow's *See It Now* programs have been lauded and celebrated in scholarship, popular histories, oral histories, and movies as a rare moment of courage during the Red Scare and as the crowning achievement of Murrow, considered now to have been the patron saint of broadcast news. Influential *New York Times* television critic Jack Gould called the broadcast "crusading journalism of high responsibility and genuine courage."[36]

Over the past few decades, as more scholars dug into the primary sources and other evidence, they have dialed back the impact of the *See It Now* programs on McCarthy's fall from power later in 1954. McCarthy was already losing influence by the time of the broadcast, and several CBS affiliates did not run the program. In an Elmo Roper survey for CBS about the broadcast, roughly the same percentage of viewers changed their minds about both McCarthy and Murrow after the program (21 versus 25 percent), with the change more negative than positive for both men, but McCarthy's negative change was much higher than Murrow's (82 versus 54 percent). Concerning Murrow himself, media historian Gary Edgerton said his myth became larger and more noble than the actual person, becoming "the electronic media's hero for self-justification." In the boundary work of broadcast journalism, Edward R. Murrow became the epitome of ethical, fearless reporting.[37]

Real Life Soap Operas

The second set of broadcasts started a month after the *See It Now* McCarthy program. McCarthy and his chief counsel, Roy Cohn, had been putting relentless pressure on the US Army to get special treatment for one of McCarthy's staff members, G. David Schine, when he was drafted into the army. The conflict resulted in Senate hearings that stretched on for weeks. NBC and CBS had popular daytime television programming they did not want to cancel, so they opted to show highlights later in the day. The two struggling TV networks, ABC and DuMont, offered continuous live coverage.

The reasons for the hearings may have been obscure, but Americans had already displayed their interest in watching live government proceedings much like a recurring soap opera, learning the main characters and watching for drama and plot twists.

Three years earlier, Tennessee senator Estes Kefauver chaired a committee looking into organized crime. At a hearing in New Orleans, he allowed a station to cover the proceedings live, complete with testimony by suspected mob leaders. The audience reaction was immediate. The unpredictability of live television and the parade of interesting characters made for popular viewing during a period of the day when many stations would have been showing a test pattern. As the committee moved to other cities with live television coverage, the hearings became sensations in Detroit, San Francisco, and Los Angeles.

In March 1951, Kefauver brought the hearings to New York, and they became must-see television for those who had sets. Particularly memorable was mob boss Frank Costello, who did not want his face shown, so cameras zeroed in on his hands as he nervously fidgeted with items on the table during his testimony. Roughly twenty to thirty million people watched at least some of the coverage, with many viewers following the characters and deciding on guilt or innocence depending on how the people appeared on television. Even Senator Kefauver became a pop culture sensation during the hearings. *New York Herald Tribune* critic John Crosby worried about the next live coverage event when the topic might be more controversial than organized crime, when "we'll have to judge the proceeding not on the physical attractions or personal problems of the witnesses, but, of all things, on what they have to say."[38]

Even though the Army-McCarthy hearings ran only three years after the Kefauver mob hearings, the influence on the American public was much more pronounced because of the dramatic expansion of television's reach in that period. Manufacturers sold millions more sets, more cities had television stations, and a network connected stations from the East Coast to the West Coast. The televised Army-McCarthy hearings ran from April until June 1954, and those broadcasts revealed McCarthy's full bullying personality and willingness to hurt innocent people.

In the hearings, McCarthy was upstaged by an even more colorful character, chief Army counsel Joseph Welch, who used a savvy homespun demeanor throughout the hearings to lure McCarthy into showing his dark side. After McCarthy accused one of Welch's law firm colleagues of communist sympathies, the attorney uttered the famous line, "Have you no sense of decency, sir, at long last? Have you no sense of decency?" McCarthy's fall from power was accentuated later in 1954 when the US Senate finally voted to censure him.[39]

The *See It Now* programs and Army-McCarthy hearings are considered the two key television nonfiction moments in revealing McCarthy's true character and the evils of the Red Scare. One of the themes of Cold War media research was that television allowed the viewers to see the *real* McCarthy and they rejected him. During television's decades of experimentation, one of the promises had been that sight and sound would allow citizens to pull back the curtain on politics and look their leaders in the eye. The American people would see into their souls and know who was real and who was not. The downfall of McCarthy in the same year as the *See It Now* and Army-McCarthy broadcasts fit into that television x-ray narrative.[40]

The Importance of Existence

Those two depictions of McCarthy and television are accurate when focusing just on *See It Now* and the Army-McCarthy hearings. But too often, those programs represent *all* of television and the Cold War, and too often the rise and fall of McCarthy are used to represent *all* of the Cold War, or at least the Red Scare portion of that era.

One obvious but usually overlooked or unspoken reason for the emphasis on *See It Now* and the Army-McCarthy broadcasts at the exclusion of the rest of television is the fact that those programs were recorded and have been made available for viewing during the ensuing half-century. As noted, most of television news and public affairs programming from the 1940s to 1960s was either not recorded, recorded and later discarded, or only available today behind a network pay wall or hidden in an archive with limited viewing options. Since *See It Now* was a prestigious, big-budget program for CBS, as well as a vehicle for its most popular news person, Edward R. Murrow, the program was not only recorded but has been made available in various formats over the decades.

The Army-McCarthy hearings traveled a more circuitous path to present-day acknowledgment. In 1954, even though both CBS and NBC opted against live coverage of the hearings, those networks recorded the live hearings and edited them into highlights for later news programs. When filmmaker Emile de Antonio wanted to use the coverage in a 1964 documentary, he found out that only CBS had saved all the kinescopes from the hearings. He edited the kinescopes into a documentary, *Point of Order!*, that received considerable attention. *Point of Order!* also ran on television and was later released on home video. These days, excerpts and full versions of both *Point of Order!* and *See It Now* can be found on video sharing sites, including YouTube—if you can find them before media company lawyers force their removal.[41]

While the full McCarthy treatment on 1950s American television may never be known, scholars are searching wider than the usual programs to reveal the senator as a popular guest on a variety of public affairs programming. Television in the 1950s was filled with forums, political interview programs, and talk shows, inexpensive formats for fulfilling the stations' FCC obligations to present news and public affairs programming. Politicians, including McCarthy, loved those programs. They were seen as an effective, free way to gain exposure. On these programs, the journalists were not always deferential to McCarthy, and they sometimes asked him tough questions about his views and methods. The senator appeared to enjoy tough exchanges with reporters in these formats.[42]

Unearthing other examples of McCarthy's television appearances or even his portrayals is helpful to an extent. Keeping McCarthy on center stage when studying journalism and television and the Cold War, however, allows for an easy exit when McCarthy falls from grace. The end of McCarthy was obviously not the end of the Cold War or the Red Scare.

Anticommunism beyond McCarthy

The Tunnel is a product of Reuven Frank's beliefs about the Cold War and the "democracy versus communism" theme after more than fifteen years as a professional journalist. During most of those years, communism was considered the number-one threat to America. For sociologist Herbert Gans, while journalists might aim for the idea of objectivity, their work is based on "a picture of nation and society as it ought to be." These "enduring values" are not overt, but they underpin the empirical information in news stories. They are usually shared by sources and the audience. For much of the American journalism community, especially those relying on government officials and politicians as sources, "freedom over communism" worked as an enduring value and foundation upon which news stories were conceived and executed.[43]

Switching from the internal threat of McCarthy and the Red Scare to the external threat of creeping communism around the world orchestrated from Moscow, journalists had an even more difficult time presenting alternative viewpoints. If reporters did not have the time or inclination to investigate Red Scare accusations and charges in the United States, what chance would there be that journalists would challenge American foreign policy platforms and beliefs by giving equal weight to the enemies of the United States?

James Aronson worked for mainstream newspapers before the Cold War, including the *New York Herald Tribune*, *New York Post*, and *New York Times*, and later founded the left-wing publication *National Guardian*. Like Frank, Aronson graduated from the Columbia University Graduate School of Journalism. Over the years, Aronson sparred with his editors because he felt they were presenting a limited worldview, determined by government and business leaders. Because of his affiliation with *National Guardian* during the 1950s, he was a frequent target of Red Scare pressure and threats.

Aronson felt McCarthy was just a tool to institutionalize the domestic fear of communism, and one reason for McCarthy's downfall was that the establishment no longer needed him. Aronson believed most journalists simply accepted the government and business leaders' opinions on foreign policy and passed them along as fact: "The American press does not reflect the American mind—it reflects the views of established power which in turn seeks to mold the American mind to accept its prejudices." Pivoting from "the press" to the television industry, media historian J. Fred MacDonald presented a common portrayal of a medium beholden to the government for the broadcast license, not wanting to create controversy, and genuinely believing in the fight against communism. Therefore, broadcasters were "eager to demonstrate their loyalty and to continue the struggle against those they felt would destroy the American way of life, offered their facilities and energies in the crusade."[44]

These views are common in analyses of journalism and television and the Cold War. They align with the influential work by Ed Herman and Noam Chomsky later in the Cold War, *Manufacturing Consent*, chronicling journalism's agreement with the US government on foreign policy issues. Herman and Chomsky considered anticommunism as a control filter, in which "issues tend to be framed in terms of a dichotomized world of Communist and anti-Communist powers, with gains and losses allocated to contesting sides, and rooting for 'our side' considered an entirely legitimate news practice." Chapter 6 more fully explores the relationship between the government and American journalists during the Cold War.[45]

Just as is evident with the more nuanced McCarthy scholarship over the past decades, the idea of television as a "co-conspirator in the conformities and repressions of Cold War America," is softening as scholars move beyond the usual historical broadcasts and dig into more complicated historical moments and ideas. In his book *Cold War, Cool Medium*, media historian Thomas Doherty draws from the usual McCarthy broadcasts but also brings in interview programs, forums, news coverage of atomic bomb tests, fiction programs dealing with Cold War issues, and the live spectacle of television, including the Army-McCarthy hearings. Doherty defines the Cold War and television connection as a constantly evolving "cultural pact," with each side renegotiating its role depending on the year and the events. While television may not have been trying to challenge the government, it also had an insatiable need for content, which allowed the medium to explore ideas and opinions beyond the typical Cold War ideology. Overall, Doherty credits television for making the United States a "more open and tolerant place" in the 1950s and 1960s.[46]

Bringing the focus back down to the individual journalists, either in print or in broadcast news, another key point is to move beyond the caricature of Americans as naïve followers of a simplistic Cold War mentality. The cartoon images of Bert the Turtle and school children trying to protect themselves from an atomic bomb blast in the 1951 educational film *Duck and Cover* conjure up ideas of a long-ago unsophisticated period when people blithely went along with their government's simplistic views of "us versus them." The Cold War is seen as a guileless period before Americans (including journalists) wised up and started asking serious questions of their government. Even with the government's efforts to present a unified message against communism, the Soviet Union and the United States did present a very real and serious threat to each other. At the start of 1958, a Gallup Poll showed that fewer than a quarter of Americans expected the "fear of war" to decrease during the year, while more than 60 percent thought it would increase or stay the same.[47]

Reuven Frank made the switch to television the same year Joseph McCarthy first made headlines by accusing the State Department of harboring communists. As Frank enthusiastically welcomed the challenge of adapting news and public affairs to a sight and sound medium with daily deadlines, the stories he was writing and producing increasingly involved the threats of the Cold War, both within the country and from enemies abroad.

Television News Expansion in the 1950s

Television news had become both a local and national experience by the early 1950s, at least for people who lived within range of a television signal. Local stations presented a variety of news and public affairs programs, in formats ranging from newsreels, newscasters on set, to live interviews. The networks, based out of New York City, also broadcast a number of news programs, some targeted at the local New York audience and others for the growing network of affiliated stations.

The network newscasts still ran for fifteen minutes Monday through Friday. John Cameron Swayze was the face of the *Camel News Caravan* on NBC while Douglas Edwards fronted *Douglas Edwards with the News* on CBS. DuMont had a few short-lived network newscasts in this period, and ABC countered with John Charles Daly as newscaster starting in the fall of 1953. Through the summer of 1955, CBS's nightly network newscast ran at 7:30 p.m. with NBC starting at 7:45 p.m. Later that year, CBS moved to 6:45 p.m., which NBC did as well two years later.[48]

In 1951, the same year that Frank took over as chief writer of the *Camel News Caravan*, NBC hired William McAndrew from its Washington, DC, station to oversee television news at the network. Frank considered McAndrew one of his most important mentors and worked under him until McAndrew's death in 1968. The year after McAndrew's arrival, NBC News combined radio and television news operations in the main NBC offices at 30 Rockefeller Plaza. Film editing stayed at 106th and Park because the network still had concerns about the flammability of moving picture film.

Longer-Form Productions

The fifteen-minute nightly format proved to be too confining for Frank's ambitions. After his experience working on the Korean War special that never aired, he wanted to try longer-format programs. At first, these opportunities were sporadic and often had a heavy Cold War component. When Soviet leader Joseph Stalin died in 1953, Frank produced a Sunday afternoon half-hour program, *Before and After Stalin*, which included both live and filmed elements, highlighted by rare films of the Soviet leader. Later that year, Frank wrote and produced *Berlin-Window on Fear*, once again relying heavily on historic film.

The next year, Frank garnered attention for a special he produced on life in prison for Nazi war criminals. NBC European film photographer Gary Stindt, who would later oversee *The Tunnel* project, secretly shot film of Rudolf Hess, Albert Speer, Walther Funk, and other Nazis living in the Spandau Prison in Berlin. Stindt captured the notorious World War II enemies walking in the prison yard, tending gardens, and engaging in other mundane activities, scenes that were accentuated with historic film from World War II and the Nuremberg trials. Sigma Delta Chi (predecessor of the Society of Professional Journalists) honored Frank with a "television news writing" award for *Road to Spandau*.[49]

In what became a recurring theme in Frank's career, he used the success of *Road to Spandau* to briefly escape from daily television news to concentrate on longer-form projects. In 1954, he worked with reporter Joseph C. Harsch on a short-lived, weekly, thirty-minute public affairs program, *Background*. Two years later, he was asked to produce another half-hour weekly program, *Outlook*, with a veteran broadcaster who had just joined NBC, Chet Huntley.

Television and Presidential Election Coverage

NBC turned to Frank to produce the 1956 political conventions and election night coverage. Starting with radio earlier in the century and transferring over to television, the broadcast network news departments considered political conventions and election night broadcasts as an opportunity to reach a wider audience. The conventions and election nights provided a rare chance to produce programming during the popular primetime hours, so the networks relied on their top journalists and showcased the latest technology. In the era before state primaries and caucuses became so prominent in selecting presidential candidates, the party conventions were filled with intrigue and surprising developments. In short, the conventions were newsworthy.

The 1948 political conventions had been a key moment in the development of televised news and public affairs. NBC partnered with *Life* magazine for the most extensive convention coverage in 1948. Over at CBS, a very reluctant Edward R. Murrow helped on the television coverage along with his radio work, paired with Quincy Howe and Douglas Edwards on the television side. ABC, DuMont, and several local stations also covered the 1948 conventions and the dramatic fall campaign as incumbent Harry Truman won a surprise victory over Republican Thomas Dewey. For both Edwards at CBS and Swayze at NBC, their work on the 1948 conventions broadcasts helped convince management and sponsors to install them as permanent newscasters for the daily newscasts.[50]

By the 1952 election season, television was already an established medium in many cities, especially in the East and Midwest. The Republican convention provided drama as World War II hero Dwight Eisenhower outmaneuvered party insider Senator Robert Taft for the nomination and went on to easily beat Democrat Adlai Stevenson in the general election.

At CBS, "the Murrow Boys" were still resisting television in favor of radio. CBS gave the key position in the CBS television coverage to a fairly new employee, Walter Cronkite. Cronkite became a household name because of his work on the 1952 conventions and election night coverage. Over at NBC, radio was also still the preferred medium for many of the broadcast journalists. The network turned to Bill Henry, who was not even a full-time NBC employee. Henry had extensive experience as a print journalist and did an adequate job on convention coverage that year.

Huntley and Brinkley

When Frank was put in charge of the 1956 convention coverage, he felt NBC needed to showcase one of its own television news broadcasters, partly to try and dampen some of the enthusiasm for Cronkite over at CBS. As NBC news managers tossed out names, Frank pushed for David Brinkley, the long-time Washington correspondent for NBC radio and television. Other executives preferred NBC's newest hire, Chet Huntley. Since Frank worked as managing editor on Huntley's *Outlook* weekly program, he already knew Huntley's value to the network. At some point in the deliberations, one of the executives suggested two other people share the convention duties. As soon as the possibility of two people was raised, Frank immediately pushed for Huntley and Brinkley.

Chet Huntley and David Brinkley were a successful match. Huntley had a dour, serious look and had been hired by NBC partly as an answer to Edward R. Murrow. By contrast, Brinkley was a Washington insider, with a sparse writing style and deadpan delivery that often poked fun at the absurdities of government and politics. The 1956 conventions provided less intrigue than usual since Eisenhower was a popular president running for reelection and the Democrats chose Adlai Stevenson again for a repeat of the 1952 campaign. Huntley and Brinkley on NBC proved to be a popular choice with media critics and viewers, similar to the reaction Cronkite had received four years earlier.[51]

The success of Huntley and Brinkley on convention coverage also solved another problem for upper NBC management. NBC president Sylvester "Pat" Weaver had never liked John Cameron Swayze as the news broadcaster for the NBC nightly newscast. Weaver had been a charismatic and polarizing leader for NBC, launching such popular franchises as *Today* and *The Tonight Show*. He also helped break the power of advertising agencies over programming by relegating the advertisers to individual commercials, spot advertising, instead of buying an entire time period, which had been the tradition dating back to radio.[52]

For both NBC and CBS, the main network newscasters had been chosen in the late 1940s, when the more important news broadcasters worked in radio. John Cameron Swayze's persona harkened back to an earlier era, relying on catchphrases including "hopscotching the world for headlines" and ending each broadcast with "Glad we could get together." He always wore a fresh carnation. For various reasons, Edwards and Swayze had never really been accepted by other broadcast journalists at their networks, but as television grew as a medium, the fifteen-minute newscasts became a popular way for viewers to catch up on the news each evening. In the early 1950s, the NBC newscast also benefited from the Camel cigarette sponsorship money as well as NBC's stronger set of local affiliates, resulting in higher ratings than CBS, making the decision to replace Swayze more difficult.[53]

By 1955, Camel had backed off total sponsorship of the newscast, relinquishing two days a week to a car company. Regular viewers during this period saw both the *Camel News Caravan* and the *Plymouth News Caravan*, depending on the day of the week. As advertising dollars decreased, NBC cut the budget of the nightly newscast, at the same time the CBS newscast with Edwards was gaining viewers. The buzz over Huntley and Brinkley in the summer of 1956 allowed NBC to remove Swayze from the newscast and move in the Huntley-Brinkley team. NBC News president William McAndrew asked Frank to serve as executive producer, pulling him back into daily television news.

A Functional Friendship

The dual newscaster format was rare, especially in network news at that time, but the added complexity involved broadcasting from two cities each night. David Brinkley built his reputation on Washington coverage and he was not interested in moving to New York. NBC let Brinkley keep his Washington beat and he continued to broadcast from that city while Huntley handled the majority of the newscast from the New York studio. The logistical issues involved in switching back and forth from two locations each night inadvertently led to a few of the reasons the *Huntley-Brinkley Report* became part of the popular culture of that era.

The perception of the symbiosis between the two newscasters in separate cities started as quick solutions to technology issues. NBC had to use AT&T's coaxial cable lines to link the New York and Washington portions of the new *Huntley-Brinkley Report*. What seemed to be a simple task of splitting the live broadcast between NBC News in Washington and New York in reality involved a telephone company employee who had to manually switch the newscast between the two cities. Since that person was not in the NBC control room, NBC had to come up with an easy cue to let AT&T know it was time to change cities. When the newscast needed to switch from New York to Washington, Huntley would say "David" to let AT&T know to immediately switch. When it was time to come back to New York, Brinkley would end his story and say "Chet."[54]

The most mimicked and remembered part of the *Huntley-Brinkley Report* was conceived in the frantic deadline stress and panic during the first day of the new multi-city format. Someone casually asked Frank how the program would end. He had not thought about that. With two men in different locations, how could they convey the idea of a team and wrap up the program quickly, since they only had fifteen minutes for the entire newscast?

Frank put a piece of paper into his typewriter and banged out:

CHET (NY): Good night, David.
DAVID (WX): Good night, Chet.
CHET (NY): And good night for NBC News.[55]

That signoff became the signature for the *Huntley-Brinkley Report*. At first, neither broadcaster liked it. Brinkley and Huntley thought it made them sound like "sissies." The two men felt they should be talking to the audience, and not to each other. Frank told Brinkley and Huntley that if they could come up with a quick way to end the program involving both of them, he would change it. They never did.

While the reason for saying the first names was purely functional, this simple exchange indicated a friendship, or at least a partnership, which resonated with those who watched the newscast. In audience surveys in later years, many viewers inferred a friendship between Huntley and Brinkley. Many did not realize they were not sitting next to each other.[56]

The change in newscasters happened so fast that Swayze fronted the last *NBC News Caravan* on Friday, October 26, 1956, and the *NBC News with Chet Huntley and David Brinkley* premiered on Monday, October 29, 1956, with only the weekend for rehearsals. Frank considered the premiere of the new format and newscasters on that Monday evening as "the worst evening news program in the history of American network television."[57] Frank's team did not have a structure in place and NBC did not have the resources to handle the amount of news on that first day, including Israeli troops attacking the Suez Canal and the Soviet Union sending tanks in to Hungary to stop an uprising in that country.

The first year of the new format was far from a success. Several of the NBC affiliates chose not to run the program. Even President Eisenhower let NBC know he thought it was a mistake to get rid of Swayze. The newscast also did not measure up in the category that really mattered in American television: commercial sponsorship. For several months, the *Huntley-Brinkley Report* had no sponsors and Frank said there was strong talk of canceling the effort.

Civil Rights

If the Cold War was the most pervasive story of American network television's first decades, the struggle for civil rights after World War II provided the medium an important issue that often had a strong visual component, just as network television news was expanding its reach through more affiliates and more homes and apartments with televisions. The unanimous Supreme Court ruling against school segregation in 1954, *Brown vs. Board of Education,* set in motion a series of events across the South, as white political and business leaders resisted the court's call for integration and equal educational opportunities. Other court rulings pushed back against other forms of segregation in the South.

When Rosa Parks refused to give up her seat on a city bus in Montgomery, Alabama, in December 1955, her action sparked a boycott of city buses in that city that lasted over a year. All through 1956, newspapers, radio, and television newscasts covered the latest developments in the volatile issue, launching Dr. Martin Luther King Jr. to national prominence as a leader of the boycott. The Montgomery issue also brought a local TV news director to the attention of NBC news executives in New York. Frank McGee ran the newsroom for WSFA-TV, the NBC affiliate in Montgomery, a station that had just started broadcasting a year before the bus boycott. McGee handled the coverage so well that NBC hired him to join the network news department.[58]

The next year, NBC sent John Chancellor and McGee to Little Rock, Arkansas, when Governor Orval Faubus called out troops to keep African American students from entering Little Rock Central High School, in defiance of the *Brown vs. Board of Education* ruling. The television cameras captured the images of National Guard troops blocking the door, while the nine African American students were forced to walk through a crowd of angry white students and parents. NBC could not initially broadcast live from Little Rock, so the network had to charter a plane to Oklahoma City each day in order for Chancellor to get his film to New York and appear on the *Huntley-Brinkley Report.*

These stories brought the stark images of segregation and anger into the homes of Americans all across the country. For people in the north, this level of oppression was no longer a vague notion but very real scenes playing out in their living rooms every night. The civil rights leaders, including Dr. King, recognized that they could gain the support of more Americans if the images they saw on television showed African Americans in a positive light. They advocated nonviolent protests, often prompting the segregationists and law enforcement into violent acts of their own, just by the protestors' act of free speech and assembly. Network news coverage of the civil rights protests across the country in the 1950s and 1960s brought a new level of awareness to the long-simmering issues. City leaders and television station owners in the South felt the network news was being unfair and deliberately making segregationists look bad. Some affiliates would not run the network news when they knew there would be coverage of civil rights protests.

Historians acknowledge the importance of the images appearing on television sets across the country, but also point out that television news covered the civil rights struggle from a fairly narrow perspective. Much as television receives too much blame for simplistic Cold War coverage, many accounts of civil rights coverage ignore the complexities of how the issues were covered. Reporters almost always focused on Dr. King, even at events when he played a peripheral role. Beyond King, reporters were not always inclined to interview other African Americans, especially if their messages were more extreme or demanded quicker change.[59]

In February 1959, Chet Huntley caused a controversy when he ended a civil rights piece on his Sunday public affairs program, *Chet Huntley Reporting*, by comparing the NAACP to the Ku Klux Klan and other white supremacist groups. Huntley said it might be time for the NAACP to disband because it was not fair to chastise white militant groups if "militant Negro leadership," including the NAACP, was allowed to continue. Civil rights leaders complained to NBC and were allowed to appear on the next week's program to debate a segregationist.[60]

Famed World War II correspondent Howard K. Smith lost his job at CBS over what he wanted to say about segregation. Smith and producer David Lowe were working on a *CBS Reports* documentary on Birmingham, Alabama, and Smith wanted to end the program by quoting Edmund Burke on how evil can triumph when "good men do nothing." CBS management forced him to remove the quote. After an angry confrontation with CBS chairman William Paley, Smith left CBS and moved over to ABC.[61]

Even with the timidity of the networks and reporters to allow more diverse voices into the civil rights debate, television was uniquely suited to bring the images and sounds of the protests, confrontations, and violence into American homes, starting in the South in the 1950s and early 1960s, and moving north later in the decade. "Television brought black people, imaginatively at least, into white people's living rooms," wrote historian Aniko Bodroghkozy. "The people in those living rooms, whether they lived in the urban North or the more rural South, had to come to terms with these television images."[62]

Strategic News Emphasis

The *Huntley-Brinkley Report* survived its rocky first years, Frank believed, partly because no one came up with a better alternative and because FCC rules demand stations offer news and public affairs programs. A series of events in 1958 helped push the nightly newscast into a more prominent place within the network as well as with the viewers. Most importantly, Texaco agreed to sponsor the newscast for three years, bringing in needed resources for covering the news. The sponsorship also signaled to the NBC affiliates that the newscast had a future, so several more stations decided to run the newscast. During the year, the *Huntley-Brinkley Report* caught up with CBS's *Douglas Edwards with the News* in audience size. Both newscasts were now running at 6:45 p.m. on the East Coast.[63]

NBC made a change at the top in 1958 that would benefit the television news efforts. President Pat Weaver was pushed out and eventually replaced with Robert Kintner from ABC. Kintner was a former newspaper reporter who had worked his way up from public relations to the presidency of the fledgling ABC network. The FCC freeze on new television licenses from 1948 to 1952 had the unintended effect of cementing CBS and NBC's position in television while making it impossible for DuMont and ABC to add the necessary affiliates for financially successful network television during that critical period. DuMont shut down in 1955. United Paramount Theaters saved ABC when it bought the network and brought in needed capital. Kintner ran ABC with a much smaller budget than CBS and NBC and emphasized filmed programs over live broadcasts.[64]

When Kintner came to NBC in 1958, CBS was clearly the ratings leader in both entertainment and news programs. Since entertainment programs were so expensive to produce, Kintner thought he could spark a turnaround first with news and public affairs. If he could get viewers to consider NBC a top news source, they might also stick around for entertainment programs. While at ABC, Kintner was praised for making the money-losing decision to run the entire Army-McCarthy hearings (along with DuMont), while CBS and NBC stuck with profitable daytime programs.[65]

Before Kintner, NBC News had a hard time preempting entertainment programs for breaking news events or special reports. NBC management was restructured to make it easier for NBC News president William McAndrew to ask Kintner for approval of network programming interruptions for major stories. Kintner became obsessed with outdoing CBS in news coverage. When CBS promoted an eight-part series on President Eisenhower, Kintner announced NBC would do a nine-part series before he even told his news staff. If both networks were covering a live event, he expected to NBC to stay on longer than CBS. This strategy initially cost NBC money because each time an entertainment show was preempted, NBC lost that advertising revenue. "Those early years with Kintner emphasized news programs as never before, or since, on any network," remembered Frank. "There was money for reporters; there was money for documentaries; there was money for special programs."[66]

Government Pressure for More News and Public Affairs

While Kintner was emphasizing news to help entertainment programming, the dramatic growth in news, public affairs, and documentary programming on all American network television in the early 1960s was also a defensive move by television executives to avoid additional government regulations.

At the end of the 1955–1956 television season, CBS pulled *See It Now* out of its coveted Tuesday 10:30 p.m. timeslot, partly because Alcoa had walked away as sponsor and other advertisers steered clear of the controversial program, but also because that primetime half-hour was now worth a lot of money to CBS. By that year, more than seven in ten households had at least one television set. For the networks, television had overtaken radio in popularity and revenue.

Sales of television sets showed no signs of slowing down. While *See It Now* continued on an occasional basis for a few more years, that summer CBS inserted a new program into the Tuesday 10:00 p.m. timeslot, *The $64,000 Question*.

Quiz shows had long been a staple of radio and television because they were cheap to produce. *$64,000 Question* upped the drama by offering a generous cash prize and allowing contestants to keep playing, week after week, building up audience interest. Networks started adding and dropping various quiz show formats, looking for the right combination to attract a large audience.

NBC launched its own primetime quiz show, *Twenty-One*, in the fall of 1956. The producers of *Twenty-One* came up with a smart contestant, Herb Stempel, who kept winning, but they did not think he had strong enough audience appeal. Their solution was to bring in Charles Van Doren, a telegenic Columbia University instructor with an impressive literary lineage. They gave him the answers to defeat Stempel. Van Doren spent fifteen weeks on *Twenty-One*, landing him on the cover of *Time* magazine and a three-year contract at NBC.

Stempel said the game was rigged, prompting a New York grand jury investigation. Van Doren and others lied to the grand jury, but later Van Doren admitted the fraud to a congressional subcommittee. At the same time, the radio industry was hit with a payola scandal, with top disc jockeys taking bribes to play specific songs. These deceptions fed into growing unease in Washington and among elites that American broadcasting, especially television, was straying too far from its public service responsibilities. The threat of new regulations, which might slightly reduce the fire hose of profits, could always get the attention of the major networks.[67]

News Programming Instead of Regulations

Long-time network executives knew the drill. When educators and other broadcast reformers tried to revise the system for awarding radio licenses in the early 1930s, the networks added in more public affairs programs to convince Washington they were worthy stewards of the public airwaves. After the Communications Act of 1934 was signed, protecting their privileged status, the networks gradually removed the nonsponsored programs in favor of the profitable entertainment programs. When the FCC once again questioned the networks' commitment to public affairs programming in its 1946 *Blue Book* report, a brief period of important audio documentaries ensued, until regulation threats dissipated.[68]

In 1959, executives from the main networks met and agreed to start scheduling more public affairs programming. The short-term loss of entertainment advertising revenue was seen as more economical than new government regulations. When he took office in 1961, President John F. Kennedy initially kept up the pressure on the networks. Just months into his administration, his choice for FCC chairman, Newton Minow, gave a tough speech to the very group that wanted to hear it the least, the National Association of Broadcasters (NAB), the lobbying group that eviscerated the champions of the *Blue Book* in the 1940s and any other attempts at regulation or reform. While the speech is best known for his description of American television as a "vast wasteland," broadcasters at that speech were chilled by his threat of potentially pulling licenses: "There is nothing permanent or sacred about a broadcast license."[69]

Television at the Start of the 1960s

By the start of the 1960s, eighty countries had television service, with more than two thousand stations and one hundred million sets. The audience was growing by 30 percent a year. The two parts of the world that were still in the beginning stages of television were Africa and India.

In 1961, BBC producer Richard Cawston visited twenty countries to see how television was diffusing around the world. Cawston compared "the television mushroom" to the "nuclear bomb, if only because of the fantastic rate at which television has grown and spread throughout the world." Most countries either turned the medium over to commercial interests or ran it as a government propaganda service. Very few took the British approach of a taxpayer-funded service without heavy government oversight. Japan had emerged as one of the leaders in television, especially in the manufacturing of transmitting equipment and television sets.[70]

Cawston said that overall he was disappointed with the programming he saw around the world. Other than sports programs, he did not feel the broadcasts reflected the culture of the home country because the two popular funding models did not encourage good television. "Unfortunately, commercial interests are tempted to concentrate on cheap entertainment," wrote Cawston, "while governments may be mainly concerned with propaganda or prestige."[71]

One country dominated the television programming around the world: the United States. Since World War II slowed growth elsewhere, the US television service was well ahead of other countries by the early 1960s. Between television and Hollywood productions, American-made programs were popular worldwide. Many countries found it economical to include American productions on their television schedule instead of trying to produce all their own programming.

By 1962, more than forty-eight million American households had at least one television set, meaning only one out of every ten homes was not watching the medium. More than six hundred stations now blanketed the country. The coveted VHF signals (channels 2–13) had become wildly profitable in most cases, and Congress would soon pass regulations to help the weaker UHF (channels 14 and up) channels have a better chance at success. Since television had become the most popular medium in the nation, television news and public affairs had already passed radio and magazines in terms of audience use, and surveys would soon show it be a more popular part of American life than reading the newspaper.

The 1960 American presidential election provided optimism that television could become a positive tool in a representative democracy. Across the country, 57 percent of newspapers endorsed the Republican nominee, Vice President Richard Nixon, while only 16 percent supported the Democratic nominee, Senator John F. Kennedy, which mirrored much of the twentieth century as newspaper owners usually supported the Republican candidate. The Republicans outspent the Democrats as well. For this election, however, the two candidates agreed to four debates on national television. The popularity of the presidential debates between Nixon and Kennedy surprised everyone.

Nine out of every ten homes in the country watched at least part of the four debates and tuned into the election night coverage of the very close race. More than half of the people who watched the debates said the broadcasts helped influence their vote. Nixon had a television strategy that has received less attention but was very effective that year. When he campaigned in different cities, he would go to the local stations and take questions from reporters. His calm and reasoned responses to tough questions showed the viewers a seasoned politician.

More importantly, the 1960 election had the largest turnout in history, close to 65 percent of eligible voters, up 5 percent from 1956. Rowland Evans Jr., a political reporter for the *New York Herald Tribune*, believed television "heightens interest and curiosity" in the election. Instead of the usual party-line or political machine voting patterns, Evans felt television brought out "the independent vote of the man who goes to the polls because his interest has become engaged."[72]

NBC Television News Dominance

While all three television networks collaborated on the presidential debates, they competed for viewers for the political conventions, election night coverage, and all news coverage in between—on the nightly newscasts, public affairs programs, documentaries, and special broadcasts. In those areas, NBC had emerged as the clear favorite among the American viewers.

More people watched NBC's 1960 political conventions and election night coverage than both CBS and ABC combined. More than eighteen million viewers were tuning in to the nightly *Huntley-Brinkley Report*. When the NBC nightly newscast won its second Peabody Award for television news in 1960, the judges said the newscast had "dominated the news division of television so completely in the past year that it would be unthinkable" to honor any other program: "For banishing the voice of doom from news broadcasting they deserve the thanks of everybody who likes to hear the day's headlines," wrote the Peabody judges, "but doesn't relish the prospect of being scared to death while he's digesting them."[73]

NBC's success forced both ABC and CBS to make major changes in their television news operations. ABC turned to James Hagerty, President Eisenhower's press secretary, to run its news organization. At CBS, the network also changed top news leadership. In 1962, CBS moved Douglas Edwards off the nightly newscast in favor of Walter Cronkite.

Print media critics then and historical accounts since tend to credit the NBC television news popularity in this era to the two newscasters and their on-air chemistry. *Newsweek* referred to Chet Huntley and David Brinkley as the "gold dust twins." At a John F. Kennedy inaugural ball, Frank Sinatra and Milton Berle turned a line from the popular song "Love and Marriage" into "Huntley-Brinkley, one is glum, the other quite twinkly."[74] The two men had become part of pop culture, on the level of television and movie stars, a first for television news.

But behind the scenes, both on the *Huntley-Brinkley Report* and on political coverage, Reuven Frank was in charge. Even at the height of their careers, after Walter Cronkite demanded the "managing editor" title when he took over the *CBS Evening News*, Huntley and Brinkley never tried to usurp

Frank's power. The three men certainly did not always agree on issues, but the two newscasters remained comfortable with their long-time producer having the final say on their broadcasts.

Frank acknowledged the "show business" appeal of Huntley and Brinkley, but he was convinced NBC News was popular for not just two men, but because of the approach that they were taking in presenting the news. Huntley and Brinkley may have been the most prominent faces on the programs, but Frank had built a television news staff that covered the stories around the world through a unique mix of moving pictures, sounds, and words. It is not an anomaly that *The Tunnel* is one of Reuven Frank's major achievements in television news and yet did not involve either Huntley or Brinkley.

From the time he was choosing photographs for the front page of the *Newark Evening News* through the dozen years in television, Reuven Frank had been absorbing a myriad of ideas and approaches in presenting the important events and issues through a mix of pictures, sounds, and words. Frank faced an uphill battle in getting print and radio journalists to move beyond their allegiance to words and sounds to stress the importance of the images, concentrating on ways to visualize the news.

In 1962–1963, Reuven Frank produced two documents that crystalized all he had learned about the power of television in presenting events and issues. One was a film documentary and the other was a written memo. The documentary was *The Tunnel* and the memo was a manifesto on how journalists should best utilize the tools of images, sounds, and words to maximize the communication impact of television.

Frank's ideas, much like the early decades of television, came from a variety of sources: newspapers, magazines, still photography, newsreels, documentaries, Hollywood movies, and radio. The next chapter once again travels through Frank's career leading up to *The Tunnel*. This time, though, the focus is on the visuals and the mix of sounds and images that he felt best suited the medium. Because, as Reuven Frank had discovered, television's emphasis was not always on the pictures.

It would be interesting if Reuven Frank in 1962 could have revisited 1947 to interview the piano player in the Newark bar who hated television. In that era, the entertainer was interested in "husband and wives, fellows and girls, not audiences." Fifteen years later, that young *Newark Evening News* reporter produced newscasts and public affairs programs that commanded the largest audiences in journalism history.[75]

CHAPTER THREE

The Transmission of Experience

IN THE 1960s and 1970s, a feud began between two camps of American print journalism. A group of New York newspaper and magazine feature writers felt they had come up with a fresh, imaginative way to write their stories. They confidently referred to their approach as *new journalism*, positioning their work against what they considered old-fashioned, inverted pyramid, neutral-voice reporting. The leader of the new journalism group, Tom Wolfe, relished the controversy, calling the approach not just better journalism, but "the most important literature being written in America today."[1]

What made this journalism new was the inclusion of techniques that were normally associated with literature and other fiction writing, including the author's voice, narrative structure, and other devices, that Wolfe said were used "to excite the reader both intellectually and emotionally." The new journalism movement would spark debate over the next decades, as print journalists argued over the methods and even the idea that this was really a new development.[2]

During this period, Reuven Frank was promoting many of the same ideas, through his actions as a producer and, in his words, as a manager at NBC News. Frank did not call his views new journalism or even *new television*; he called it television news. Building on a dozen years in television, preceded by his print journalism career, Frank had settled on some basic ideas that he felt elevated television as a medium to convey the latest news and important issues.

Frank realized television served a different function from the printed word in journalism. "The highest power of television journalism," wrote Frank, "is not in the transmission of information but in the transmission of experience." Newspapers might be best at information, but television could excel at conveying experience. Using the right combination of moving pictures, other images, audio, and spoken words could help the viewers feel as if they are a part of the story, to help build interest in the topic.[3]

Frank's ideas on television news as the "transmission of experience" did not arrive as an epiphany, nor was he following Wolfe's new journalism. Frank's views evolved after years of writing and producing journalism on different formats. Since he transitioned relatively early to American commercial television, he was confronted with few set standards and absolutes on how to best utilize the live sight and sound medium as a journalistic platform. He experimented. He adapted.

Frank's accumulated knowledge on the strengths and weaknesses of television as a vehicle for nonfiction productions coalesced in two key documents in 1962–1963. The first is *The Tunnel* documentary, one of his proudest achievements in a long career in television news. The second is the memo initially sparked by a request from his boss to justify the potential expansion of the *Huntley-Brinkley Report*. Frank's response started as an eleven-page letter. He later expanded it to a thirty-two-page memo to his staff in 1963 when NBC News prepared for the longer newscast. Eventually, the memo spread to network and local television news reporters, producers, photographers, and editors. It became a touchstone for generations of visual journalists, quoted and reprinted over the years, both by people who supported and those who were critical of television news. Frank's manifesto never had a formal title, but over time it became known as the "transmission of experience" memo or simply "the bible."[4]

The Tunnel and the "transmission of experience" memo appear to be disconnected broadcast news documents, but the structure and success of *The Tunnel* as well as the popularity of the *Huntley-Brinkley Report* and, by extension, television news are all indelibly intertwined. His boss's directive to justify television news came just four days after *The Tunnel* broadcast, as Frank was being praised for his vision and courage, and in a period when the *Huntley-Brinkley Report* was the most honored and watched nightly network newscast. Frank had always been a confident man, but at this moment in his career, he had good reason to believe he had figured out how television could be an important journalistic platform, both critically and in attracting a sizable audience.

Connecting a Documentary and a Staff Memorandum

Reuven Frank's experience producing *The Tunnel* documentary is the cornerstone of the "bible" memo. The memo may have been specifically addressing the newscast format, but the ideas and direct instructions in the document reflect all forms of nonfiction television, from public affairs programs to documentaries.

The memo is important not just for its vision of effective television news, but also for its confidence. Frank exudes a bravado in his writing that had been absent for much of television news up until that point. Television journalism had been in the shadow of print and radio news since its emergence (explored in chapter 5) and was often on the defensive against journalism critics from other media. Reuven Frank was writing from a position of strength because of the success of both *The Tunnel* and the *Huntley-Brinkley Report*. He did not apologize for the differences between print and television news, nor accept the common journalism belief that television news was inferior. Instead, he acknowledged the differences while highlighting television's advantages as an information medium.

To better understand the specifics of the "transmission of experience" memo, a deeper exploration is needed on the influences and restrictions that faced Reuven Frank and all of television news in the years leading up to *The Tunnel* and the memo. The last chapter chronicled the unprecedented growth of television as a medium in the United States during the Cold War and its acceptance by most of the American public, both as an entertainment and information medium. How, specifically, did television journalists utilize the unique characteristics of the medium, a combination of moving pictures, audio, words—mostly presented live—into the living rooms of American homes and apartments?

When Frank moved into television in 1950, ideas were starting to coalesce around some of the strengths of the medium as a journalistic platform. Unfortunately, the economics of American television usually did not support the type and amount of programming that journalists wanted to provide. Television journalists had to experiment with different versions of live sight-sound communications within a fairly limited budget until the expansion of the medium and government pressure freed up more resources.

The historical view is followed here by a deep read of the "transmission of experience" memo for its similarities to the new journalism movement in print and how Frank felt television could best use its strengths as a news format that was already on a par with newspapers and magazines in audience size and trust.

After the deep read of the memo, *The Tunnel* documentary itself is analyzed for its structure and production, and how it fits into journalism at the height of the Cold War. The documentary is compared with the "transmission of experience" memo to show how Reuven Frank's thoughts on daily television news were intertwined with his experiences on *The Tunnel* production.

With *The Tunnel*, Frank employed the lessons of visuals and audio he had learned after a dozen years in television. The production of that documentary crystallized his fermenting ideas about news on television. To put it simply, *The Tunnel* was a key audio-visual justification for the later written document.

Theater Newsreels

Newsreels are mostly forgotten or ignored in academic scholarship, especially in journalism or nonfiction film histories, while their influence on television news is obvious but at the same time mostly unacknowledged. Before the newscast structure that endures today took hold in the late 1940s and early 1950s, the format that signaled a serious commitment to covering a community on television was the newsreel. Given new media's penchant for mimicking what came before, the format was a predictable choice. People had been watching moving pictures of current events in the theater for three decades by the start of commercial television in the United States in 1941. The influence is hidden because the newsreels did not have a good reputation among journalists and the elite. Newsreels were considered contrived and sensational. Since Hollywood studios controlled the newsreels, they were not considered real journalism.[5]

The antecedents and development of newsreels are explored in the next chapter, but at the height of the moviegoing experience in the 1930s and 1940s, using ticket sales as a measure, anywhere from 37 to 74 percent of Americans saw at least one newsreel a week, depending on whether people went to the movies once or twice weekly. Even on the low end of this estimate, the number represents as large a percentage of the American public as would watch network television newscasts in the 1960s.[6]

While the main newsreels were subsidiaries of the top Hollywood studios of the time, their production process was modeled on a newspaper newsroom. Cameras crews were assigned to cover stories to be edited and assembled into a twice-weekly package. Newsreel length ranged from seven to ten minutes and each edition included from six to a dozen separate stories. The newsreels were packaged as one part of the moviegoing experience, along with cartoons, coming attractions, and the main feature.

The theater newsreel production and distribution has been compared to an assembly line process. The format was established early in its development and rarely deviated over the next half-century. Stories would be edited together in a loose structure with the most current or serious news at the beginning, and lighter topics, including women's fashions, sports, and interesting people or events, at the end. In the silent film era, the stories were delineated with title cards providing textual context. When movies and theaters moved into the sound era, the newsreels added an off-camera narrator who spoke with a dramatic "voice of God" tone.

Sound cameras were much more expensive, heavier, and therefore less mobile than silent camera equipment. Newsreels adopted the economic strategy of using smaller, silent film cameras on most stories and reserving the sound cameras for interviews, press conferences, and other staged or pre-scheduled events. The silent film was then enhanced with dramatic music or sound effects during the editing process.

Because the American newsreels developed and continued under the Hollywood studio system, the newsreel photographers and editors followed the shooting and editing cues of the fiction filmmakers, using sequential editing and numerous close-ups, which often required staging or directed behavior.

The content of the newsreels was determined by the structure, ownership, and distribution system involved in the format. Since the narrator was never seen on camera and the use of graphics was limited, every story had to include at least one scene that could be captured by a moving picture camera. Stories without an obvious visual element were usually ignored. The Hollywood studios and movie theater owners were convinced people came to the movies to escape their problems, so the audience did not want to be depressed by the news. Newsreel editors learned to avoid negative stories or controversial issues. Finally, while the newsreel assembly-line process and attention to a quick turnaround of film meant a reliable system of getting the most important film onto the next edition, the distribution system favored the bigger cities first, with smaller towns and theaters often waiting up to a month to receive a print. Therefore, the newsreel editors gravitated to stories that would still be interesting weeks later.[7]

Since the theater newsreels were not the main reason people went to the movies, it is hard to gauge their impact. The studios must have believed part of their overall success could be attributed to the newsreel because they did not eliminate that expensive part of their movie package until well after television arrived and movie attendance plummeted.

One measure of the newsreel's popularity is that for a few decades, theaters devoted to newsreels carved out a niche in the United States and Europe. The newsreel theaters would feature the latest editions from the different studios and run them on a continuous loop. People could come and go on their schedule. At their height in the 1930s, roughly thirty newsreel theaters had opened around the United States.[8]

The newsreel audience was not passive. The crowd would cheer or boo people on the screen as part of the experience. The newsreels gave the public their first chance to view national and world leaders speaking in their own voice, and in action, week after week. While sitting in the movie theater, Americans witnessed moving images of Franklin Roosevelt, Charles Lindbergh, Adolf Hitler, Winston Churchill, and many other public figures.

With alliances around the world, the newsreels also constituted the first global broadcasting system, decades before satellites and cable news channels. While the newsreels might avoid controversial national issues, they often featured important stories from other countries, especially if US interests were involved.

Just as the newsreels' impact on American viewers in the first half of the twentieth century has been underplayed, the format's impact on television news is rarely acknowledged. The influence, though, is unmistakable, both on the industry and on the individual level. Many newsreel veterans moved over to television, hired for their knowledge of the logistics of photographing events around the world and getting the film developed and edited as quickly as possible.

Newsreel photographers worked in the growing tradition of Hollywood fiction films, so they were versed on the most effective camera shots and sequences for audience appeal. They knew how to capture and edit disasters, press conferences, government hearings, sporting events, and other stories on moving picture film. Television needed that kind of experience.

Newsreels and Television

When Reuven Frank moved to television in 1950, NBC had a much stronger newsreel influence than CBS, mainly because of the work of Paul Alley, who had started the network newsreel operation in the mid-1940s. Frank had conflicted views on the newsreel tradition at NBC. On one hand, the experience in the screening room watching people discuss unedited film convinced him to quit his newspaper job. Frank's insights into television's ability to transmit experiences through visuals and sounds began with his early work at NBC. On the other hand, he considered himself first and foremost a journalist.

On one of Frank's first days as writer and editor of an NBC network newscast, he received an early lesson on the differences between newsreel conventions and what he considered journalistic priorities. Four of the six NBC cameramen working that day had spent hours filming the New York City St. Patrick's Day Parade. They had already started working on a film piece for that night's network newscast. Frank told them he had no room in the fifteen-minute program for a local parade, "and in the camera room there was horror, 'what do you mean you don't want pictures of the parade?' I said it's been on TV all day." Parades had long been a staple of the theater newsreels, so the newsreel veterans could not understand why he would reject their work so easily.[9]

While Frank was drawn to television because of the opportunity to work with moving images, he was often dismissive about what he learned from newsreel veterans at NBC, allowing only that "some of them knew how to make pictures and put pictures together." For Frank, the collaborative process mostly involved trying to get newsreel people to understand journalism: "they had a lot to unlearn . . . and we had a lot to learn. So we had to learn together. We had to learn what they did and they had to learn why we were doing what we did."[10]

The theater newsreel format may have been consistent, to the point of rigidity and criticism, but television news at the start of the 1950s was much harder to pin down in terms of structure. Unfortunately, many of the decisions on how to present news and public affairs on television were predicated on economic factors rather than the most effective use of the medium.

Television News Economics and Formats

When Reuven Frank moved to NBC television news in 1950, he joined a small but growing group of people in the United States who were experimenting with the best ways to exploit the live sight-and-sound format of television to present news and public affairs, given the economic constraints of the advertiser-funded model. With the variety of approaches of presenting the news in this early period of experimentation, the only commonalities of a television news program were that they were live and in a recurring timeslot of fifteen and sometimes thirty minutes. When Professor Harry Heath of Iowa State College tried to categorize the types of television news programs in a 1950 survey, he came up with six formats, in order of their popularity with the audience: remote coverage, newsreels (local and national), still-picture casts, headline shows, television "newspapers," and ticker-tape programs.[11]

As early as 1950, it was already clear that television's strength was in the live coverage of special events. Sports was the most popular format for live broadcasts. The audience also tuned in for political conventions, United Nation ceremonies, parades, and other newsworthy events. The Kefauver crime hearings in 1951 as well as the Army-McCarthy hearings in 1954 showed the public was fascinated with watching real events unfold live on television. A survey of local stations in 1950 showed that 46 percent of live remotes involved sports, 23 percent involved meetings and hearings, and 20 percent of remote coverage dealt with disasters.[12]

Heath admitted that even though remote coverage had the "highest potential" for news presentation, the cost and complexity of live coverage made it unfeasible for regularly scheduled programs. Remote coverage involved hours, or days, of preparation, one or two large trucks, as well as a sizable technical crew. Rudy Bretz of WPIX in New York estimated it would cost $200,000 a year to have remote equipment and crew on standby for breaking news events. CBS, and especially NBC, had the money and resources to switch live to affiliated stations' studios for breaking news, but even this practice was limited because of the expense. In reality, live coverage of an event was a separate program category from daily or weekly news and did not become a regular part of an American newscast until the proliferation of microwave technology and electronic news gathering (ENG) in the late 1960s and 1970s.[13]

The next category on the Iowa State list of popular television news formats was the national and local newsreel. In the 1950s, CBS and NBC, as well as the theatrical newsreel companies, sold syndicated newsreels to local television stations. Those stations could run the newsreels as provided or they could customize the reels through selective editing or by using a local narrator. These national and international newsreels became popular because the stations did not have to invest much manpower into presenting these productions. The programs looked much like the newsreels the American public had been watching in theaters for decades, with an unseen narrator explaining the filmed stories that were edited together in one package, usually accompanied by music and sound effects since most of the film was shot without sound.

Conversely, the local newsreel was the most ambitious format a station could attempt in 1950, and few stations invested in such an elaborate local news program. According to Heath, "Newsreels set a vigorous pace, demand a narrative that doesn't overstate what can clearly be seen and completely comprehended, plus strong human interest." As early as 1947, WFIL started producing a newsreel for its Philadelphia audience. The next year, WPIX in New York created quite a splash by blanketing the area with film cameras, using planes, helicopters, and remote film developing to get moving pictures quickly from the scene to the screen. WBAP in Fort Worth and WGN in Chicago also created newsreels for their communities. Unfortunately, these local newsreels rarely attracted the audience or advertising money necessary to support the staff to produce the programs.[14]

By 1950, people working in television news had already learned a hard lesson: the staff and budget needed to present news effectively was larger than station owners and advertisers would fund. If news programs had been considered "entertainment," they would have been quickly canceled in favor of formats with higher audiences and lower costs. Since the Federal Communication Commission (FCC) demanded news and public affairs programs as part of the license requirements, stations were forced to provide those programs. The usual approach was to spend as little money as possible on the regularly scheduled news broadcasts since they were not as popular with advertisers. Heath estimated that the fewest number of people needed to staff a newsreel program was five. In 1950, more than 30 percent of the stations did not have a single person specifically dedicated to the television news effort. Another 32 percent reported only one or two people working in news.[15]

With limited staff and resources, the proliferation of the final four formats in the Iowa State survey (still-picture casts, headline shows, television "newspapers," and ticker tape programs) is obvious. Still-picture casts consisted of a man reading the news on camera supplemented solely with still photographs received from the wire services. These were the same photographs available to newspapers and magazines. Headline shows also involved a newscaster reading the news on camera, with the headline of each story flashing on the screen.

Television "newspapers" had been an experimental format dating back to the mid-1940s when stations would partner with a newspaper and produce a visualized, moving-picture version of newspaper sections. These tended to be special one-time broadcasts. The stripped-down 1950s version of the television newspaper was a graphic mock-up of a newspaper format with headlines, copy, and sections. The viewer had to read the stories on the screen while soft music played in the background. Ticker-tape news, supplied by United Press and other companies, is similar to today's news ticker. Stories scrolled across the bottom of the screen or in some cases would take up the entire screen and move from bottom to top. A few stations even admitted in the Iowa State survey that their local news efforts consisted of nothing more than one man, on camera, reading news stories supplied by the wire services, with little extra effort to provide visuals.[16]

The Iowa State survey categories were a bit limiting because some stations used a combination of techniques, even within the same program. The University of Missouri also conducted a television news survey in 1950, and more than 70 percent of the stations reported they were using live or filmed interviews in their news and public affairs programs. More than 30 percent were using graphics and almost 10 percent included animated graphics.[17]

With such low-budget approaches to news, it is not surprising that another survey at the start of the 1950s, when roughly 10 percent of the country owned television sets, indicated viewers liked all types of programs better on television than radio, except for news. Heath was hopeful that as television started to make more money, the low budget approaches to news would disappear: "It is illogical to ask a viewer to strain to read when he can read with less effort and in greater detail in newspapers and magazines. It is illogical to ask him to watch another man read the news to him."[18]

On the other end of the budget spectrum from the man reading the news on camera on a local station were the network newscasts on CBS, NBC, and, to a lesser extent, ABC and DuMont. While the budgets and staffs of television network news efforts in 1950 paled in comparison with entertainment programs, or even radio news, they were the apex in television news operations. CBS's *Douglas Edwards with the News* involved 150 staff hours of work every day, including "at least half a dozen newsmen [who] are in on the planning and producing of the show." NBC's *Camel News Caravan* had a similar operation, and at that point, a larger budget because of the advertising sponsorship. One term used to describe the network news format was "hybrid" because the newscasts included different visualization methods, including live reports from affiliates, film, graphics, and interviews. The hybrid format, which today we call the television newscast, was created by the CBS television crew in the early 1940s and then adopted by NBC in 1949.[19]

Nonvisual Influences on Television News

The development of television news in the 1950s was not only hampered by advertiser indifference, but also by the prior experiences of those who worked in the medium. In the United States, NBC and CBS were two of the biggest players in the development of television. Since these companies were built on radio and that medium brought in the major profits until the early 1950s, television developed in radio's shadow and was subjected to the ideas and experiences of people from an aural medium.

Newspaper companies also owned a significant number of both television and radio stations. In 1950, newspapers owned 41 percent of all television stations, 23 percent of AM radio stations, and 35 percent of FM stations. With the high cost of programming, television news expenses could be minimized by using newspaper or radio staff to produce the newscasts. In most cases, journalists or executives from newspapers or radio had little background or interest in visual communication.[20]

In a 1950 survey of people working in television news, two-thirds of "television newsmen" came out of radio (42 percent) and newspapers (24 percent). Fifteen percent started after graduation from a journalism school, 9 percent from photography, 3 percent from newsreels, and 3 percent from "dramatics." This survey may be skewed because in this era, people shooting or editing film may not have been considered part of the television news effort. [21]

Reuven Frank's Visual Maturation

Both NBC and CBS had settled on the hybrid newscast by 1950, but the NBC newscast that Reuven Frank joined borrowed more heavily from the theater newsreel tradition, which was one reason for his unhappiness with the format. The newscast usually began with the top story of the day, and if it involved the US government, David Brinkley would often present the story live from the Washington newsroom. Other stories would be visualized by film and interviews from press conferences, meetings, and anywhere else they could get their film cameras.

NBC ran fashion segments with an unseen female narrator, a tradition taken from the newsreels. The newscast would also include sports stories and scores, along with a periodic weather forecast. Feature stories on antique car shows, parades, and other newsreel staples were often used toward the end of the newscast.

Over the years, Frank and others at NBC were able to eliminate many of the newsreel staples. By the launch of the format with Chet Huntley and David Brinkley in 1956, the newscast focused on as much of the top stories and original reporting that the staff size, budget, and fifteen-minute timeslot could handle. While Frank rejected the newsreel traditions, he was experimenting with telling stories visually and finding ways to make the news more compelling for the growing audience for television news.

As chronicled in the last chapter, Frank sought out opportunities throughout the 1950s to produce half-hour specials, weekly public affairs programs, documentaries, political party convention coverage, and election night returns. For most of the decade, he juggled these additional projects in addition to his work on the nightly newscast. He was able to escape from the restraints of the nightly newscasts periodically, but he was then called back to revamp the format. The first instance happened when NBC asked Frank to create and produce what became the *Huntley-Brinkley Report* in 1956. He was finally able to step away from daily production of that newscast in 1962, just as he was working on *The Tunnel*. By the end of the year, he knew he would be dragged right back into the daily grind, as the two top networks started making plans to double the length of their newscasts.

Thirty-Minute Newscast

Expanding the length of the nightly network newscast had long been the wish of those working in network television news. The fifteen-minute format was a throwback to radio news and limited the ability to bring together moving pictures, sounds, graphics, and words. The restrictive length often forced the newscast into a mere digest of the news, which was not a satisfying format for many of the journalists working in television news. Frank had never been shy about criticizing both the length and timeslot of the network newscast: "The quarter-hour succeeded despite itself because the audience wanted news, not because the audience wanted 15 minutes of news with dinner."[22]

Scheduling the network newscast in the early evening was not a strategic move, but instead resulted from a gradual compromise between the popular network prime time hours and the local station afternoon hours. Networks did not want to schedule newscasts when the audience size was the largest because of the greater audience potential of entertainment programs. Local stations, especially in larger cities, had already taken fifteen or even thirty minutes in the post-prime time 11:00 p.m. EST hour for local news, as well as portions of the 5:00 p.m.–6:30 p.m. EST timeslot for their early evening news. These decisions pushed the network news into the period after the local early news and before primetime evening hours.[23]

People who had been advocating for a longer newscast had to contend with those same two powerful forces: network executives and local affiliates. The networks made most of their money on entertainment programs, so executives bristled at providing precious air time for news and public affairs programs. The quiz show scandals and the renewed interest of the Kennedy administration in forcing the industry to schedule more public affairs programming provided extra muscle for the longer newscast argument. Since NBC president Robert Kintner embraced a strategy of using news and public affairs to build an audience for primetime entertainment programs, he could also be seen as an ally.

The affiliates were another matter. The local stations fought any expansion of the network schedule because the move would mean less time for local commercials. In most cities, the network and local news ran adjacent to each other in a news block. Expanding network news to thirty minutes would force many local stations to change their local news schedule as well as forfeit another fifteen minutes of air time close to primetime evening hours. The length of the program was one issue. How to best utilize those minutes on a sight and sound medium became a more contested topic.

New Journalism

While Frank was working on *The Tunnel* in 1962, a few blocks away from Frank's office in 30 Rockefeller Plaza in midtown Manhattan, *New York Herald Tribune* reporter Tom Wolfe was experiencing his new journalism epiphany. Wolfe framed the beginning of this movement as a friendly competition between feature writers at his *Herald Tribune* along with other New York newspapers and magazines, including the *New Yorker*. In short, those reporters decided that it "was possible to write accurate non-fiction with techniques usually associated with short stories and novels."[24]

New journalism was much more time-consuming than traditional reporting because the journalists not only had to get the usual information, but then add in the "subjective or emotional life of the characters." The only way to capture those moments was to spend considerable time with the subjects, as Wolfe put it, to "*be there* when dramatic scenes took place to the get the dialogue, the gestures, the facial expressions, the details of the environment."[25]

The 1960s' new journalism movement included Wolfe, Jimmy Breslin, Dick Schaap, Gay Talese, Joan Didion, George Plimpton, and many others, depending on who compiled the list. Truman Capote caused a sensation with his 1966 book *In Cold Blood,* chronicling the brutal murder of a Kansas farm family, following the suspects from their trial to eventual hanging. Hunter S. Thompson took the concept to the extreme, joining a Hells Angels motorcycle gang as a reporter for several months, writing in the first person, and eventually getting beaten up by the members for what he wrote.

Over time, new journalism gave way to a slightly more precise term, *literary journalism*. The name change allowed Wolfe and his style of writing to be encompassed in a larger, more historical, subset of nonfiction writing that included techniques normally found in fiction writing, most notably the narrative format.[26]

Journalism on Television

None of the ideas that the new journalism movement was pushing seemed very radical to Reuven Frank. He had been blending ideas of traditional journalism and narrative film for years as he adapted to television news. By the end of 1962, he was thrust into a project that forced him to put down his ideas on paper.

In December, CBS announced that it would double the length of its nightly newscast from fifteen to thirty minutes in 1963, forcing NBC to do the same. NBC News president William McAndrew turned to Frank to shepherd NBC's expected newscast expansion. But first, McAndrew wanted a rationale on why the newscast should be expanded and what it would look like.

This request came just four days after *The Tunnel* finally ran on NBC and Reuven Frank was still reveling in the compliments from that struggle. Frank's response to the need for, and format of, a thirty-minute network newscast started as an eleven-page letter to his boss in early January 1963. When NBC made formal plans to expand the newscast by September 1963, Frank was assigned to oversee the expansion. He reworked and expanded the original memo into a thirty-two-page manifesto for the NBC News staff, with help from colleague John Chancellor.

By 1963, Frank had more than a dozen years of experience in daily television news, roughly nine continuous years of weekly half-hour program producing, several long form documentaries, and three years' experience on a city daily newspaper. His ideas, reflections, observations, insights, complaints, and other ruminations in these two written documents not only provide the structure and rationale for a half-hour newscast, but are also clearly driven by the lessons he learned during his months producing and fighting for *The Tunnel*, and how to apply those lessons to all of television news.

The two written documents were originally composed for a small, specific audience, and not for public consumption. The letter was clearly providing his boss a rationale for the expansion that could be taken to NBC executives as well as to help convince affiliates to give up the extra fifteen minutes. The memo was written for the NBC News staff, especially those who still favored radio over television, as Frank attempted to show them the strengths of television news. The ideas and examples in the memo resonated so strongly that it eventually found its way to television journalists at other networks, at local stations, and into books and articles.

96 CHAPTER THREE

Taken together, Frank's documentary and the subsequent memos on the strength and potential of television news provide a unique perspective on this critical juncture in American journalism and media history as television emerged as the most popular and trusted source for the public, a position it would hold well past the turn of the next century.

The rest of the chapter is devoted to analyzing the two written documents and the documentary for Frank's vision on how to best practice journalism on the live sight-and-sound format. First, Frank's ideas on the best use of television as a news medium, as a primer for those who would be working on the expanded NBC *Huntley-Brinkley Report,* followed by the linkages between the two written documents and *The Tunnel* documentary that had consumed Frank during the previous year.

The News in Television News

To understand the context of the memo and why it has resonated with so many television journalists over the decades, a disconnect must be acknowledged between the public, academic, and in many cases historical view of the *Huntley-Brinkley Report* and the perception of reporters, photographers, editors, writers, and others who work in television news. This distinction is explored more fully in chapter 5, but a brief explanation here might preclude some questions later. The *Huntley-Brinkley Report* was the flagship NBC newscast from 1956 until 1970 when Chet Huntley retired. For most of those years, the *Huntley-Brinkley Report* was the most watched and honored network news program in the country, even when it competed against Walter Cronkite at CBS, who took over the *CBS Evening News* in 1962.

The disconnect lies in the reason for the success of the *Huntley-Brinkley Report.* In the popular press at the time, and in many academic and anecdotal histories of this period, the public embraced Huntley and Brinkley and their unique two-city co-newscaster arrangement. Huntley and Brinkley became television celebrities, along with Milton Berle, Lucille Ball, and others. For television writers then, and many historical accounts since, the *Huntley-Brinkley Report* success had little to do with journalism or informing the public, and was all about the two men.[27]

Frank clearly knew that his two newscasters and the format had connected with the public. He went along with the efforts to get Huntley and Brinkley involved in weekly public affairs programs and in breaking news situations.

As a producer, however, he believed the audience turned the nightly newscast into a viewing habit because of the stories they covered and how those stories were presented to the public. Huntley and Brinkley might get them to watch, but the coverage kept them returning.

As evidence, Frank never mentioned the two newscasters in his eleven-page letter to McAndrew, and they are referenced only once in the thirty-two-page memo to the staff. Clearly, the value of Huntley and Brinkley was implicit, but Frank did not believe the newscasters were the key to effective television news.

Converting Print and Radio Journalists

The "transmission of experience" memo goes into deep detail and has an edgy feel to it partly because of the *specific* audience Reuven Frank had in mind when writing the guide to the expanded newscast. His dozen years in television as that medium emerged, preceded by a few years at a newspaper, meant Frank had worked with people with a wide range of backgrounds and views on journalism. Since NBC had started out as a radio company and then added television, most of the news staff until the mid-1950s came from a print or audio background. Even as television clearly emerged as the more dominant medium, those who favored radio clung to their format and, when asked to report for television, gave little thought to the added visual component of what they were doing.

When Frank was creating and producing the fifteen-minute *Huntley-Brinkley Report*, as well as his various documentaries and public affairs programs, he had been able to put together a team within NBC News that mostly agreed with his vision on the importance of the visuals, as well as the audio and the words. Frank and his team learned together over the years how to expand the communication potential of television news.

That group was just a small part of the growing NBC News operation on both television and radio. By expanding to thirty minutes, Frank was going to have to include the rest of the NBC News staff, many of whom had not adapted well to the visual format. As a result, the "transmission of experience" memo included not only the structure and logistics, but also specifics on the best and worst practices of television news. Frank was trying to convince the rest of the NBC News staff that the *Huntley-Brinkley Report*'s success was not just because of the two newscasters, but the result of understanding how television was different from radio and print.

Transmission of Experience

For Reuven Frank, the most important point he tried to instill in the staff was that while newspapers and television news both produced journalism, the two formats had different strengths. Unfortunately for those working in television news, the printed word had centuries of history as the primary, or at least preferred, format for disseminating information, coupled with a few decades of radio journalism. With such a strong preference for words on paper by the elite, including the academy, coupled with a strong twentieth-century push by print journalists, publishers, and journalistic organizations, journalism's default was the printed word, with all other formats judged on how close they came to the newspaper and magazine approach to covering and presenting the news.

As a veteran of both formats, Frank delineated between the printed word's ability to convey information, with television's more visceral reaction among its viewers. He called television's strength "the transmission of experience." Television could not match newspapers for presenting a series of facts and figures that the readers could casually consume and reread if interested. Since television was a linear viewing experience, the viewer could not stop to ponder a fact or viewpoint without missing whatever came next. Therefore, too much spoken information could easily overwhelm the viewer's ability to process.[28]

When television journalists produced an effective combination of images, spoken words, natural sounds, and other visual information, the medium could provide a more personal connection to the news. Using two important issues of the early 1960s, Frank differentiated the two media: "*The Washington Post* can explain that the mainland Chinese are living on 1200 calories a day. Television can show hunger. *The Kansas City Star* can feature a study of the trend toward larger farms in the Midwest; we can watch a farmer and his family while his farm is being auctioned."[29]

In 1962, these insights would not be particularly enlightening to anyone working in documentary or fiction film. For journalists with a print or audio background, Frank was asking them to make a radical change to how they researched and reported a story. In short, Frank's vision of effective television news required a different skill set than print or radio journalism.

He ran into heavy resistance within NBC. In the memo, Frank gives specific instances of bad television stories that had run on NBC, without mentioning names. He also provides examples of effective ways of approaching a story from a visual perspective.

Frank was not only asking the NBC News journalists to think visually first; he also wanted them to strive for a structure for each story that would draw in the viewers and get them to care about the issue, whether it affected them directly or if it was happening halfway around the world. In one of the most important paragraphs in that memo, Frank urged the staff to borrow techniques often considered part of fiction writing or film producing: "Every news story should, without a sacrifice of probity or responsibility, display the attributes of fiction, of drama. It should have structure and conflict, problem and denouement, rising action and falling action, a beginning, a middle and an end. These are not only the essentials of drama; they are the essential of narrative. We are in the business of narrative because we are in the business of communication."[30] In essence, he wanted his staff to become storytellers. Frank's experience producing *The Tunnel* documentary is clearly part of his thinking when he wrote this section of the "transmission of experience" memo. Frank's insights into effective television journalism are quite similar to what Tom Wolfe and the other feature reporters in New York were discovering during the same period.

NBC correspondent Linda Ellerbee would later describe Frank's ideas on television news to be both "obvious, and radical." While the idea of using narrative techniques in documentaries or print feature stories was not new in 1962, suggesting this approach to daily journalism prompted strong responses, both in print and television. Narrative structure is a long way from the preferred print journalism "inverted pyramid" approach that positioned the most important information in the beginning and lesser details deeper in the story in case it had to be cut for space. Suggesting fiction techniques for daily journalism provided ammunition for people who already believed television was, in essence, an entertainment medium, and not suited for serious information.[31]

Television Authority and Responsibility

The unbelievable growth of television in the United States in the 1950s and early 1960s brought about an important change in how Reuven Frank and many in television news approached their responsibility to the audience watching those daily newscasts. Many of the people in television news came out of a newspaper background and most considered newspapers, as well as radio, as the primary source of news in a community. Television journalists believed their viewers had already read at least one newspaper before they watched the newscast. Therefore, 1950s television news producers did not feel the obligation to cover all the news, especially with the fifteen-minute limitation. They could skip stories that worked better in a print format and concentrate on issues and events that had a more visual component.

By the early 1960s, Frank and other television news veterans realized that a growing number of viewers were using television as their primary source of news, not a supplement. These viewers included people who stopped or cut back on reading newspapers and, more importantly, people who had never read the paper regularly but instead had started to follow the news because of television's widespread adoption and format for presenting the news.

This realization meant a shift in how television news producers decided what stories to include in the newscast. "Our excitement at the novelty of pictures as their own news medium was no longer justification enough," remembered Frank. "For better or for worse, to too many people, what we did was The News." Frank felt a strong obligation to cover all the important stories, even those that might work better in a text format. Because of its audience size and loyalty, Frank believed TV news was "now accepted as authoritative, and this authority sustains it where it cannot rely on the impact of picture, and cannot shirk the mandate to inform comprehensively."[32]

One big question by the early 1960s that did not have a clear answer was why so many people were watching television news. The default, mostly unspoken reason was that the television medium had become the most pervasive format in the United States, so television news benefited from that reach. Television ratings clearly showed that on average many more people watched entertainment programming than news, mirroring listening habits when radio was the top format. Under FCC rules, networks and local stations had to offer news programming, and it was often scheduled at the same time on the different stations, so people had little choice than to watch the news if they wanted to watch television, especially at the dinner hour.

Rarely in the print press did anyone acknowledge that the sight and sound format could be more effective at communicating the news, for certain issues, and for people who did not have a newspaper reading habit. People might not be watching television news because they had to, but because they preferred that format. As a believer in the format, Frank wanted to make sure his staff did not take the audience for granted. Over the short history of American television, various formats had cyclical popularity trends, gaining and losing favor, including live anthologies, comedies, westerns, and variety shows. While television news and informational programming usually attracted a smaller audience than entertainment programs, the audience kept pace with the increase in stations and viewers. Frank was convinced that a large part of the American population considered television as an authority on the news and that the bond "is delicate and can easily be destroyed because it is essentially the result of a trust," a prescient view considering the political and public backlash against network television news later in the 1960s.[33]

Shared Experience

In 1962, the act of watching television was known as appointment viewing. Home recording would not become popular for a few more decades. If people wanted to watch a specific program, they had to be in front of the set at the moment it was broadcast. Families sat together to watch their favorite shows. Friends and strangers gathered at the bar to watch sports. Those groups were linked with all the other people around the country watching that program at the same time. Much like radio earlier in the century, the liveness of television provided a shared experience. For Frank, the potential of helping the viewers experience a story through effective use of visuals, sounds, and words provided an even more vivid and lasting shared memory of the world's top issues. As examples in the memo, Frank listed major world events that had happened since he started producing the *Huntley-Brinkley Report*: the Hungarian revolution and Suez Crisis in 1956; the civil rights school standoff in Little Rock, Arkansas; the building of the Berlin Wall; the 1960 Democratic primaries; and Soviet leader Nikita Khrushchev's 1959 visit to the United States. He not only considered these stories that television covered well, but also that television news was now providing a communal memory: "There are events which exist in the American mind and recollection primarily because they were reported on regular television news programs. We have found a dimension of information which is not contained in words alone."[34]

Producing a Television "Experience"

Frank's "bible" memo had both big picture ideas and minute details on how to move television news more toward its strength in the "transmission of experience." For most reporters, Frank's ideas on how to report and produce a television news story in collaboration with producers, photojournalists, lighting technicians, sound engineers, and editors was no easy transition from the individualistic work in print or radio.

Print and radio reporters were used to writing a story or script, which was either printed on paper or read into a microphone, depending on the format. Many of these reporters made the transition to television without an understanding of, or respect for, the visuals. Instead of editing in moving pictures that would illustrate the specific story, the reporters would merely read or ad-lib parts of their script on camera, which prompted Frank to remind them sarcastically, "A reporter's head is not our logotype."[35]

Instead, Frank advocated shooting and editing the film first, then writing just enough words to add understanding to the pictures. This method forced reporters to work closely with the photographers and other members of the production team. By editing the images first, the reporter needed to match the words to the pictures, not the other way around. He urged the film photographers and editors to look for the small details that would connect the audience to the story: "A street sign in a foreign language, a store selling strange goods, the clothes of bystanders, a main street with cars parked down the center, these can take the viewer to the place of the event."[36]

Natural Sound

Another key element in the push to transmit an experience is the sound of a scene. A moving image of a location is one part of the experience and the sound of that location can be just as valuable. The sound could be traffic noise, birds chirping, or even heavy artillery in battle. Frank felt that providing the viewer with both the sights and sounds of a scene allowed for a better chance for immersion: "Sound can establish the environment of your event. So can picture. Very few events we trouble to cover are not enhanced by including a feeling of where they took place."[37]

Economic and technological roadblocks had relegated the capturing of sound to an exception instead of the rule during the first six decades of nonfiction moving pictures, from newsreels and documentaries to television news. Cameras that recorded both pictures and sound at the same time, sync sound, were expensive, heavy, and difficult to use away from an electrical source. Silent film cameras were smaller, less expensive, and could be easily used in the field. Most American television news and public affairs in the

1950s followed the newsreel practice of limiting sound camera use for scheduled interviews, speeches, and other staged events, such as press conferences and government hearings. On location pictures were shot without sound. Music or sound effects would be added in later.

On *The Tunnel*, the camera crew chose to shoot most of the film without sound because of the confined space in the tunnel, which made it difficult to include audio equipment. They did specifically record the sound once in the tunnel, to let the viewer hear the sounds of footsteps and other surface noises just feet above the tunnel.

As Frank wrote his memo in 1963, portable sync sound cameras were available and in use, but they were not yet the standard at NBC. "One day, every cameraman will come with a portable camera synchronized by remote control to a high-fidelity portable tape recorder. That day has not yet come." He encouraged reporters to bring a separate audio recorder for natural sound, as long as that practice did not conflict with union restrictions on technology use. But he had to warn the reporter not to talk continuously while recording sound because that would ruin the effect of capturing the sounds of the scene.[38]

Overall, he expected all members of the team to respect the role of the individuals. Reporters in a hurry should not rush film crews in setting up the camera, lights, and audio, especially for indoor filming where proper lighting was needed for usable film. He reminded the film crews that their images had to be well lit, in focus, and with clear audio, and also, just as important, the images needed to relate directly to the story they were trying to tell. In a not-so-subtle dig at the *cinéma vérité* movement becoming popular in that period (discussed in the next chapter), Frank reminded the film crews they chose to work as journalists: "It may not work in the art film houses, but that's a choice you made long ago."[39]

Interviews

In the 1990s, a sub-strand of political communication research gained attention for its damning evidence on the stark changes in how television newscasts covered political campaigns over the decades. Two studies, by Kiku Adatto and Daniel Hallin, comparing network coverage of the 1968 and 1988 presidential campaign coverage emphasized the dramatic decrease in the length of candidate sound bites on television newscasts over the two decades. Adatto found that Richard Nixon and Hubert Humphrey spoke for 42.3 seconds on average compared to 9.8 seconds given to George Bush and Michael Dukakis; Hallin's results were nearly the same, with a decrease from 43.1 seconds for candidates' soundbites in 1968 to only 8.9 seconds in 1988.[40]

Adatto said the shorter soundbites illustrated "television's growing impatience with political speech." Hallin perceived the 1968 coverage to be about the future of the nation but by 1988, he warned that the coverage "no longer conveys that sense of seriousness."[41]

The method and results resonated among elites and the academy because of the numbers-oriented social science approach popular in communication research and because of its negative assessment of television's role in the election process. The studies have been referenced over the subsequent quarter-century, with several scholars replicating or expanding on the method.[42]

These studies often included possible reasons for the change, including television's transition from film to electronic news gathering, which allowed for much easier and quicker editing; the increasing distrust in government leaders because of deceit over the Vietnam War and other issues; and criticism of all journalists for their lack of skepticism and context in earlier political coverage.

If the soundbite scholars are looking for another scapegoat for the decrease in newscast interview air time, they should look back farther to the "transmission of experience" memo. Frank hated long interview clips in the network newscasts, not just for politicians, but for everyone.[43]

Frank felt reporters often used the interview as a "crutch," letting the question and answers fill up too much of the story. Instead, he pushed reporters and producers to find important visuals about the topic and pare down the interview to some key points. Frank likened the long interview (one to two minutes in the early 1960s) in a news story to taking a print reporter's scribbled notes and just printing them in the paper. "Getting a picture of an event as it happens takes effort and luck, sometimes a lot of both. Neither is needed to back some hapless eyewitness, or even participant, against a wall and let him tell what happened. It is too easy to consider this an adequate substitute." Given his blunt nature, Frank made it even clearer why interviews often did not help the viewer better understand an issue or event. "Most people are dull. That is, they communicate ineptly. If they are dull, their description of interesting events will be dull."[44]

Most of the soundbite length research is devoted to campaign coverage, which is only one type of story covered in a network newscast. Frank did not make an exception for politicians. He did not believe the interview length could be equated with the amount of insight or knowledge gained by the viewer. "Those who communicate eptly—politicians, actors, and the like—tend to be self-serving." Frank felt the effective communicators could easily sidestep the issue to promote their own interests. The journalists needed to keep the report, and the interview clips, focused on the particular topic.[45]

He also reminded the staff that his views on favoring the visuals and story focus over interview length was mainly geared toward the newscasts. The networks all had their Sunday morning talk programs on which politicians and other leaders could speak at length without interruption. But even by 1962, Frank felt *Meet the Press, Face the Nation,* and the other political talk shows were geared more toward the Washington establishment than the average viewer.

Reuven Frank's Thirty-Minute Newscast Vision

The half-hour television newscast was not a new innovation in 1963. A few local stations had already expanded beyond the fifteen-minute benchmark. Frank had not been impressed with what he had seen in the longer newscasts, and he wanted to use this opportunity at NBC to do more than just expand the digest format to include more stories. Frank considered the nightly newscast a unique experience, different from reading the newspapers or even watching breaking news on television, partly because of the shared experience of millions of Americans watching at the same time every night: "a feeling of one-time-only which draws an incredible number of Americans to their sets at a given time each night against the distraction of kids, cartoons, cooking, and martinis."[46]

Since the *Huntley-Brinkley Report* started in 1956 with limited fanfare and a budget to match, Frank had become accustomed to making the best with a small staff and finding a way to make even the poorly executed stories fit into the newscast. Now, he wanted the network to build a large, international news staff that would generate so many stories that he could pick and choose the best material each night and eliminate the rest. He felt the key to improving quality involved journalists competing for a chance to have their work featured on the nightly newscast.

Instead of more stories, he wanted to use the extra time to showcase the longer-form work he had been doing in the weekly *Chet Huntley Reporting* half-hour public affairs programs as well as in his occasional documentaries. These stories would be planned in advance, giving the crews time to research, shoot, and edit the best combinations of visuals, words, and sounds to best execute the "transmission of experience."

More specifically, Frank broke the newscast into five segments, separated by commercial breaks. The first and third segments would include the top stories of the day, much like the fifteen-minute newscast format. The final segment would be for a summary as well as any new bulletins. He wanted to reserve the second and fourth segments for the longer stories. The second segment pieces would run roughly four minutes, and the fourth segment stories could be as long as seven minutes. Network newscasts had not emphasized such in-depth pieces with any regularity since the visualizers at CBS television news in the mid-1940s.[47]

Frank felt the large nightly audience for the *Huntley-Brinkley Report* was the perfect venue for producing stories that would help viewers connect with and care about issues beyond their daily life: "We want him to feel it is he crossing the Vietnamese marsh under fire, that it is he who has just been elected, that it is he who faces the problem of learning a new trade and moving his family to a new city. It is an ideal we shall rarely achieve, but it is not absolute. It can be approached by degrees."[48]

Both CBS and NBC switched to the half-hour format in September 1963. CBS launched its expanded newscast with Walter Cronkite on Labor Day and the *Huntley-Brinkley Report* debuted the thirty-minute program the following Monday. ABC would not expand its nightly newscast to thirty minutes until 1967. Frank lost his battle to move the newscast to a later hour when more people were home from work. In most cities on the eastern time zone, NBC and CBS network newscasts ran at 6:30 p.m. or 7:00 p.m.[49]

Matching up Frank's vision with how the staff actually executed the emphasis on the "transmission of experience" is anecdotal at best since the networks rarely saved their newscasts, and the Vanderbilt Television News Archive in Nashville did not start recording and archiving newscasts until 1968. Sampling scripts, audio air checks, and some film examples from NBC newscasts in the first years after Frank's memo show a consistent effort to produce stories, or at least just scenes within a story, that attempted to transport the viewers to different places through the sights and sounds of the locations. Frank's vision of highlighting the longer form stories in the second and fourth segments did not often fit with the stories that the networks chose to present or were available on a particular day. The longer pieces did tend to run in the fourth or final segments. Overall, elements of the "transmission of experience" memo could be found both in shorter and longer stories throughout the newscast. A study of NBC network newscast stories in 1968–1969 showed that just under half of the stories reflected daily news and the rest involved less timely topics.[50]

Frank's insistence on longer stories was not unique; CBS also used the expanded newscast to include stories that moved beyond the digest format. Both networks featured exclusive filmed interviews with President John F. Kennedy on the first day of their expanded newscast, Walter Cronkite for CBS and Huntley and Brinkley for NBC. Concerning what would become one of the biggest stories of the decade, the half-hour format allowed the networks to offer more filmed coverage of the Vietnam War, just as the United States was escalating its involvement.[51]

The "transmission of experience" memo clearly had been and continued to be the blueprint for how NBC approached the expanded *Huntley-Brinkley Report*. The memo also had an impact well beyond that newscast and through the decades, as discussed later in the book. Another important connection is how much Frank's experience producing *The Tunnel* influenced the ideas in the memo itself. Frank considered *The Tunnel* the ultimate experience because instead of the usual process of filming a story that had already happened, he had moving pictures of a big event in process. When he was a print reporter, he could easily re-create an event or scene with words, but "in film, being in on the unfolding of a story is a big and unique experience. I believe there are a lot of honorable journalists who spend useful professional careers without achieving it, and I just fell into it." Frank's approach to producing *The Tunnel* and its subsequent success cemented his confidence that he knew how to communicate via television. *The Tunnel* production also reveals just how deeply Frank and the NBC crew were ingrained in Cold War ideology, even as they specifically worked to avoid that trap.[52]

"Transmission of Experience" and *The Tunnel*

One of the reasons *The Tunnel* experience was such an epiphany on visual communication for Frank was the unorthodox way he had to produce that documentary. Normally, as producer, he would be determining the direction of the project and the visual opportunities all throughout the process, coming up with the different elements and structure as the work progressed. Because of the secrecy of the tunnel dig, he had to rely on his staff to tell him what was happening in their periodic meetings in other European cities as the dig progressed. Frank had ideas on how he wanted to include the different ways people had been trying to get out of East Germany, including escaping through sewers, jumping the wall, and swimming the rivers and canals. He felt the student tunnel project would be one element of a larger story.

Instead of his usual practice of guiding and adapting his projects with each interview and film shoot during the process, Frank and editor Gerald Polikoff sat through an exhaustive session of twenty hours of film when they arrived in West Berlin in September 1962, as the diggers were ready to open up the tunnel for escape. From Thursday afternoon until midnight and Friday morning to mid-afternoon, Frank was overwhelmed and stunned by the images that flashed by, projected on the screen. "When I saw the film of the digging," wrote Frank, "I threw out the sewers, the other tunnels, everything we had planned in those melodramatic meetings in Paris and London. I threw out the plan for what would have been a pretty good documentary surveying means of escape from East Berlin."[53]

He realized the student tunnel project *was* the story. Frank recognized he had a personal story that would represent the oppression of the wall and the determination of people to find a way to escape to freedom. The images on that screen represented the essence of the Cold War ideology: the suffocation of communism juxtaposed with the freedom of democracy and capitalism. "We knew we had found what we had always insisted the best journalism should be: the specific event which illuminates the general condition of man, an action taking place in a defined and identifiable time and place which is an adventure of the human spirit."[54]

The secrecy and logistics also helped Frank focus his documentary on the diggers and the tunnel. He did not think it would be safe to try and transport all twenty hours of film back to New York, so he chose to edit a rough cut of the documentary in Berlin, to "a workable length," and brought that version back to New York for revisions and script writing.[55]

Narrative Structure

As discussed earlier, one of the key points in the "transmission of experience" memo, which dovetails with the new journalism movement starting at the same time in New York, was Frank's insistence that television news should embrace some methods that are usually linked to fiction writing and filmmaking: "We are in the business of narrative because we are in the business of communication."[56]

The Tunnel has an obvious narrative structure. By throwing out all his other ideas for the documentary, Frank was able to reduce the issue to a basic story with identifiable characters, built-in drama, and a dramatic conclusion. He chose to tell the story in chronological order, starting with the ideas for the tunnel project, through the process, and ending with the escape and a post-escape party. In the first half of the documentary, the audience is introduced to the student diggers, Luigi Spina, Domenico Sesta, and Wolf Schroedter, and one of their classmates, Peter Schmidt, who had been stuck on the East side of the wall since the border was closed. The audience is introduced to other diggers throughout the documentary.

While he watched the hours of film for the first time, Frank was struck by the difficult, exhausting, and tedious nature of digging a tunnel. He believed the documentary needed to help the viewers feel like they are crouched underground, in a confined three-by-three-foot space digging forward and maneuvering the shovelful of dirt back into the tunnel. The tunnel was so small that Peter Dehmel had to lie on his stomach with the camera in front of him while his brother Klaus positioned himself on top of his brother to shine the light on the digger ahead. Frank was also fascinated by the process of moving the dirt out of the tunnel and hiding it in the building.

To show the monotony of digging and hauling dirt, Frank felt he had to allow considerable time for that part of the process. As Anderton says in the documentary, "Tunnels are romantic.... Hauling dirt is not." Four times during the ninety-minute documentary, *The Tunnel* features scenes of the diggers sweating in the dark hole making incremental progress with each shovelful.[57]

For some of television's critics, Frank's insistence on spending so much time on the digging process hurt the overall impact of the film. Donald Kirkley of *The Sun* felt the emphasis on the engineering of the tunnel took away from the human story. Frank later admitted he could have easily produced an hour documentary by cutting out some of the digging segments: "It would have moved, would have had much more pace, but it would have been false to the premise," insisted Frank. "There would not have been the feeling of digging in a space 3 feet by 3 feet." This producing decision highlights a short-lived time in American network television when a news producer could command thirty extra minutes of primetime programming merely to help the viewer experience a monotonous activity.[58]

"What Must They Be Leaving to Risk This?"

Since NBC first scheduled *The Tunnel* to run on October 31, 1962, Frank had roughly six weeks from the end of filming to produce the documentary. For the first three weeks after the escape, NBC's involvement in the tunnel stayed a secret from Western media and the US State Department. The project was not postponed until October 24, at the height of the Cuban Missile Crisis. During those weeks, Anderton and Frank worked on the script, while Frank and Polikoff refined the edited film. Frank also contracted with jazz double bass player Eddie Safranski to write and record a score for the program, since most of the film was silent.

The Tunnel, by subject matter alone, is a product of the Cold War. Both the film and premise are black and white. The theme and execution of the project reflect the prevailing ideas in the United States of good versus evil, democracy versus communism. As a producer friend watched a rough cut of *The Tunnel*, he turned to Frank, saying, "What must they be leaving to risk this?" Frank borrowed that line and inserted it at a key point in the escape footage.[59] For Frank, the Berlin Wall represented a graphic symbol of the dangers of communism. If you have to forcibly keep your people in your community and in your system of governing, something must be seriously wrong. The extraordinary risks and planning undertaken by those student diggers, as well all of those other successful, unsuccessful, and even fatal attempts to get out of East Germany, became a visual representation of the inherent flaws of communism, a key component of Cold War ideology since the end of World War II. Frank did not define it as ideology. He considered it reality and he now had the images and story to present to the public as only television could, as a "transmission of experience."

In addition to Cold War ideology, the logistics and politics of filming East and West Berlin may have helped to enhance the image of East Berlin as a sad, depressing space versus the ease of life on the West side of the wall. Most of the documentary is shot in the tunnel, with various segments showing the above ground spaces immediately on each side of the wall in Berlin, especially along Bernauer Strasse and Shönholzer Strasse, streets that ran parallel to the wall.

East Berlin officials rarely let Western film crews into their part of the city, so the majority of the images of East Germany in *The Tunnel* are filmed from above on the Western side of the wall. This logistical limitation helped reinforce the idea of communism as repressive and inferior to democracy. By filming East Berlin from the Western side, the NBC film crew was forced to use telescoped images, through a zoom lens, to provide images of East Berlin. This caused the images to look like surveillance footage, with no ability to show faces or close-ups.

This strategy also meant NBC would mostly be showing images of East Berlin within a block or so from the wall itself. Because of the heavy presence of police and the forced abandonment of some buildings near the wall, as well as the death strips where would-be escapees could be shot on sight, people in East Berlin stayed away from the streets adjacent to the border. As a result, the East Berlin scenes in view from a camera in West Berlin revealed a lifeless place, which was emphasized in the images and script.

In one section of the documentary, Frank makes a direct comparison between life in East and West Berlin, using images from the area along Bernauer Strasse on both sides of the wall. Because of the wall's proximity, Bernauer Strasse had become a popular tourist stop for West Berlin. NBC filmed crowds of people strolling up and down the street, buying postcards in gift shops. A wooden platform had been built so people could climb up and look over the wall into East Berlin.

East Berlin is represented by the space directly beyond the wall, with an empty street and a close-up image of a weed growing in a cracked sidewalk. The doors and windows of the buildings are bricked up to keep people from jumping over the wall. In other shots, zoomed in from the Western side, faceless people are huddled in line with a lonely streetcar slowly going by. We are told that for East Berliners, "leisure time was spent standing in line" waiting for food and packages.[60]

The only upbeat images of East Germany were not filmed by NBC but by tunnel organizer Domenico Sesta. He smuggled a camera across the border to Wilhelmshagen, in the suburbs of East Berlin, to film Peter Schmidt and his family. Schmidt was a classmate at West Berlin's Technical University until the wall trapped him and his family in East Germany. The images show a country scene, with a child playing in the tall grass outside the house, a sharp contrast to the bleak East Berlin city scenes seen throughout the rest of *The Tunnel* documentary.

The Tunnel Script

Since Peter and Klaus Dehmel had filmed such powerful images of the tunnel project and escape, Frank did not want the script to take away from the simplicity of the visual story. As he suggested in the "transmission of experience" memo the best method for producing television stories, the moving images for *The Tunnel* were edited first, and then a script was crafted to complement the visuals. As Frank and Anderton wrote the words the correspondent would voice for the documentary, their goal was to use words sparingly: "Part of our reaction was the extreme, almost mannered, simplicity of the script—incidentally, the most complicated type of script to write."[61]

It was not difficult to portray the wall (and communism) as evil. *The Tunnel* script was quite blunt on the symbolism: "To live in West Berlin means to live always in the presence of menace." For East Germans, "each stone is meant to keep you out . . . each strand of barbed wire to catch you and hold you." Moving beyond the wall, existence in a communist state is considered to be without virtue or mercy. In the script, the words function and (lack of) grace are employed twice. When describing why Peter Schmidt wanted to get his family out of East Berlin, even though the images show a young child playing in the grass with family, we are reminded they live "the functional, graceless life of communism." While peeking in on East Berlin just past the wall through the telescoped camera shots, Anderton observes that "the life you saw when you looked to the east was not only a life of poverty, but it was lived without grace. It seemed to be life only as a function." These phrases were not attributed to an expert or a Western government official; they were presented as observable facts.[62]

While these two descriptions about life under communism may seem fairly mild considering the fervor surround the Cold War in the early 1960s, they are worth considering because the writer boasted how *The Tunnel* had avoided the usual Cold War clichés. A year after the documentary ran on NBC, Frank said he and Anderton specifically vowed to avoid political positions while working on the script. "There were to be no slogans in the script at all," wrote Frank. "Never once in the script were the words 'free world' used." He was clearly aware of journalism's tendency to follow the government's lead on Cold War comparisons, but he felt he had avoided that trap.[63]

Escape

Frank felt he could avoid Cold War slogans in the script because the images conveyed the powerful message of the dangers and hard work people would endure to help others escape communism, embodied in "What they must be leaving to risk this." The first hour of the documentary focused on the risks, hard monotonous labor, logistics, and setbacks involved in digging the tunnel under the Berlin Wall. The final thirty minutes comprised the tense moments leading to the escape and the dramatic images of the families coming up out of the dark, wet, tunnel in West Berlin. As the film presents nighttime scenes of the streets outside the Eastern terminus of the tunnel and the empty tunnel shaft on the Western side, the narration describes who will be escaping in what order. This information allows Frank to limit the narration during the escape scenes, with Eddie Safranski's ominous score providing the sound to accompany the silent film of women, babies, children, and men slowly emerging up the wooden ladder to the dark basement. We see women with torn hosiery from crawling through the tunnel. We see mothers taking the dirty, wet clothing off their children and washing the youngsters in a tub. We see husbands reunited with wives and children. The limited narration emphasizes the risks involved in escaping. "To escape through a tunnel is as risky as to build one. What lies ahead is unknown. The couriers were strangers. The rendezvous could have been a trap."[64]

The emphasis throughout *The Tunnel* is on the individual story meant to symbolize a larger truth. Frank could avoid Cold War posturing because the story itself emphasizes that point. The first line voiced by an unseen NBC announcer at the start of *The Tunnel* noted the broadcast would be "a document on human courage in seeking freedom." Piers Anderton makes it even clearer when he appears on camera before the opening credits, saying that "this is the story about those people and that tunnel." The personal story is emphasized throughout *The Tunnel* all the way to the final escape scenes. The viewer watches as one of the diggers climbs down the ladder to help up his family, including a baby born while his wife had been detained in a communist prison. Out of the darkness, a crying baby appears in a man's arms. The baby's mouth is wide open as the father holds the child at the bottom of the ladder and the shot is frozen on the screen. Anderton concludes the escape scene with the line, "Tonight, for the first time, he held his baby."[65]

Interviews

One of the most obvious influences from *The Tunnel* experience for the "transmission of experience" memo is Frank's dismissive attitude toward on-camera interviews on television. The memo was written not long after his award-winning documentary filled ninety minutes of network prime time without a single on-camera interview. In *The Tunnel*, Piers Anderton talks on camera twice, just before the opening credits, and then toward the end of the broadcast to sum up some of the key facts concerning the escape. We never hear any of the diggers or the escapees speak during the program. Instead, Anderton's narration fills in details about their lives and their motivations for digging or escaping through the tunnel.

Frank even boasted about the lack of interviews in *The Tunnel*: "An interview is somebody talking about something you wish you could have covered." He felt he had all the images and drama he needed and did not have to rely on interviews as a crutch. *The Tunnel* was a rare project in which the journalists did not need the government for information or background. This would become an important distinction when NBC fought with the US government over the documentary (as chronicled in chapter 6). By limiting the story to that specific tunnel, Frank already had all the images and background to produce the documentary. He could skip the usual self-serving government interviews with their Cold War slogans he was trying to avoid.[66]

Frank was not entirely forthright about the lack of interviews. One of the main impediments to interviewing the diggers was that the two organizers who were willing to talk, Spina and Sesta, did not speak English. Any interviews would have to be translated into English, through subtitles or an off-screen narrator voicing the English translation. Frank admitted this reality after the broadcast: "If an interview in German with a heavy Italian accent would have been useful, perhaps we should have used it."[67]

In reality, *The Tunnel* does include one obvious interview. During a lull in digging because of water in the tunnel, Anderton talked with Domenico Sesta about his reasons for getting involved in the project. Technically, it does not count as an on-camera interview because sound was not recorded, but we see various shots of Anderton and Sesta sitting and talking in the tunnel basement. Interestingly, Sesta's comments, paraphrased by Anderton in the narration, include the opinions in the documentary that stray the furthest from Cold War ethos of good democracy versus evil communism.

Sesta grew up in Italy. His father died fighting in the Spanish Civil War and his mother died soon after that. The script paraphrases Sesta telling Anderton that he had no use for any governments: "Politics is a game between capitalism and communism.... The man in the street wins nothing in this game." Sesta even separates the idea of communism from the actions of the East Germans, as paraphrased by Anderton: "The East German rulers are swine not because they are communists, but because they keep people living frightful lives. People should live in happiness, not by an idiotic theory of a future one hundred years from now." Even though *The Tunnel*'s overall impression pitted communism against democracy, the writers were able to insert a more complicated view through the words of one of the principal people in the story.[68]

The Memo's Enduring Legacy

The "transmission of experience" memo moved beyond the NBC newsroom and became a subject for debate, much as Wolfe's claims of the superiority of new journalism sparked spirited discussion among print journalists in the next decade. A. William Bluem recognized the significance of the memo but chose not to integrate it into his arguments in his influential 1965 book, *Documentary in American Television*. Instead, Bluem included the entire memo as an appendix, noting how it connects the work of the television journalist and the documentarian.[69]

During the next decade, when academic researchers finally began to take notice of television news, analyzing both the content and the process, Reuven Frank's memo was scrutinized for how it compared to traditional journalism, or even reality. Edward Jay Epstein spent time at NBC News watching how they produced the news for his book *News from Nowhere*. Epstein quotes liberally from the "transmission of experience" memo throughout the book, often using Frank's words to show that the nightly news was not a mirror of society but a heavily produced product, constrained by money and technology. Epstein felt Frank's insistence on employing the elements of fiction, including conflict and narrative, forced his staff into finding images that would fit specific formulas and stereotype to support the narrative, which he calls "resurrecting reality." Epstein is even critical of Frank's emphasis on longer stories with more context because those pieces meant the newscast would have less daily news.[70]

Epstein's views contrast sharply with television critics who reviewed *The Tunnel* when it ran in December 1962. Those critics could not comment on the memo since it hadn't been written yet, but they picked up on Frank's efforts to produce a real event with the structure of a fictional movie. According to *Variety*, "Few if any of tv's action-adventure episodics have managed to pack the suspense and drama that was inherent in this painstakingly (and painfully) produced documentary." Cecil Smith of the *Los Angeles Times* thought that if Alfred Hitchcock had directed a similar movie, it would have been powerful and suspenseful, but the fact that *The Tunnel* was "filmed during the actual digging of the tunnel and the escape of the refugees made it 100 times so." Cynthia Lowry of the *Harford Courant* called the program television at its best because it "showed refugees—real people, not actors—crawling covered with mud and exhausted from a narrow tunnel."[71]

Video Storytelling Influence

For those who believed in the communicative power of television for news and public affairs, the Frank memo became a touchstone for effective storytelling. The emphasis on the visuals and the teamwork necessary between the reporter and photographer especially resonated with television news photographers. Television members of the National Press Photographers Association increasingly experimented with effective methods for visual storytelling, especially at local television stations with a financial commitment to news and a willingness to explore new techniques. The focus on the "transmission of experience" method was most often found in timeless or feature stories because of the work involved in crafting those type of television pieces. At CBS, reporter Charles Kuralt and cameraman Izzy Bleckman carved out a niche with their "On the Road" segments that offered a counter to all the negative news coming out of Vietnam in the late 1960s. Steve Hartman resurrected the "On the Road" segment in 2011. Bob Dotson filled a similar role for NBC with his "American Stories" into the twenty-first century.[72]

The photographers, reporters, producers, and other visual journalists who believed in this approach came together (and still do) every year at the NPPA TV News Workshop at the University of Oklahoma to compare stories and influence the next generation. While this group was (and is) a small subset of all those working in television news, its work can be seen on television newscasts across the country.

Although Frank's vision and work for television news may have resonated with many in the industry, the accolades did not cross over into other media or practices. Even with the common ideas in the "transmission of experience" memo and the new journalism approach to print journalism, Frank and television news in general are rarely mentioned in connection with the debates over the use of fiction techniques in journalism sparked by the new journalism movement. Expanding to journalism as a whole, the reception and impact of *The Tunnel* in 1962 was mixed, with many journalists dismissing the documentary, and most of television news, as inferior to print journalism. Even with Frank's success with and devotion to the documentary format, his work is rarely acknowledged in the area of documentary film studies. The complicated and divisive relationship between television and documentaries is the focus of the next chapter.

CHAPTER FOUR
Journalist vs. Filmmaker

The Tunnel and the Elusive Definition of Documentary Films

IN 1971, JAPAN's Nippon Television Network invited Reuven Frank to be the keynote speaker at the International Documentary Symposium in Tokyo. Even though he was now NBC News president and had produced and overseen many documentaries in the intervening years, Frank chose to screen *The Tunnel* at the symposium. He considered that program to be his most satisfying attempt to utilize the "structural rules and artistic aims of fiction without violating the factual principles of reporting."[1]

In his keynote speech, Frank admitted he did not have a good definition for what constituted a documentary. He felt that so many different types of nonfiction film production came under the umbrella of documentary to the point that the term had little meaning.

To emphasize the different approaches, he specifically mentioned two types of documentaries: those produced by journalists and those produced by people he called "film-makers." While he admitted the editing process is a subjective activity in all documentaries, with "the film-maker there is always the temptation to improve and polish, sometimes even at the expense of the story, or, more dangerous, the facts." Over the years, Frank said, NBC had more success in training journalists to be documentary producers than in guiding documentary filmmakers to adhere to journalistic practices.[2]

In his speech, Frank said he had little use for documentary producers who demanded their own vision and approach. He reminded the international audience that American television is regulated by and must answer to the government on its practices. Documentary producers who were not transparent on their approach and editing, at least to their bosses, reflected poorly on the organization: "A network may resent and resist an elected official's interference, intimidation and prying. It must never be in the position of having to answer a question with 'we don't know.' That is a luxury reserved to other people, perhaps to other places."[3]

Frank's dismissive attitude toward a certain group of documentarians reveals the contradictions and disagreements at the heart of early 1960s American television documentaries. Since the networks devoted more resources and air time to news and public affairs, this period has been called the golden age of television documentaries in the United States. The expansion happened so quickly that the networks had to look beyond their own staff to produce all of these programs.[4]

The critical juncture at the heart of *The Tunnel* and the "transmission of experience" memo not only involved television in relation to radio and print media; it also involves a brief period when nonfiction filmmakers from a variety of backgrounds came together to produce documentaries for American television. As Frank noted, defining the term "documentary" is an elusive task, and each person brought his or her training and background to that definition.

This blending of ideas of what constitutes a documentary film not only resulted in innovation but also tension, as was obvious in Reuven Frank's symposium speech. By the early 1960s, documentary filmmaking had a tradition almost twice as long as commercial television, with its own set of iconic work, rules, and debates, often concurrent but separated from television and journalism practices.

Reuven Frank's embrace of communication practices from a variety of sources, including print journalism and "documentary" films, was responsible for his important work, including *The Tunnel* and the *Huntley-Brinkley Report*. This approach, though, also brought him criticism, or a lack of acceptance, for the very reason that he was blending practices from different media fields.

Media History and Practices as Boundary Work

Erik Barnouw worked in network radio in the mid-twentieth century, including as a radio documentary producer. He later founded the Film Division at Columbia University and was respected by both practitioners and scholars in the second half of the century. Barnouw wrote an exhaustive and influential three-volume set on the history of American broadcasting. He later condensed his television history into a single volume. In his television history, *Tube of Plenty*, NBC's *The Tunnel* warrants more than two pages and a photograph.[5]

During the same period, Barnouw was working on a history of documentary film. In his book *Documentary: A History of the Non-fiction Film*, there is no mention of *The Tunnel* or Reuven Frank, for that matter. Barnouw does not ignore television or the 1960s; instead he focuses on other filmmakers and other work of that period. The reasons why the same scholar would highlight *The Tunnel* in television history but ignore it in documentary film history can be found in an exploration of the histories and traditions of the various media formats.[6]

The concept of boundary work is helpful in understanding the passion involved in the defense of the various ways to define these long-form nonfiction films. Boundary work involves the rhetoric and practices used by professions and other groups of people who are attempting to define their niche. It is important to remember that boundary work involves more than just the work itself, what people *do,* but also what *they say they do.* To protect professional boundaries, these groups also criticize those who are attempting to usurp their authority. In the case of documentary work, the different groups had their own definitions, so the rhetoric revolved around what projects could truly be defined as documentaries and what work should not be included.[7]

The history of a profession or group is key to its boundary work. The rationale for the boundaries determining inclusion or exclusion are usually based on previous work in the field. The groups look to iconic people and projects to justify their expertise. These examples can include either positive or negative lessons; in the case of documentaries, they could be producers or films that symbolize the highest achievement, or they could represent practices not acceptable within the group. Over time, once-accepted or even once-lauded practices can become cautionary tales of unprofessional work to be avoided, or vice versa.

To understand the reactions to Reuven Frank's work, including *The Tunnel*, as well as the tensions at play in network television when documentarians from different backgrounds were thrown together and had to negotiate projects in the early 1960s, a wider lens is needed to understand the influences and historical touchstones. Media practices and boundary work starting at the end of the nineteenth century play a role in how people viewed Frank's work in 1962 and beyond.

Documentary film history was a fairly well-defined academic field during the later period of Reuven Frank's career, with a shared set of important films and filmmakers in the twentieth century. Within that discipline, boundary work involved people or projects under periodic debate over legacy and contribution. Within documentary film in the first half of the twentieth century, several different motivations and approaches were at play, causing internal debates about the proper role of the nonfiction film.

Most of the people working in television news did not come out of a documentary film background and had limited knowledge of the accepted practices and beliefs. Their influences and examples came from a variety of sources, including journalism practice, newspapers, magazines, still photography, motion pictures, and radio. Each of these areas played a role in shaping the people producing long-form films during American television's golden age of documentaries. An exploration of these different media practices in the first half of the twentieth century will help illuminate both Frank's work and the reception to his approach.

Early Film

One attribute that almost all documentary practitioners and scholars can agree on is that the format is not fiction. But even that delineation takes on incredible nuance in the twentieth century in areas such as re-creations, the use of actors, shooting and editing practices, and even deception. To understand the fiction and nonfiction approaches taken in early film, the work and orientations of a few of the film pioneers provide an admittedly simplified starting point for the later definitions and separations of film genres.

The Lumière brothers, Auguste and Louis, of Lyon, France, and Thomas Edison's laboratory staff in New Jersey are considered two of the key inventors and proponents of moving pictures. The Lumières recognized film's potential to bring viewers pictures of distant lands, so they designed their camera, the *cinématographe,* to be mobile, sending photographers out into the world to film places and events. The Edison group, led by inventor William Kennedy-Laurie Dickson, initially designed its camera, the *kinetograph,* as a stationary device, thereby demanding that subjects such as vaudeville acts and other performers be brought to their Orange, New Jersey, studio for performances that would work in the roughly twenty-second, silent-film format. Edison himself thought the money would not be made on the films themselves, but on selling or leasing his *kinetoscope* viewing machines to arcades and other amusement locations.

Eventually the Lumières, Edison, and the dozens of other film companies that formed around the turn of the century realized the public liked all types of films, including historic scenes, faraway places, short fiction, and vaudeville performances. The individual arcade machine was soon replaced by a large screen for a communal viewing experience.

In 1896, motion picture viewers could see both American presidential candidates, Republican William McKinley and Democrat William Jennings Bryan. At least four film companies captured McKinley's inaugural parade the next year. Also in 1897, several film companies attended Queen Victoria's Diamond Jubilee celebration in June, and film of the royal family in ceremonies and private moments became a popular subject for British audiences. Pope Leo XIII allowed film cameras into the Vatican in 1898.

Filmmakers faced an early dilemma. Movie goers loved seeing newsworthy events and exotic locations, but these types of films pushed the limits of technology and budgets. Even with more mobile cameras, the possibility of filming an important event as it happened involved considerable time, expense, and luck. In the cases of war coverage, there was danger involved as well. The limitations of the early film cameras, the audience's interest in events as they happened, and the theatrical antecedents influencing and involved in early moving pictures led early filmmakers to make decisions that would haunt nonfiction moving pictures for the next century and beyond.[8]

Re-creations, Deception, and Fiction

In 1898, the Vitagraph film company sent a crew to the Spanish-American War in Cuba. The photographers who accompanied Teddy Roosevelt and his Rough Riders dutifully filmed scenes of the group slowly working its way through underbrush and avoiding enemy fire. When they returned to the United States, however, their film did not match Roosevelt's exciting and valorous charge up San Juan Hill as described in the print press.

Since the public clearly wanted more war films and they wanted exciting images, companies began staging scenes in the United States and presenting them as authentic battle scenes, or at least not clearly labeling them as re-creations. Vitagraph built a miniature diorama of the Battle of Santiago Bay, with cardboard cutouts of American and Spanish ships, using people off-camera to blow cigar and cigarette smoke into the scene.[9]

Another early example involved William Dickson. After leaving Edison, he worked for Biograph in its London office and lugged his massive camera to South Africa for the Boer War in 1899. His camera was so large that he had to haul it around in a cart, which made it very difficult and dangerous to capture battle scenes. Dickson missed the moment when Lord Roberts raised the British flag in Pretoria, so he faked the flag ceremony. His deception was quickly discovered. Albert Smith of Vitagraph made Dickson's deception seem quaint. He convinced British soldiers to wear Boer clothes so he could reenact battle scenes that he had not been allowed to film.[10]

Early film scholar Raymond Fielding believed every motion picture company in this period faked at least some of their supposed real films because they "saw as their primary role and function not so much to provide accurate information for educational, political, or social action as to provide sensational visualizations of attention-compelling news events."[11]

The first two decades of the twentieth century saw dramatic changes in the direction and structure of moving pictures, especially in the United States. Filmmakers moved beyond the ten to fifteen minutes that could be contained on one reel of film, giving way to a description of film length by the number of reels needed. By 1906, American film production companies were favoring fiction films, or "story film productions," over nonfiction productions. With story films, the action could be easily controlled with actors on a set, allowing companies to churn out more films for a growing audience wanting new material. As a result, most of the innovation and advancements in the United States involved fiction movies, from more complex editing to longer lengths. In 1915, D. W. Griffith directed his famous and controversial work *Birth of a Nation*, which was the first American film to span twelve reels, for a running time of close to three hours.[12]

Newsreels

While the top American companies moved away from nonfiction films in this period, those productions were still popular in Europe, especially in France, partly because of the Lumière brothers' original vision. As fiction films became more complicated, the skills needed to produce and shoot on a set diverged from the attributes of a roving film photographer. Nonfiction motion pictures—news films—took on more of a journalistic tone and structure. When news films were edited together in a package, the resulting film was called a newsreel.[13]

Charles Pathé started the first regular newsreel in France and expanded first to England, and then to the United States in 1911. The American version, *Pathé's Weekly*, was released every Wednesday and called itself "an illustrated magazine on film," signaling the first regular newsreel in the United States. A handful of newsreel companies came and went in that decade, but the ones that survived, in addition to *Pathé*, were part of larger media companies, including Hearst, Universal, and Fox. The newsreels took on a fairly consistent structure and schedule that had little variation over the next half-century, as described in the previous chapter.[14]

Documentaries

Although documentaries and other nonfiction films took on many forms and approaches in the first half of the twentieth country in countries around the world, this exploration is limited to the people and productions that most likely influenced Reuven Frank and the people he worked with prior to *The Tunnel*. Because of the dominance of Hollywood fiction films in this period and the limited distribution of nonfiction films, the work under consideration is mostly from Europe, the Soviet Union, and the United States.

For the most part, the canon of early documentaries is structured around specific people or particular movements. Another important factor in the early development of a documentary film history is that some of the key figures not only made films but wrote extensively about nonfiction films and traveled to other countries, influencing like-minded filmmakers. With a relatively small subset of filmmakers interested in documentaries in these countries, they shared ideas and approaches from different people and places and came up with a fairly consistent timeline and list of important films, even if they did not always agree on the merits of the influences.

While the work from the Lumière brothers to the start of newsreels is often presented as an influence, one traditional starting point in documentary film history is *Nanook of the North* in 1922. Robert Flaherty spent a few years filming the Inuit people near the Arctic Circle and then decided to build his story around one man, whom he called Nanook. Flaherty employed the shooting and editing practices that had become popular in fiction movies but had not yet been used extensively in nonfiction film. *Nanook of the North* became a surprise hit with American audiences, on a par with popular silent fiction movies of the year.[15]

Subsequent revelations about Flaherty's work reveal many ethical decisions he made that would not be acceptable in later definitions of nonfiction film. Flaherty wanted to portray the Inuit people as he imagined they lived before the influence of European explorers. He convinced Nanook and others to wear only traditional clothing, and in some key hunting scenes he encouraged them to use spears, even though guns were their preferred weapons by the early twentieth century.[16]

Because of *Nanook*'s success and the merging of the fiction elements of character development, sequential shooting and editing, and other elements of the grammar of fiction films that had already become standard by the early 1920s, Flaherty has been heralded as a father of documentary film. In *Nanook*, he created what Lewis Jacobs called "the classic progenitor of the documentary idiom."[17]

In the century since *Nanook of the North*, many documentarians and scholars have moved Flaherty more into the area of travel films, or travelogues, and instead look to movements and individuals in the Soviet Union and Europe in the 1920s and 1930s as a more accurate starting point.[18]

The Bolshevik Revolution in Russia and the creation of the Soviet Union sparked a period of influential filmmaking. Sergei Eisenstein caused a stir in the film world with his 1925 silent classic *Battleship Potemkin*. This fictionalized version of rebellion against Russian authorities included his advanced editing techniques, montage, that showed the power of image juxtaposition in the silent film era. Another pioneer, Dziga Vertov, started in the genre of newsreels, producing the Soviet weekly newsreel. Vertov considered the camera as an improvement on the human eye and wanted to use cinema as "a new perception of the world." He called his nonfiction style *kino pravda*, or film truth, and brought together a group of filmmakers to work on reality films. Vertov's *Man with a Movie Camera* (1929), on a day in the life of the

Soviet Union, is considered one of the great nonfiction silent movies for its experimental cinematic style.[19]

In Europe, just a few years after the Soviet documentary film movement, Scotland's John Grierson also championed the idea of nonfiction film with a point-of-view and a purpose, "propaganda in the public interest." Grierson came to the United States in 1924 to study the effect of propaganda in the press on public opinion. He reviewed films for *The Sun* and is credited with first using the term "documentary," interestingly, in a review of Robert's Flaherty's follow-up, *Moana*, in 1926. Grierson and Flaherty eventually worked on a film together, *Industrial Britain*, but the former was always critical of the latter for not taking a stand in his travel films.[20]

Later in the decade, Grierson moved back to Great Britain and brought together like-minded people into a government-funded film collective, the E. M. B. (Empire Marketing Board) Film Unit, to promote various causes and interests. His directorial debut, *Drifters* (1929), chronicled the North Sea herring fishermen and brought him the same kind of attention in England Flaherty received in the United States for *Nanook*. Grierson then spent much of his time encouraging and promoting other filmmakers in his unit, including Basil Wright, Harry Watt, Paul Rotha, and Alberto Cavalcanti. The British documentary work in this period is marked by attention to both social purpose and experimentation in shooting and editing.[21]

Other than Flaherty, the United States was not seen as fertile ground for documentary films until the mid- to late 1930s. Given the sway of Grierson's insistence on a point of view or social purpose, in this period of documentary film, using actors or other fiction elements in telling a larger truth was a lesser evil than using the camera just to take people places or show them the latest events without taking sides.

In the United States, the film industry, now collectively called Hollywood, created a vertical oligarchy in filmmaking, with the studios controlling everything from the actors and scripts to what movies could be shown at the local theaters. In this environment, the twice-weekly newsreels became the most popular nonfiction genre because the studios owned the newsreels. Independent filmmakers with a message had little chance at funding and an even slimmer chance of getting their work shown at the neighborhood theater.

Since Grierson's insistence on film as propaganda gained favor in the documentary film community and that group solely focused on moving pictures, the documentary film history canon and perceived influences are often limited to film with a point of view. Understanding the divisions in 1960s American television documentarians, and the reasons why *The Tunnel* is remembered or ignored to this day, requires an understanding of the broader media influences, especially in the United States. The New York City that Reuven Frank moved to in 1940 was bursting with interesting and new approaches to all forms of communication, especially in the area of pictures and sound.

Broader Influences

Film was certainly not the only new platform or innovative approach to an existing medium in the first half of the twentieth century. Radio programming included documentaries, analysis programs, and other news broadcasts. Still photography could be considered artistic or factual, and also as a tool for social awareness and change. Nonfiction filmmakers were working on newsreels and travel films, or with independent groups attempting to crack the Hollywood theater stranglehold. Some even experimented with early television.

Each of these areas eventually built up a set of standard practices and ethics, and the people who worked in those areas brought those ideas and convictions to their later work. The boundary work of establishing the rules and criteria of each medium and format and, just as importantly, marginalizing people and productions that threatened the autonomy of a specific group resulted in either helpful collaboration or intense divisions. Changes over time in practices and ethics within each group also caused debate and instances of turning against once-accepted approaches.

As these media workers changed formats or approaches with new job opportunities, the cross-pollination of previous experiences created tensions, wariness, and eventually interesting new approaches in these workplaces or independent groups. These experiences helped influence the direction of television news and documentaries in the postwar period.

Radio

American radio stations in the mid-twentieth century had to present a percentage of news and public affairs programming to ensure their licenses would be renewed. The role and scope of nonfiction programming, including documentaries, depended on audience interest and how closely the government was monitoring radio public interest programming.²²

Similar to all new media in their formative years, radio looked to proven genres on existing platforms for programming ideas. Radio borrowed generously from vaudeville, Broadway, newspapers, magazines, books, and movies. Brief newscasts were often read straight from the news cooperatives (Associated Press, International News Service, United Press) set up to share news among members. Newspaper columnists and reporters were hired to talk about their careers and reflect on the news of the day.²³

American network radio in general by the mid-1930s had been taken over by the sponsors and advertising agencies, with more deference to the sponsor's message than creative uses of the aural format. Radio historian R. LeRoy Bannerman said listeners heard "burlesque comedy, tinny music, stiff and blatant drama," which he dubbed "a mosaic of awkward moments." When radio reformers gained some traction in trying to set aside signals for more serious programming, the networks put more effort and money into non-sponsored programs. This sparked interest from theater and literary people who wanted to adapt and expand their work on the aural medium. In most cases, these productions would be audio adaptations of books or plays, often with hints at current events. One reason that Orson Welles's historic *War of the Worlds* broadcast on CBS in 1938 was so memorable, even if the hysteria it supposedly caused has been exaggerated over the decades, was his *Mercury Theatre of the Air* crew's inventive mash-up of a science-fiction novel and the popular, breathless, and frantic style of radio breaking news of that era. Another important program for experimentation was CBS's *Columbia Workshop,* a low-budget weekly offering that allowed writers including Irving Reis, William Robson, and Norman Corwin, a radio outlet for their creativity.²⁴

March of Time—Radio Version

Only one American newsreel receives somewhat positive, or at least mixed, reviews in documentary films histories: *March of Time.* In true emerging media fashion, the project had nothing to do with moving pictures when it began; instead it started as a collaboration between a new medium and a new format in an old medium. America's first weekly newsmagazine, *Time,* launched in 1923. Cincinnati radio station WLW convinced the publisher to create an aural version of the newsmagazine, using actors to re-create the top news stories. By 1931, *March of Time* was a weekly radio documentary on CBS, with top stage and radio actors, thousands of sound effects, and a twenty-one-piece orchestra. Broadcast news historian Edward Bliss called *March of Time* "the first important documentary series on radio," and even though the half-hour program involved actors, re-creations, and occasional historical revisions, Bliss said the program had a "paradoxical striving for accuracy," with meticulous research into the re-created events. The *March of Time* radio program ran until 1945, and its fusion of fiction techniques (actors, music, dramatic scripts, and narration by Westbrook Van Voorhis) and real-life events became the standard for American radio documentaries through the 1940s. Generations of media professionals used *March of Time* as a historic touchstone, a role model in the early years and often an object of scorn, especially among journalists, later in the century.[25]

Still Photography

Reuven Frank's transition to television started with his interest in how photographs influenced the look of the newspaper page. He was a not a news photographer himself, but, like many other journalists, he was learning about the importance of the visuals. When Frank started his newspaper career after World War II, the news photograph had already found its place in most publications. In the previous century, however, the photograph was often considered less valuable than illustrations and artwork. Visual magazines in the late nineteenth century, including *Harper's Weekly* and *Leslie's Illustrated Weekly*, used the photograph as a starting point and then let the illustrators and artists re-create the scene with added detail, providing more context than just the frozen moment in time. American newspapers publishers were wary of the major change, and the extra cost involved, in including photographs in a format that had always relied mostly on text. *National Geographic* started featuring photographs extensively in the first decade of the twentieth century, but it took another ten years before the *New York Illustrated Daily News* began heavily using photographs as part of its tabloid format, borrowing its visual approach from the British paper, the *Daily Mirror*. Small and innovative papers tended to experiment with visuals while established operations were slower to add photographs.[26]

In Kevin Barnhurst and John Nerone's *Form of News*, the rise of realism and modernism in the twentieth century elevated the status of the photograph in journalism. The news picture removed the reporter and the artist as photography "bases its claim to authority on immediacy, on the conviction that nothing intervenes between a reader and a scene." This transformation in the role of the news photograph was happening at the same time as the establishment of the theater newsreel.[27]

The tabloid's embrace of the news photograph, especially in New York City, was complete by the late 1920s, when the city's *Daily News*, *Daily Mirror*, and *Evening Graphic* all heavily covered the case of Ruth Snyder, convicted of conspiring with her boyfriend to murder her husband. *Daily News* photographer Tom Howard capped the coverage by sneaking a camera into the execution chamber and taking a picture of Snyder as she was electrocuted, resulting in a full, front-page picture with the caption "Dead!" That edition sold an extra half-million copies.[28]

Life

Another major influence on the people who would later move into television news and documentaries, especially those with a journalism background, was Henry Luce's *Life* magazine, launched in 1936. After starting *Time* magazine in 1923, Luce added *Fortune* seven years later. *Life* began as an idea of showing people and world events through photography. With *Life*, Luce flipped the usual template of print publications by featuring the photographs and limiting the text to captions to help explain the images, especially in the first years. Several of the photo essays even looked like the successive frames of moving pictures, with dancers and other visual scenes depicted in a series of panels. *Life* hired some of the best photographers of the era, including Margaret Bourke-White and Alfred Eisenstadt.

Life caught the public's attention on a level that surprised even the publisher and his staff. They had predicted a quarter-million subscribers for the first year, but the number jumped past a million in just four months. Later television pioneers including Reuven Frank, Fred Friendly, and Don Hewitt said their visions for various television ventures, including *See It Now* and *60 Minutes*, started with the idea of transforming *Life* magazine into a television program.[29]

Photography as Persuasion

The idea of the photograph as an unmediated moment in time proved to be too limiting for many photographers. Since its invention and proliferation in the nineteenth century, photography had been promoted as an art form, as a medium to be explored, for a variety of motives. A Denmark immigrant, Jacob Riis, worked as a journalist and wrote about the horrible living conditions in New York City's slums. When he felt words were not enough, he started experimenting with flash photography, so he could take pictures at night of the people in their squalid conditions. Some of his work was published, but he also gave lectures, using his photographs as lantern slides. In 1890, he put out a photography book, *How the Other Half Lives*, which sparked a movement in using photography for social action.[30]

Another influential photographer in New York in the first decades of the twentieth century was Clarence White. White taught the first photography class at Columbia University and later founded his own school, the Clarence White School of Photography. White, Alfred Stieglitz, and many of their contemporaries considered their work an art form, and the people and their work intermingled with other artists and art galleries in the city. As a teacher, White inspired and influenced a number of photographers who had their own ideas on how to use the medium.[31]

New Deal Images

The Depression mobilized people who felt that visualizations of the devastation and misery caused by the financial crisis would help more people understand the extent of the problem. The government began to fund some of these projects in the 1930s through President Franklin Roosevelt's various New Deal programs.

One of the most successful visual efforts involved the Resettlement Administration (RA), later known as the Farm Security Administration (FSA). Roy Stryker hired photographers, both still and moving picture, to document rural poverty, including the Dust Bowl in the Plains states. Walker Evans, Dorothea Lange, Carl Mydans and other still photographers produced images that have represented the suffering of that era for later generations. Lange, who studied under Clarence White, took the most iconic photo in this period, "Migrant Mother," of a desperate, starving mother in a migrant camp, with her young children clinging to her with their faces hidden. Evans later teamed up with writer James Agee for a text-photography project on white tenement farmers in the South, *Let Us Now Praise Famous Men*.[32]

In New York City in the 1930s, a group of photographers formed the Workers Film and Photo League to share ideas and find outlets for their work. They already considered Hollywood films "mass hypnosis," and as the group helped each other survive during the Depression, they realized that all lives were interconnected. Many people were sharing in the struggle. Instead of emulating Hollywood, Leo Hurwitz said the group realized that "ordinary people could use film and photography with more relevance and purpose than the professionals." During the 1930s, leading up to US involvement in World War II, this loose connection of photographers and other artists at various points and under various names (including Nykino and Frontier Films) included Hurwitz, Margaret Bourke-White, Paul Strand, Ralph Steiner, Pare Lorentz, Willard Van Dyke, Elia Kazan, Ricky Leacock, Henri Cartier-Bresson, Paul Robeson, John Dos Passos, Lillian Hellman, and Archibald MacLeish. They set up their own classes to teach each other film and editing techniques. They watched the significant documentaries from the Soviet Union, England, and Germany. They were able to buy cheap 35 mm silent cameras when Hollywood transitioned to sound movies. They also experimented with a new smaller silent 16 mm format that was promoted as a way to get film cameras into the hands of nonprofessionals.[33]

The Plow That Broke the Plains

The New York collection of photographers, writers, and artists helped create one of the first American documentaries included in the canon of documentary film history since Flaherty's *Nanook of the North*. The New Deal Resettlement Association program turned to the New York Film and Photo League[34] group to work on a documentary on the ravages of the Dust Bowl. The government hired Pare Lorentz to produce the film. Lorentz sent Leo Hurwitz, Paul Strand, and Ralph Steiner to Montana, Texas, and Wyoming to film the ruined land and the farmers who were forced to leave their homes and head west as migrant workers. The beautifully framed images of the blowing sand, abandoned houses, failed crops, and desperate people in *The Plow That Broke the Plains* (1936) mirrored the still photography of the RA/

FSA group. Since sound film cameras were expensive and not very mobile, documentary filmmakers enhanced their silent film with an orchestra score, in this case composed by Virgil Thomson. Borrowing from the newsreel format, Lorentz wrote a dramatic script and Thomas Chalmers narrated in the "voice of God" manner popular with *March of Time* and other newsreels.

Even with the popularity of *The Plow That Broke the Plains* in documentary circles, the motives of the funding source and the artists clashed during the project. Hurwitz, Strand, and Steiner shot the film with the idea that capitalism was to blame for the Dust Bowl. They wrote a script and demanded Lorentz use it. As producer, Lorentz was following the government vision that a more modern method of farming would have protected the top soil, so he fired the three men and filled in their work with Hollywood stock footage and some staged scenes. *The Plow That Broke the Plains* had trouble finding an audience since Hollywood had control of most movie theaters around the country. One New York theater that did run Lorentz's film even promoted it as "The Picture They Dared Us to Show!"[35]

With the success of his first film, the government asked Lorentz to produce a documentary, *The River,* on the need for more dams and water management to prevent flooding. For this film, he used Willard Van Dyke, Floyd Crosby, and Stacy Woodard as cinematographers. The documentary starts with the many rivers that flow into the Mississippi River and builds toward dramatic scenes of the major flooding of the Ohio River in 1937. Lorentz's rhythmic script, Thomas Chalmers narration, and Virgil Thomson's score combined to make a memorable film. Cultural Critic Gilbert Seldes lamented that Lorentz's previous film had been shut out of most theaters and declared to *Scribners* readers that "I now feel free to urge them with all the vehemence and authority I may possess to demand the showing of this picture at their local movie houses."[36]

March of Time—Film Version

The one American nonfiction film series that did reach a wide audience already had made its mark as a radio documentary. In 1935, *March of Time* debuted as theater documentary, under the direction of newsreel veteran Louis de Rochemont. Continuing the emphasis on re-creations from the radio version, de Rochemont had the idea of mixing in newsreel footage and creating a narrative in the telling of the current event or issue. The producers also found that in some cases the people involved in events were better at the re-creations than actors. Audience members watched General Douglas MacArthur, Father Charles Coughlin, Senator Huey Long, and many other public figures act out events depicted in the newsreel. For documentary historian A. William Bluem, the confident use of re-creations "stretched the limits of journalism" by acknowledging that pictures, just like words, were really just symbols of reality.[37]

The theater version started with multiple stories within each production, in keeping with the newsreel format, eventually evolving into a fifteen- to twenty-minute film on a single topic, at a rate of about one a month. In the period before the United States entered the war, *March of Time* was shown in 9,000 theaters, reaching twenty million people a week.

March of Time also separated itself from other newsreels by taking on controversial topics. In the years leading up to World War II, the producers tackled topics including the rise of Hitler and Nazism in Germany, the US Neutrality Act, the work of the Tennessee Valley Authority, and opposition to Roosevelt's New Deal programs. Because of its willingness to go beyond the scheduled events of other newsreels, *March of Time* became the target of local censorship boards that periodically would refuse to show specific segments, depending on the topic. The motion picture industry was so impressed with the format that *March of Time* was awarded an honorary Academy Award in 1937 for revolutionizing the newsreel.

Television

People interested in documentary films in New York City in the late 1930s and 1940s also explored the possibilities of another new medium: television. Documentary film, as well as other media, histories rarely make this connection because the work these people produced, especially before America's entry into World War II, usually did not look like documentary films, and often did not even involve any specific end product. Just the act of bringing together a diverse group of people, many interested in visual communication, resulted in collaboration and experimentation, as well as connections that would influence both television and documentary films in subsequent decades.

In 1937, CBS hired cultural critic Gilbert Seldes to create and oversee its experimental television operation. Seldes first came to prominence with his

1924 book *The 7 Lively Arts*, arguing that American arts forms including Broadway theater, jazz music, and cartoons were just as important as the high culture of classical music and ballet. In the 1930s, Seldes soured on the timidity of the newsreels and the crass commercialization of American radio, and he approached the CBS position as a chance to develop television as a more meaningful communication source.[38]

Seldes, and the small staff he hired, had years to experiment since CBS would not offer a regular television service until 1941. Seldes brought together men and women from a variety of backgrounds. They would take film cameras to events and scenes, develop the film, and watch the results on the small screens of the early electronic television era. In television history, the most remembered person in this group was Broadway director Worthington "Tony" Miner, who was later credited for helping create the live anthology genre on television, most notably in the program *Studio One*, that premiered on CBS in the late 1940s.[39]

Another member of the group, Robert Bendick, brought a strong photography background. He attended Clarence White's photography school and published his work in top magazines including *National Geographic*, *Life*, and *Look* before transitioning to moving picture films. During World War II, Bendick joined the Combat Camera unit of the Army Air Corps, taking on the dangerous work of filming the bombs dropping out of the planes and later returning to film the damage. When Bendick returned to CBS after the war, he was put in charge of all news and special events for a few years. Later, he was producer for NBC's *Today Show* and was one of the key people involved in the development of the *Cinerama* widescreen movie format.[40]

While Bendick was filming bombing runs in World War II, CBS hired a documentary veteran to run its television news operation. Leo Hurwitz had been part of the New York *Film and Photo League* and was one of the cameramen on Pare Lorentz's *The Plow That Broke the Plains* project who wanted to use the film as an indictment of capitalism. Hurwitz was also a driving force in Frontier Films, which produced 1942's *Native Land*, which was a human rights documentary intended to counter the *March of Time* newsreels. When Frontier Films disbanded, Hurwitz joined CBS television news and insisted the staff understand the concepts in shooting and editing film, a rare edict in journalism at the time, a vocation still firmly rooted in print and aural communication.[41]

Two other early CBS television staff members, Edward Anhalt and Rudy Bretz, helped on *The City*, a documentary by Paul Strand and Willard Van

Dyke that received critical praise when it premiered at the New York World's Fair in 1939.

When Rudy Bretz started working for CBS, Seldes sent him to the World's Fair to watch documentary screenings and write critiques, with an eye toward television techniques. With this task, Bretz had the rare opportunity of viewing some of the most celebrated filmmakers and documentaries of the period from around the world, sometimes attending multiple screenings of select films. He called Paul Rotha's *Shipyard* "one of the best of the technically clever British Documentaries"; found Joris Ivens and Henri Storck's coal mining film *Borinage* to depict "living conditions such as I have never before seen pictured were here shown, and in a very exciting manner"; said of Frontier Films' *People of the Cumberland*, "It seems to cover too great a field however and falls apart somewhat in doing so"; and described Basil Wright and John Grierson's *Song of Ceylon* as "the idyllically beautiful film of Ceylon which aquires [sic] deeper significance at each viewing."[42]

Even when the government allowed commercial television in July 1941, only a few thousand television sets existed in the New York City area that could receive the WCBW (later WCBS) signal. The network was basking in the publicity and success of its World War II European radio coverage led by Edward R. Murrow, so the television service received little attention and funding, considered mostly as a placeholder for the medium's potential. The autonomy afforded by a lack of expectations allowed the television staff to pursue its own ideas, albeit with very limited funding.

In general, Gilbert Seldes focused on the cultural and public information programming, while Worthington Miner explored ways to translate his Broadway experience to television. The small staff was forced to collaborate on almost all programs because they did not have enough people to specialize. Anhalt would help the news programs by taking his film camera out to capture events in the area. Bretz experimented with animated graphics so the newscasts could visualize the progress of battles in World War II, since CBS television did not have any reporters or access to much war film.

After the Pearl Harbor attack in December 1941, American television lost most of its experienced technicians and equipment to the war effort, forcing most stations, including CBS, to shut down their studios until the Allies were able to start beating back the German forces. While the war slowed down the development of television around the world, the collective emphasis on winning the war resulted in the production of strong nationalistic propaganda films in many of the nations involved in the conflict. In the United States, Hollywood's enthusiastic response to government war requests resulted in top fiction directors and other technical staff intermingling with documentarians, allowing for a cross-pollination of ideas that would also influence postwar, nonfiction, moving picture efforts.

World War II Propaganda Films

The first films connected to World War II to gain international attention were produced before Germany began its assault on Europe. Adolf Hitler handpicked German actress-turned-director Leni Riefenstahl to capture the 1934 Nazi Party rally in Nuremberg, providing a staff of 120 and full access to all locations for the best camera shots. In the film, *Triumph of the Will*, released the next year, Riefenstahl purposefully avoided a narrator and written script, relying instead on a strong musical score, natural sound from the rally, and excerpts of speeches by Hitler and other Nazi leaders. The film is considered a masterpiece, credited with both stirring up nationalistic pride in her home country and scaring other countries wary of Hitler's growing power. She followed it up with two films shot at the 1936 Olympic games in Berlin, mostly avoiding politics and instead celebrating the human body.

With strong documentary and newsreel traditions in both Great Britain and the Soviet Union, those countries were able to make the transition to war propaganda films early in the conflict. While John Grierson had moved to Canada in 1939 to help organize film efforts in that country, the filmmakers he had brought together and encouraged carried on his vision as England faced the Nazi threat. In the Soviet Union, the *kino pravda* movement, started by Dziga Vertov, also started producing war propaganda films, some of which were influential in the United States in painting a more sympathetic picture of the country. For all the countries involved, the newsreels focused on the war, with clear messages for the audiences of the righteousness of the cause.

In the United States, the military asked one of Hollywood's top directors, Frank Capra, to create films to explain to the American soldiers why they were fighting the war. Capra had never produced a documentary, so he watched the work of Riefenstahl as well as propaganda films from the Soviet Union, Japan, Great Britain, and other countries. He brought together top Hollywood people as well as documentarians, including brief stints by both Robert Flaherty and Joris Ivens, at the old Twentieth Century–Fox buildings in Hollywood.

The collection of films, known as the Why We Fight series, showcased Capra's ability to personalize a subject and present it in an understandable way. Most of the Why We Fight films were compilations of footage from other sources, combined with artwork and graphics often created by the Disney studio. Capra effectively used Riefenstahl's *Triumph of the Will* images to illustrate the sinister and dangerous side of Hitler. While the films were produced for the military, President Franklin Roosevelt was so impressed with the first installment, *Prelude to War,* that he said all Americans should see it. The films were considered a major success in helping American soldiers both understand the politics and machinations that led the United States to enter the war, as well as to demonize the enemies.[43]

Another example of Hollywood and nonfiction film people working on propaganda productions was the First Motion Picture Unit (FMPU) of the Army Air Corps. The group took over the old Hal Roach studios and included Ronald Reagan, Clark Gable, and other Hollywood actors and directors. The FMPU also utilized the film shot by members of the various Combat Camera Units, including CBS's Robert Bendick, tasked with filming the bombing raids throughout the war.[44]

World War II signaled the growing importance of capturing events as they happened, as visual evidence of the importance of the cause. Battle and bombing preparations now included attention to how the exercise would be captured visually. These films were used internally for military purposes and also provided to newsreel producers in Allied countries to keep their citizens interested and to show the progress of the war. Writing just after the war, French film theorist André Bazin felt Capra, through the Why We Fight series, had created a new genre: the "edited ideological documentary," in which most of the scenes had been filmed for other purposes but appropriated for a specific message.[45]

World War II gave nonfiction filmmakers, both in documentaries and newsreels, a clear purpose and propaganda message, resulting in some of the strongest work of the first half-century of moving pictures. Another important result of the war mobilization, especially in the United States, was the bringing together of both fiction and nonfiction filmmakers. Top Hollywood directors, actors, and crews adapted their storytelling skills beyond providing an escape from real life, using the impact of film of real events to persuade an audience of the importance of the cause. Nonfiction filmmakers, especially documentarians, learned from the experts in film fiction in Hollywood, and for once were able to work on projects with ample, reliable funding. Just as economists worried what would happen to the American economy once the need for tanks, planes, and other military goods stopped at the end of World War II, documentarians wondered where they would find their funding and their audience once the nationalistic fervor subsided.

Documentaries after World War II

The postwar years proved to be a tough period for motion pictures as viewers in cities with television stations started staying home instead of heading to their nearest movie theater. In the United States after the war, documentaries mostly disappeared from the movie screens. Theater owners said they could not find quality nonfiction films to run. Documentarians and distributors blamed theater owners for pushing out nonfiction in favor of double features, 3D movies, and widescreen productions, in a panicked effort to compete with television. "The brave disciples of the late Robert Flaherty," wrote *New York Times* theater critic Bosley Crowther, "are lonely and scattered to the winds." A decade after the war, British documentarian Paul Rotha blamed successive British governments for misusing and then dismantling the documentary unit started by John Grierson and expanded during World War II.[46]

Radio Documentary

By contrast, in the United States, the network audio documentary enjoyed a brief period of attention and funding just after the war. With the popularity of the radio war reporting in Europe and Asia, as well as the antifascism broadcasts produced in the United States, the reporters and producers felt they could turn their talents toward problems and opportunities at home. While industry leaders and economists were hoping television would spur postwar financial growth, confusion over standards held back the medium for a few years while the most experienced network journalists and producers still favored the audio format.

This sensibility coincided with government pressure for more news programming. In the last year of the war, the FCC announced a study to see if radio stations really delivered on their promises of news and public affairs programming. In 1946, the FCC released the report, known as the *Blue Book*, which threatened revoking licenses if stations did not take their public service responsibilities seriously. While the industry, led by the powerful lobbying organization the National Association of Broadcasters (NAB), beat back any attempts at serious reform, for a few years the industry was willing to spend a little money on documentaries to calm down government regulators.[47]

In his book *Radio Utopia*, Matthew Ehrlich calls the 1945–1951 period "a brief heyday that vividly reflected the social and cultural climate of the times." Network documentaries tackled important issues including nuclear power, venereal disease, poverty, juvenile delinquency, and treatment of African Americans.[48]

At CBS, Edward R. Murrow returned to New York after the war in an administrative role and a seat on the CBS Board of Directors. As part of the deal, Murrow negotiated a new documentary unit for CBS News, led by Robert Heller. The other networks and some local stations also emphasized longer-form news programs.

CBS's Norman Corwin had been celebrated for his patriotic war productions, and after the war he embraced the idea of world peace by traveling around the world and recording interviews, a novel concept in this period, for *One World Flight*.

The structure and tone of many of these documentaries reflected the format made popular by *March of Time*. While the radio broadcast ended in 1945, the newsreel version lasted until 1951. Like *March of Time*, network documentaries used a mix of actors and re-creations with a growing number of live and recorded interviews with the real people involved in the topic. In a continued mix of entertainment and news formats, producers turned to well-known actors and entertainers to host the programs, as a way to connect to the audience. On the issue of atomic power, CBS used actress Agnes Moorehead for its 1947 broadcast *Sunny Side of the Atom*. Bob Hope hosted NBC's 1951 production on the same topic, *The Quick and the Dead*.[49]

The network radio documentary started to lose favor in the early 1950s with the rise of television. Congress and the Truman administration had become more business-friendly while the threats of license forfeiture lessened. The rapidly changing international climate, switching from antifascism to anticommunism during this same period, also resulted in social justice topics to be shelved as the focus turned to Cold War issues. Three of the top CBS documentary producers not only fell out of favor, but Norman Corwin, Robert Heller, and Robert Lewis Shayon ended up on the dreaded *Red*

Channels list of people in the broadcasting industry with potential communist sympathies. Inclusion on this list usually meant immediate banishment.

Hear It Now

One exception to the decline of network radio documentaries was an ambitious weekly series that premiered in 1950. While the program only lasted six months, that production led to one of the most important documentary efforts in American broadcasting history. Fred Friendly started his career at his local station in Providence, Rhode Island, and then became fascinated with recording interviews and sounds during his time in military communication during World War II. After the war, his interest in audio recordings led to a partnership with Edward R. Murrow on a series of surprisingly successful record albums of historic speeches, some real and some re-created, called *I Can Hear It Now*. He also created and produced *Who Said That?*, a marginally successful radio and television quiz show for NBC. After producing the atomic power radio documentary *The Quick and the Dead*, for NBC in 1950, CBS hired Friendly to shore up its radio documentary efforts.

Friendly had bigger ambitions. He wanted to continue his partnership with Murrow on a documentary series. Friendly brought his love of audio recordings and Murrow brought his journalistic gravitas while CBS paved the way for an expensive public affairs program featuring its most famous news personality. Borrowing the title from their record album project, *Hear It Now* premiered in December 1950.[50]

Each week, Murrow and Friendly presented important issues and lifestyle stories through recorded interviews and natural sounds, an ambitious effort in this era. In an attempt to fit in with his new CBS News colleagues, Friendly disavowed his earlier use of actors and re-creations in documentary production. He and Murrow boasted that all recordings were of real people and real events, an attribute he would champion for the rest of his career. For Friendly, *March of Time* became a symbol of misguided and deceptive practices not acceptable in journalistic documentaries.[51]

Given the top story of 1950 and 1951 and the devotion to recording real events during *Hear it Now*'s short run, Friendly was fortunate to have Murrow as his newscaster since Murrow could command the budget necessary to travel to Korea and cover the war. *Hear It Now* avoided the battle stories and focused on the individuals, the soldiers fighting the war. When *Hear It Now* went on summer hiatus in June 1951, Murrow told the audience they would be back for another season in a few months.

American Television Documentaries

Little attention has been paid to American television documentary efforts prior to the explosion of productions in the early 1960s, with the exception of a few key network programs, leaving the impression the medium mostly ignored the format during the 1940s and 1950s. In reality, as a whole, network and local television experimented with a variety of different ways to present information on the new medium, especially in the early years before the networks established a firm scheduling structure and coaxial cable and radio relays linked all cities together for a shared network experience. While the main Hollywood studios mostly avoided television in the early years, considering the medium a competitor, smaller film companies and individuals saw opportunities for televised film productions. Jerry Fairbanks was an early advocate for television films, often instructional in nature. NBC even turned over its *NBC Television Newsreel* to Fairbanks during the mid-1940s, before creating its own television news operation.

One local television documentary example was an ambitious 1948 television production at the *Baltimore Sun*'s WMAR. During World War II, reporter Philip Heiser had witnessed the raising of the flag at Iwo Jima, captured by Joe Rosenthal in an iconic photograph of the war. The US government brought home the three survivors from the photograph and paraded them around the country to pump up support for the war. In *Three Men from Suribachi*, WMAR tracked down the veterans and filmed unvarnished interviews about postwar life. Native American Ira Hayes was back on the Pima Indian reservation near Phoenix and lamented being treated as an inferior again after years serving alongside his Marine brothers. Rene Gagnon of Manchester, New Hampshire, wondered about all those good jobs he had been promised when the government promoted him as a hero. Because *Three Men from Suribachi* was broadcast a few months before AT&T opened up a commercial coaxial cable network, the program was seen only in Baltimore and New York City.[52]

See It Now

Most journalism and broadcast histories give the impression that Edward R. Murrow's transition from radio to television was natural. The new medium had just been waiting for someone of his stature to give it a try. While this view appears to anoint Murrow with a journalistic acumen unbounded by format, in reality, Murrow and Fred Friendly had to exhibit an extraordinary amount of humility and flexibility to succeed on the new medium. Instead of imposing their will on the staff, they purposefully, and by chance, brought together experts from all forms of nonfiction communication.

Only five months separated the last edition of radio's *Hear It Now* and the premiere of television's *See It Now* in November 1951. That summer, CBS finally convinced Murrow to give television a serious try, the offer sweetened by Alcoa's sponsorship deal. Friendly and Murrow kept intact much of the *Hear It Now* staff, which included people with radio and print backgrounds. Even with the bad reputation of Hollywood newsreels, they hired Hearst's *News of the Day* staff to shoot and edit their program.

Friendly and Murrow's lack of visual communication experience became a strength because they were not constrained by film conventions. Most newsreel, documentary, and television films were shot with silent cameras because of their mobility compared to sound cameras. With their love of recorded sound and their generous budget, Friendly and Murrow convinced the newsreel veterans to drag the heavy 35 mm sound cameras around the world, including in the mountains of South Korea. The on-location sound added an important element missing in most news films of the era.[53]

Murrow and Friendly proved to be a great management team, Friendly with the boundless energy and ideas and Murrow with the ability to smooth out his partner's rough edges and keep the program focused. The two men also had the humility to let their staff bring in the strengths from their various communication backgrounds, especially on the visual side. While journalists still viewed newsreels as a failed format, Murrow and Friendly were quick to praise the work of the individual newsreel veterans on their staff, including photographers Martin Barnett, Charlie Mack, Bill McClure, and Leo Rossi. *See It Now* also benefited from dedicated network air time and a virtually unlimited budget.[54]

They did not waste these advantages. *See It Now* is best known for its series of courageous broadcasts involving the Red Scare and an entire program devoted to Senator Joseph McCarthy. *See It Now* also tackled a number of stories on segregation in the United States as well as apartheid in South Africa, immigration, and the devastation of polio. *See It Now* ran as a weekly series for four years, including a few years in primetime. The pressures from anticommunists and the lure of cheaper entertainment programming scared away advertisers and network executives, and *See It Now* was relegated to occasional programs for a few years before its cancellation in 1958.

During the early years of *See It Now,* Reuven Frank and the rest of NBC and ABC television news staffs looked at the CBS program with envy, wishing they had the power to command regular air time and resources for productions lasting longer than the fifteen-minute nightly newscasts. As chronicled in previous chapters, Frank occasionally produced half-hour specials on issues that usually had a Cold War theme. The most popular format of that period was the compilation film, made popular by Capra's Why We Fight series.

At NBC, Pete Salomon edited together government World War II films for the series, *Victory at Sea,* starting in 1952. *Victory at Sea*'s message of the United States as "an international warrior in a global crusade for freedom" was popular with both viewers and critics. That success led to Salomon's *Project 20* series of compilation documentaries that ran the rest of the decade.[55]

CBS had its own compilation series, *Twentieth Century,* in this period. In addition, CBS transferred its *You Are There* radio series to television for four years in the 1950s, with Walter Cronkite appearing as a modern-day reporter covering historical events, complete with actors and sets. While the pro-American premise was meant to be acceptable to all viewers, producer Charlie Russell secretly hired blacklisted writers who found ways to make subtle parallels between historic events and the evils of McCarthyism and the Red Scare. Cronkite became the CBS television news "utility man," hosting both *You Are There, Twentieth Century,* and several other peripheral programs for the network in this period before he became the main newscaster in 1962.[56]

Expansion of Television Documentaries

When government pressure after the quiz show scandal forced the networks into offering more informational programming, the increase in news and public affairs at the American television networks took on a variety of forms. The flagship evening newscasts at CBS and NBC were doubled from fifteen to thirty minutes in 1963. NBC added to its longer-form reporting staff, producing half-hour weekly programs and full-length documentaries. NBC's Washington, DC, documentary unit, originally assigned to David Brinkley, was responsible for some of the most important documentaries on the Vietnam War and unrest around the world. Pete Salomon continued his *Project 20* series, and the network hired Irving Gitlin from CBS to produce NBC's prestige documentary series, *White Paper*. The network also had an Instant Specials unit to produce programs on breaking news stories.[57]

At CBS, *See It Now* was retooled as *CBS Reports*, with Fred Friendly continuing as producer but with Edward R. Murrow openly demoted to just another reporter available to work on projects. At this point, Murrow was publicly critical of his network and television in general. His 1958 speech to the Radio-Television News Directors Association during the quiz show scandal was a direct attack on the business model of favoring shareholders over citizens: "Let us have a little competition not only in selling soap, cigarettes, and automobiles, but in informing a troubled, apprehensive but receptive public." When John F. Kennedy was elected president, Murrow quietly left CBS to run the US Information Agency.[58]

While the networks were willing to lose a little profit to make room for more public affairs programming, they also were strategic in limiting the loss. In his study of network news later in the 1960s, *News from Nowhere*, Edward Jay Epstein reported that public affairs programming would be scheduled to run against popular programs on other networks and in other hard-to-sell timeslots. Documentaries in this period cost between $60,000 and $150,000, compared with an entertainment program that could range between $100,000 to $250,000 per episode. In addition, up to 40 percent of documentary costs could be charges from the network itself (studio time, office space, etc.) as part of an internal bookkeeping system. The less expensive news programming was scheduled at times when the network could not sell the time or expected a small audience.[59]

For the network news crews, the scheduling was a minor annoyance compared to the windfall of time and resources to produce news and public affairs programming. The increase in programming came very quickly, causing a dearth of public affairs program producers. At NBC, as late as 1960, Reuven Frank was one of just a handful of producers. A few years later, the network had more than twenty producers on staff. In 1962 alone, the year *The Tunnel* was broadcast, the three networks presented 400 documentaries.[60]

The networks' need for experienced nonfiction filmmakers provided an opening for those with a documentary film background. By 1960, the field of documentary films was more than twice as old as television news with a rich history of highly regarded filmmakers and approaches. Some followed the informational approach of Robert Flaherty or the British activist style of John Grierson, while others looked to the early Russian emphasis on political messages and editing through Sergei Eisenstein and Dziga Vertov. In the United States, documentarians and television news people remembered, and some worked on, Pare Lorentz's mid-1930s government-sponsored calls to action *The Plow That Broke the Plains* and *The River*, or the World War II era work including Frank Capra's Why We Fight series.

Cinéma Vérité

As noted near the start of this chapter, media historian Erik Barnouw's history of documentary films *does* include projects that aired on American television in the early 1960s, just not Reuven Frank's work. Instead, documentary film historians focus on a group of television outsiders whom supporters thought brought a fresh approach to the form.[61]

Robert Drew had worked as an independent documentary producer during the 1950s and fixated on finding an affordable and user-friendly way to shoot pictures and sound simultaneously out in the field, known as "sync sound." Even though the *See It Now* camera crews had been using 35 mm film sound cameras since the early 1950s, in documentary film studies Robert Drew is usually heralded for bringing "sync sound" to documentaries. Drew also pulled together both veteran and new documentary filmmakers who were ready to experiment with the equipment and approach. His company, Drew and Associates, started with short films, some included on one of the networks' 1950s attempts at elite programming, *Omnibus*.[62]

By the time of the 1960 election documentary *Primary*, Drew and Associates was seen as at the forefront of a new genre of documentary, *cinéma vérité* or direct cinema.[63] The key to *cinéma vérité* is capturing events without influencing the moment, defined as "the act of filming real people in uncontrolled situations."[64] Drew rejected the idea that documentaries needed to have a unifying theme or pre-planned structure: "You *do* see a specific man caught up in his own specific problems. If these problems happen to relate to a great issue, then they shed light on it. If they don't relate to a great issue, then perhaps they shed light on human nature, or man, in the way a drama would."[65] In documentary film history, the canon of American *cinéma vérité* in the United States starting in the 1960s includes Drew & Associates work (*Yanki No!, The Children Were Watching, On the Road to Button Bay*), Albert and David Maysles (*Salesman, Gimme Shelter*), D. A. Pennebaker (*Don't Look Back, Monterey Pop*), and Frederick Wiseman (*Titicut Follies, Hospital*), among others.

The Clash of Documentary Cultures in American Television

The idea of documentary independence, point of view, or lack of an overall theme caused consternation among the television documentarians who came from a journalistic background. During this period that Daniel Hallin has dubbed American journalism's "high modernism" era, journalists believed they were the experts in exploring important issues from multiple angles and avoiding their own viewpoint.[66] Their success in practicing objectivity is another matter, but it was, and is, a core tenet of American journalism. In addition, broadcast journalists were constrained by government regulation. Under the FCC's Fairness Doctrine, broadcasters had to tackle controversial subjects and they had to include diverse viewpoints. The beliefs that documentary films should have a point of view and reflect the producer or director's vision were not compatible with the views of journalists and network executives.

When ABC hired Drew and Associates, through Time Inc., to produce documentaries for the network, ABC News president and newscaster John Daly quit in protest. While Daly had no problem running a network news division at the same time he hosted a popular quiz show, *What's My Line*, on a competing network, he did not like giving control of news programs to outside producers. When Daly quit, Drew's *Yanki No!* documentary on the rise of Fidel Castro in Cuba was scheduled to air within a month, and Daly had no idea what would be in the program. His anger may have partly been about losing control over programs presented as news, but journalists were often suspicious of documentary filmmakers, worrying they had an opinion about a topic and would only film and edit the evidence to support their view.[67]

Journalist vs. Filmmaker

Reuven Frank had strong ideas of what journalism on television should look like, as noted at the start of the chapter. He did not arrive at those ideas by clinging to old journalism maxims or settling on a single approach. Instead, he lived through and seriously considered all of the mid-twentieth century ideas on how to tell stories visually. While *The Tunnel* is the documentary manifestation of what he had learned by 1962, the "transmission of experience" memo also includes clues that Frank was paying attention to changes in documentary films in this era. Many of Frank's ideas and observations in the memo may have gone right over the heads of NBC reporters who were still focused on radio, but the arguments would have been familiar to documentarians, especially in the subgenre of *cinéma vérité*.

One of the most jarring visual manifestations of *cinéma vérité* was the emphasis on filming the moment over the aesthetic of the shot. *Cinéma vérité* allowed out-of-focus, shaky, and poorly lit scenes to be included if they happened to capture an important element. This was heresy to documentary crews who would spend hours setting up lights and equipment for a more appealing image.

During this same period, television news crews still fought over the time it took to set up the camera, lights, and sound for usable film. Reporters with print or radio backgrounds would often try to rush the camera crews, resulting in poor film or audio quality that had to be scrapped. Some considered the new *cinéma vérité* approach as validation that aesthetics could be compromised for speed. In the "transmission of experience" memo, Frank used his blunt candor to dismiss that idea: "A cameraman who cannot light is not a cameraman. A reporter who insists there is enough light is a fool." But Frank did not completely dismiss *cinéma vérité* techniques because he, too, wanted to capture an event as it happens: "They are useful and effective only in the hands of the most highly-skilled cameraman."[68]

Re-creations

When Reuven Frank made the decision to structure *The Tunnel* in chronological order, he was forced to confront one of the most debated practices in broadcast journalism and documentary film: re-creations. Since NBC learned about the tunnel after the digging had already begun, the Berlin crew did not have film of the preparatory work to find the right location. Frank wanted to emphasize the different locations the students considered before settling on the Bernauer Strasse section of the wall. The NBC crew chose to film the students as they reenact their trips to various spots along the wall. The students are also shown studying maps of the city as they reenacted the decision process.

Employing fictional techniques to represent reality, such as re-creations of events or actors standing in for real people, had been a part of radio and film documentaries for decades. The World Union of Documentary definition in 1948 clearly supported re-creations: "all method of recording on celluloid any aspect of reality interpreted either by factual shooting or by sincere and justifiable reconstruction."⁶⁹ In both documentary and journalism work, the use of re-creations and actors became a running ethical debate throughout the 1940s and 1950s. By the time of *The Tunnel*, these dramatic devices were still acceptable in some genres of documentary film but had fallen into disfavor in much of network news and in the *cinéma vérité* movement.

CBS's Fred Friendly's views and practices in this area highlight the disparate and changing beliefs about what was acceptable. When he was working on the 1948 audio project with Edward R. Murrow on famous twentieth-century speeches, *I Can Hear It Now,* Friendly used actors if he could not find a recording. He even asked historic figures to reread their speeches for the project. In his NBC radio documentary on atomic power, *The Quick and the Dead,* Friendly hired Bob Hope to narrate the project. When Friendly and Murrow began their *Hear It Now* and *See It Now* programs, they specifically made a point to say they would never use re-creations or actors. Just a few months before *The Tunnel,* Friendly referred to documentary staging and reenactments as "hanky panky" in a *New Yorker* profile. In the *cinéma vérité* subfield of documentaries, the key was capturing moments as they happen, so re-creations and actors would not be considered. Even formal interviews were shunned.⁷⁰

Reuven Frank was clearly aware of the danger of deception in using reenactments. While he felt re-creations would help visualize the process of picking a tunnel site, he also valued transparency. The viewer sees the three students who organized the dig as they drive their Volkswagen bus to various Berlin locations including the Reichstag and Brandenburg Gate. They walk around the buildings, as well as along the Berlin Wall, while Anderton's narration explains the planning process: "Along this border—as they reenact here—the three students search for just the right spot." The reenactment scenes continue as the three students are shown in sequences of looking at maps and drawing circles on potential sites for the tunnel. They even chisel concrete for the camera to show the viewers how they started the actual dig. At this point, Anderton's narration clearly involves the viewer in the production decision. "Here the reenactment ends. From this point, all pictures were made as they happened."⁷¹

When Frank wrote about *The Tunnel* after it was completed, he hinted at different procedures for filming real events versus re-creations. He lamented cost and secrecy concerns forced him to limit involvement from NBC in New York: "I couldn't send an experienced director, so [reporter Piers] Anderton had to direct some re-enactments. It turned out to be a little wooden, but we had to use it because it explained so much." This implies NBC News relied on directors, in the tradition of Hollywood films, to oversee re-creations, while news cameramen and field reporters could handle real events. This practice is not discussed in Frank's "transmission of experience" memo, or in any of his writings about producing television news.[72]

Post-Escape Party

While Frank did draw attention to the re-creations in the script, there is a more egregious example of staging that Frank did not acknowledge until decades later. *The Tunnel* does not end with the dramatic images of the people escaping through the tunnel. Frank felt that would be "too simple, too anti-climactic." Instead, the final portion of the documentary was filmed at a party held four days after the escape.[73]

The script leaves the impression that the diggers and escapees set up the party, when in reality NBC paid for the event; as Frank admitted, he "laid on a heavy spread of food and whiskey." The script hints that the party was not particularly joyous because the group had already broken into factions. Some of the diggers skipped the party because they were upset more should have been done to keep the tunnel open longer so more people could escape.[74]

During the party, Peter Schmidt, the student trapped on the wrong side of the wall with his family until the escape, is goaded to get up and sing a song on his guitar. Schmidt plays an Italian song in honor of Sesta and Spina, but he sings it in an exaggerated manner for comic effect. During the song, Frank juxtaposed shots of diggers and escapees at the party with earlier images of those same people digging the tunnel or escaping from East Berlin. This is one of the few times in *The Tunnel* when the film crew recorded sound along with the images.

What makes the party deception a little more troubling is that Anderton's script criticizes Schmidt as he sings his song, calling him "a show off, or perhaps he could express his emotions only by clowning." The script does not mention that NBC paid for the whiskey that might have been responsible for how Schmidt chose to thank his rescuers. Schmidt's song, at the NBC-funded party, serves as the ending of the documentary.[75]

Frank was not the only documentary producer during this era to combine different strategies in his work on television. American network television in the early 1960s became a crucible for documentary production approaches and beliefs. While the mixing of different backgrounds brought about interesting collaborations, the individuals did not come together with a unified vision or definition of a television documentary. Instead, they mostly fell back on their individual career paths for touchstones.

The Elusive Definition of Documentary

In December 1963, a year after *The Tunnel*, the New York City chapter of the National Academy of Television Arts and Sciences (NATAS) sponsored a forum on the television documentary. The forum featured seven men from a variety of backgrounds, affiliations, and orientations to documentary film. While Frank was not involved, the main three networks (CBS, NBC, and ABC) were represented as well as Robert Drew, considered the leader of the *cinéma vérité* approach in the United States at that time. The panel also included Willard Van Dyke, who traced his documentary roots back to the pre–World War II American group of filmmakers who struggled to find an outlet for their work.[76]

The forum represented a microcosm of the decades-long debates about documentaries. The seven men could not agree on a basic definition of a documentary. Instead, they spent much of the forum engaging in boundary work, putting down stakes to denote what should or should not be considered a documentary.

Van Dyke started out the discussion by differentiating television documentaries from the work he did with Pare Lorentz (*The River* 1938), Ralph Steiner (*The City* 1939), and others before television became a mass medium. Van Dyke said his prewar group "took uncompromising opinions" on the topics they produced. He felt that television documentaries diluted the main points with "on the other hand." In a fit of nostalgia, Van Dyke said the early documentary projects had no money but a lot of time, so a greater emphasis was placed on the photography.

The television network documentary producers disputed Van Dyke's interpretation of aesthetics and intent. NBC's Lou Hazam separated television documentaries into "news-type" and "art-type," with the latter category fitting more into Van Dyke's definition. ABC's John Secondari dismissed those categories, saying the only common documentary attribute would be that "within the maximum limits of the tools that are available, a man can produce an honest work." CBS producer David Lowe, best known for *Harvest of Shame* (1960), said television and film documentaries are hard to compare but agreed with Secondari that the strongest productions start with one person's idea, "born out of individual creative art."

On the ethics of documentaries, they had differing ideas of what was acceptable, but most of the men at the symposium did not support the use of re-creations or actors. Most agreed the editing process was the part of the production where a documentarian could get carried away and stray from reality of the subject and insert too much subjectivity. Only editor Robert Collison of CBS's *The Twentieth Century* would admit to possibly manipulating events: "What you have to look for is not an idea but *the feel of truth*," reminiscent of the justification for re-creations in both *March of Time* radio and film versions. Robert Drew would not allow any instructions for people in his documentaries and David Lowe went even further, calling reenactments "a great dis-service to the entire field of documentary."

The discussion then shifted to Robert Drew's work, representing the *cinéma verité* approach. Two of his most famous productions involved President John F. Kennedy: *Primary,* which focused on the 1960 Wisconsin Democratic contest between Kennedy and Hubert Humphrey, and 1963's *Crisis: Behind a Presidential Commitment,* concerning the standoff between Alabama governor George Wallace and the US government over integrating the University of Alabama.

One of the more controversial aspects of Drew's version of *cinéma vérité* was his lack of commitment to an overarching theme or purpose: "I'm interested in one approach only, and that is to convey the excitement and drama and feeling of real life as it actually happens through film." He did not apologize if that event did not relate to a larger issue.

Because of the lack of a larger theme, Van Dyke classified Drew's work as "*film documents,* not *documentary films.*" Drew did not disagree. NBC producer Albert Wasserman marginalized Drew's style as "life-as-it-is" but "with no social purpose."

Wasserman cautioned about the need both for choosing important issues but also for the evidence to determine the structure: "The conclusions must grow out of what has been demonstrated in the body of the program, and not be the result of a personal orientation of the film-maker." Drew rejected the need for a social purpose in favor of the reality of capturing a scene as it happens. ABC's John Secondari could have been describing *The Tunnel* when he talked about the rare situation when the two approaches come together: "When you can tell a story as it unfolds, with your camera and without very much need of words, you have a documentary in the palm of your hands." The wildly divergent ideas of what constitutes a television documentary at this one symposium hints at the reasons why *The Tunnel* has been remembered or forgotten in the more than half-century since it was broadcast on NBC in 1962.

The Tunnel as a Documentary Film

The Tunnel is a powerful documentary. The production, focusing on the personal stories of a group of Berlin college students taking on the massive and dangerous digging project to help their friends get out of East Germany, tackles the overarching issue of the generation, the Cold War, and narrows it to specific people risking their lives to allow others to escape communism. The structural arc of the documentary employs a narrative form by first introducing us to the characters, then presenting the obstacles and dangers, and finally showing the payoff of the muddy and tired people crawling out of the darkness of the tunnel.

As one of American television news' most vocal proponents of the power of moving pictures and sound in helping the viewer experience an issue, Reuven Frank recognized he had a rare opportunity when he first viewed the hours of film his Berlin crew had been shooting throughout the tunnel project. Instead of a traditional documentary, he could tell the entire personal story, beginning to end (save the reenactments), with images filmed at the moment they happened. He did not need interviews to fill in the nonvisual parts or to argue the righteousness of the West's cause. The pictures would do that for him. He was proud of the sparse narration, opting instead for long segments of the images accompanied by the musical score.

The US government knew *The Tunnel* was a powerful topic, which is why officials worked so hard to kill the production (chronicled in chapter 6). Most of the print media television critics recognized Frank's efforts to tell a compelling story and likened it to a strong fiction film. The audience certainly tuned in, since it was one of the rare television documentaries to match popular entertainment programs in viewership. The television industry took notice, with *The Tunnel* winning three Emmy Awards. Frank considered *The Tunnel* to be one of his top achievements, by picking it over all his other work nine years later to be screened at an international documentary conference.

Even with the structure of and the response to *The Tunnel*, Frank's documentary is absent in most timelines of documentary history. One of the points of this chapter is to show the complicated and discordant histories of the format, depending on how one defines a documentary. *The Tunnel* combines enough ideas and approaches to allow documentary scholars to look elsewhere for iconic productions.

The Tunnel was produced during the height of the *cinéma vérité* movement in the United States, which has survived in documentary studies as the key work in the United States in this period. While *The Tunnel* demonstrates (and the "transmission of experience" memo instructs) the importance of moving pictures shot during the actual event, as well as other key tenets of *cinéma vérité*, the production also features conventional television production techniques shunned by Robert Drew and others, including a reporter guiding us through the story, both on camera and reading a narrative track. The production employs a musical score instead of an emphasis on natural sound, even though Frank apologizes in the script for the lack of sound from the scene, blaming it on the tight conditions in the tunnel that didn't allow for the audio equipment. The re-creations, although clearly identified in the narration, are also anathema to *cinéma vérité*.

Another reason to ignore Frank's work in overall documentary history timeline is the organizational structure in which he worked. Documentaries are often celebrated as the vision of one person, consistent with the auteur theory, much like a Hollywood fiction director. Therefore, a production constrained by the structure of a television network, stifled by government oversight, strays too far from the image of the crusading John Grierson, Dziga Vertov, or other documentarians who used the moving pictures to take what Van Dyke in the NATAS forum called "uncompromising positions," an approach documentary film scholar Michael Curtin refers to as "oppositional film practice."[77]

This version of documentary history ignores the reality that Grierson championed the government sponsorship approach, with the documentary producer beholden to the government viewpoint and using film skills to convey that message. Van Dyke did not mention that Pare Lorentz fired his *The Plow That Broke the Plains* crew when they did not agree with the government's version of what caused the Dust Bowl.

At CBS, Fred Friendly's documentary approach, on *See It Now* and later on *CBS Reports*, was heavily dependent on narration and the juxtaposition of interview clips (sound bites) to create tension and move along the story. While the crews spent considerable time lighting and framing the interviews for these productions, less emphasis was placed on the visuals that accompanied the narration. This approach was adapted later in the decade by Don Hewitt for his new public affairs program, *60 Minutes*. Robert Drew considered this approach "word-logic," as opposed to the picture-logic of *cinéma vérité*.[78]

By contrast, Frank's attention to and emphasis on the moving pictures of the tunnel dig and escape (albeit without the natural sound in almost all of the production), the lack of on-camera interviews, and the limited narration resulted in a powerful and unique production in television news and public affairs at the time, hence the positive reviews and industry awards. Unlike Friendly's, and later Hewitt's, productions, a viewer could not adequately experience *The Tunnel* by the audio alone. The pictures provided the main impact, much as Drew championed in *cinéma vérité*.

The Tunnel is remembered in the academic research subfield of American television documentaries. A. William Bluem's *Documentary in American Television*, published in 1965, pays special attention to Frank's ideas as well as provides a unique take on *The Tunnel*. As editor of *Television Quarterly*, Bluem had featured Frank in articles, including a piece on *The Making of the Tunnel*. As noted in chapter 3, Bluem included the "transmission of experience" memo as an appendix to the *Documentary in American Television* book, saying Frank's views are "of significance for that area of television programming where the journalist's and documentarist's functions draw near to each other."[79]

Concerning *The Tunnel*, Bluem labeled it both "art and record." He admitted the footage and narration was "pure and dispassionate reportage," which was Frank's argument. But Bluem added that because Frank had been looking for evidence of people trying to escape East Berlin, "the very selection of an event was implied the dramatization of the great theme of man's urge to be free, expression of whose universality is a true function of art."[80] In other words, Frank used the real tunnel escape to represent his feelings on the evils of communism.

Chad Raphael, in *Investigated Reporting*, also noted the dual nature of Frank's documentary. While Frank did not rely on government sources for information, the topic and approach did not challenge the Cold War western consensus, so Raphael dubbed it "media adventurism," not adversarialism. At the time of the controversy, Secretary of State Dean Rusk called *The Tunnel* project "adventurous journalism."[81]

The Tunnel does not fit neatly into one genre or production category, because Reuven Frank worked across all formats. His work straddles academic disciplines of documentary film, television, and journalism because his experience and day-to-day work did not distinguish between the formats. He used the techniques and approaches that he felt would best make an impression on the viewer depending on the topic and venue. *The Tunnel* and the "transmission of experience" memo show he was clearly impressed with some tenets of *cinéma vérité* and dismissive of other practices.

At his core, however, when asked to explain his guiding principle and reason for one approach over another, Frank identified first and foremost as a journalist. As evidenced in his Tokyo speech, Frank would dismiss other people and approaches if he felt they did not fit with his core mission as a journalist, even if the definition of journalism was never clearly articulated beyond an allegiance to the truth.

While Reuven Frank wore his journalistic badge proudly, some of the harshest criticisms and dismissals of his work, including *The Tunnel*, came from his own professional fraternity and origin, print journalism. The next chapter delves into Reuven Frank's (and all of television news') fight for acceptance from the very group from which he derived his identity, newspaper and magazine journalists and publishers, many of whom had adopted a superior air and patronizing and dismissive approach toward radio and television journalism, an attitude that has survived well into the twenty-first century.

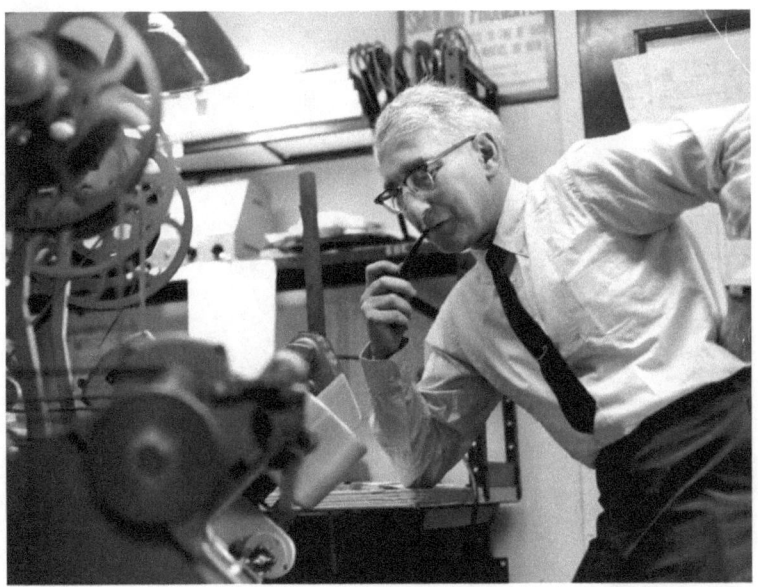

FIGURE 1. Reuven Frank moved from newspapers to television news partly because of his interest in combining words with moving images.
—*Digital Collections and Archives, Tufts University, Medford, Massachusetts.*

FIGURE 2. Reuven Frank (standing) worked on the NBC nightly newscast, the *Camel News Caravan*, during his first years at the network. Ralph Peterson (left) directed the newscast while John Cameron Swayze (right) served as the main newscaster until 1956.
—*Digital Collections and Archives, Tufts University, Medford, Massachusetts.*

FIGURE 3. Chet Huntley (left) joined NBC in 1955 and first worked with Reuven Frank (right) on a weekly public affairs program, *Outlook*. NBC paired Huntley with David Brinkley for the signature NBC nightly newscast, the *Huntley-Brinkley Report*, in 1956.
—*Digital Collections and Archives, Tufts University, Medford, Massachusetts.*

FIGURE 4. David Brinkley (left) came to NBC Radio in 1943. Reuven Frank (right) was instrumental in promoting Brinkley and Chet Huntley for political convention coverage and the NBC nightly newscast, the *Huntley-Brinkley Report*.
—*Digital Collections and Archives, Tufts University, Medford, Massachusetts.*

FIGURE 5. Tunnel organizers Wolf Schroedter and Luigi Spina reenact for *The Tunnel* documentary their search along the Berlin Wall for a proper spot to dig a tunnel to East Berlin. Domenico Sesta is hidden behind Spina.

—*NBCUniversal Archives.*

FIGURE 6. NBC Berlin correspondent Piers Anderton inside the tunnel during the 1962 escape project.
—*Special Collections and University Archives, University of Maryland, College Park, Maryland.*

FIGURE 7. NBC correspondent Piers Anderton (left) and NBC cameraman Peter Dehmel (right) talk with project organizer Domenico Sesta in the tunnel.
—*Bettmann Archives/Getty Images.*

FIGURE 8. Luigi Spina crawls through the tunnel as the diggers get close to finishing the project in September 1962, from *The Tunnel* documentary.

—*NBCUniversal Archives.*

FIGURE 9. NBC correspondent Piers Anderton at an NBC press conference on October 11, 1962, announcing *The Tunnel* documentary. The drawing, used in the documentary, shows the route of the escape tunnel under the Berlin Wall.
—*Special Collections and University Archives, University of Maryland, College Park, Maryland.*

FIGURE 10. In one of the climactic final scenes from *The Tunnel* documentary, tunnel organizer Domenico Sesta hands Annett Schmidt to NBC's Klaus Dehmel at the top of the shaft after the Schmidt family successfully escaped from East Berlin through the 140-yard tunnel.
—*NBCUniversal Archives.*

FIGURE 11. Gary Stindt, NBC chief of news film for Central Europe, standing next to the basement stairs where the tunnel project began in West Berlin.
—*Digital Collections and Archives, Tufts University, Medford, Massachusetts.*

FIGURE 12. *The Tunnel* won three Emmys in 1963, including overall program of the year. Klaus Dehmel (left) and his brother Peter (right), the camera crew on the documentary, flank producer Reuven Frank after the Emmy Awards.
—*Special Collections and University Archives, University of Maryland, College Park, Maryland.*

CHAPTER FIVE

Adventurous Laymen

Print vs. Broadcast in Journalism Boundary Work

IN OCTOBER 1962, as Reuven Frank defended the proposed NBC Berlin Wall tunnel escape documentary against strong government pressure, one of the most stinging criticisms of the project came from within his own profession. Jack Gould, the influential television critic for the *New York Times*, wrote an article accusing NBC of causing a "minor international incident" because of greed and naiveté. Gould referred to Frank and his crew as "adventurous laymen" stumbling into delicate and dangerous Cold War politics.[1]

Given Frank's allegiance to the ethos of journalism above all other professional affiliations, this sharp rebuke from a writer at one of the bastions of American journalism could be seen as a serious blow to Frank's reputation, or at least a form of betrayal within the journalism community. For Reuven Frank, the attack was not a surprise because it had become a familiar response from print journalists when confronted by the exponential growth and reach of television news. In the dozen years since he jumped from print to television journalism, Frank had personally witnessed the divide between journalists who focused on words versus those who also included audio and moving pictures.

The boundary work of print versus broadcast news dates back well before Frank became a journalist, starting roughly when radio first showed its potential in presenting news and public affairs on a platform other than words on paper. The legitimacy of radio news, and later television news, became entangled in the twentieth-century efforts to lift up American journalism from its mixed reputation as an important but ethically challenged vocation to a professional group trained to cover and present the important issues to the people. On an economic level, many newspaper and magazine publishers used the divide to try to dampen competition from newer media, through efforts ranging from government intervention to demonizing the broadcast media and its employees.

The controversy over *The Tunnel* project provides a revealing moment during the critical juncture in American journalism as the public increasingly moved its allegiance from newspapers and radio news to television, while leaders in print journalism stood firm on the superiority of their format.

Just one year after *The Tunnel*, the assassination of John F. Kennedy showcased television's ability to attract the nation's attention for four days through a combination of live reporting of the Dallas shooting and visual assurances the country could survive the shocking events. That very month, November 1963, also signaled the first time a national survey showed television had eclipsed newspapers as the most popular and trusted news format in the country. Using the lens of boundary work, the threat to the printed word's position as journalism's preeminent platform provided more emotional and heightened examples of protecting one's format by disparaging interlopers, in this case, television news.

Reuven Frank played an important role in the divide between print and broadcast news because he was the creator and producer of the most popular news program of any format at the time, the *Huntley-Brinkley Report*. Frank was also the rare television journalist who not only fully understood the potential of sight and sound journalism, but was willing to stand up for the medium and not bow down to the primacy of the printed word. With a graduate journalism degree from Columbia University and years in a newspaper newsroom, Frank clearly understood the differences between the media.

Other journalists who moved into television still based their reputation on a previous life as a print reporter. One of the key reasons Frank wrote the "transmission of experience" memo was to try and reach journalists within his own organization, NBC News, who still had not accepted the strengths of the television medium and approached their work as a print or radio journalist. With his print background, Frank did not hesitate in calling out print journalists for their hypocrisy in disparaging television news for professional decisions and practices shared between the media.

Journalism Professionalism

Frank's journalism training and career leading up to *The Tunnel* happened at a time in American journalism when a variety of initiatives had taken hold to improve the quality and image of the work, making a case for professional status. Since the First Amendment precludes journalism from creating exams, licenses, or other barriers to entry, as used in the emulated professions of law and medicine, the newspaper industry worked on other ways to differentiate and elevate its work. In the nineteenth century, printers held and reported on annual Franklin Dinners as a way to connect their work to founding father and printer Benjamin Franklin. In the twentieth century, journalism schools and programs opened across the country in an effort to standardize practices and improve the work. Frank's alma mater, Columbia University, received a major gift from notorious New York publisher Joseph Pulitzer and started a graduate program in journalism, one of the first dedicated journalism programs in the nation. Columbia also used Pulitzer's gift, at his bequest, to establish a nationwide award in the benefactor's honor.

In the spirit of modernism and the scientific method, journalists sought to position themselves as information experts, uniquely qualified to gather and present the news without opinion. This attention to objectivity became a key component of journalism's push for professional status and had become an accepted foundation of journalism when Frank began his studies and career.[2]

Journalism's push for professional status also included independent organizations and awards to guide the practitioners towards accepted behavior. Even though journalists worked for different companies and corporations, they could turn to their professional organizations, such as Sigma Delta Chi (now known as the Society of Professional Journalists), or journalism honors, including the Pulitzer Prizes and Peabody Awards, as evidence of their independent and professional status. These organizations also confronted ethical issues through codes of ethics or, in most cases, on the job training.[3]

Since Frank worked both in print and broadcast journalism, he learned quickly that the beliefs and sensibilities of journalists did not always match the owner, whether that be the publisher or chain owner of a newspaper, or the head of a radio and television network.

Newspaper Economics

In addition to the First Amendment's prohibition on licensing journalists, another major impediment blocking journalism from gaining true professional status involved the differing objectives between those reporting the news and those signing their paychecks. Journalism schools, national organizations, and codes of ethics emphasized the public service and independence model of journalism, its lofty status in the First Amendment to the Constitution, and its watchdog role on government. These ambitions did not always align with the newspaper owners.

Publishers and chains started or bought papers for a number of reasons, from gaining a powerful voice in a community, pushing their own political or economic agenda, making money, to believing in the same principles espoused by the journalism organizations. Even if publishers did not all get rich, they all had to worry about cost and competition. When the principles of a free and responsible press collided with the economics of running a newspaper, publishers had the final say. Those decisions could range from more robust reporting, sensational news, made-up stories, favoring advertisers, demeaning political or economic enemies, or any number of approaches, depending on the owner—or, later in the century in the case of highly leveraged, publicly traded companies—banks and shareholders. The journalists' recourse usually ranged between going along with the boss or finding another job.

The push toward professionalism, however, provided a platform on which both publishers and journalists could proudly stand. Gaining stature in the public's eye not only helped the individual journalists; it gave the newspapers themselves more gravitas. The push toward objectivity, the trained journalist's professional ability to cover the news "without fear or favor,"[4] also dovetailed with the move to consolidate newspapers and reduce competition.

Printed word diversity, especially in larger cities, including newspapers with a variety of political, geographical, and cultural approaches, reached its peak in the first decades of the twentieth century. World War I and the First Red Scare caused a retrenchment of viewpoints, with the government clamping down on foreign language and socialist publication through the courts and postal system restrictions. On the economic side, newspaper owners started to pursue a more inclusive approach to their news stories (if not their editorial stances) as a way to reach more readers than papers with a more targeted (Republican, Democrat, socialist, religious, labor) niche. With advertising subsidizing the true cost of printing a paper, the publications reaching the largest audiences and least controversial viewpoints could corner the coveted ad market and keep their street prices low, eventually forcing those competitors out of business that could not keep up in advertising revenue.

Publications also began combining in newspaper chains, providing economies of scale in production and even better advertising rates across the company. By promoting their journalism as "objective," newspapers could argue that they were providing readers with both sides of an issue, thereby justifying the reduced competition. By the mid-twentieth century, people in most medium-to-small cities in the United States no longer had a choice in newspaper ownership, maybe only in the time of day they received the paper.[5]

While the combination of competition, advertising, and government interference helped cut down the choices in newspapers, a new threat to the American print journalism business model appeared in the mid-1920s: radio and, in the shadows, television. This threat emerged just as American journalism was pushing hard for professional status on several fronts. The publishers saw radio as an interloper for the crucial advertising dollar, and the journalists had only known their vocation as the printed word and images. Many did not trust this new medium of delivering information. The boundary work involved in promoting the printed word and disparaging the spoken word (and later visual information) revealed the importance of publishers in defeating a new competitor and for print journalists in protecting their improving status in society.

Newspaper Response to Radio

The National Broadcasting Company (NBC) began in 1926, followed by the Radio Act of 1927, which firmed up a license system for those who wanted to start a station in the United States. By 1930, 1.3 million radio receivers were in use around the country. The American newspaper industry had a hard time mustering a unified response to radio in the 1920s and 1930s because publishers generally fell into two camps: those considering radio a threat, pushing various approaches to stifle or discredit the format, or those embracing the technology, to see how it could expand the reach of their newspapers and bring in more advertising revenue.[6]

For the newspaper owners who either did not have a chance at a license or did not want to get involved in radio, this new medium threatened their bottom line. By the early 1930s, the immediacy of radio and the reality of a mass medium became apparent. In 1932, the baby of aviation hero Charles Lindbergh was kidnapped and murdered, sparking an ongoing tragic story as the baby disappeared from his crib, eventually leading to the killer, Bruno Hauptmann, and his subsequent trial and execution. Americans with radio receivers heard the latest information hours before newspapers could print their next, or even extra, editions.

In February 1933, Joe Zangara tried to assassinate President-elect Franklin Roosevelt at a speech in Miami. Instead, Zangara's bullets hit five other people, killing Chicago mayor Anton Cermak. In newspaper tradition, Miami papers raced out extra editions on the shooting, but to little interest since the news had been on the radio for hours.[7]

The threat of radio became a contentious topic at print media organizational meetings, beyond just the redundancy of the extra edition. A downturn in advertising heightened the concern as publishers tried to figure out how much of the loss was due to radio competition and how much could be related to the economic crisis brought on by the stock market crash in 1929.

One response was to charge radio stations and networks for services newspapers had published for free. When radio gained a sizable audience in the 1920s, newspapers printed station program schedules, both as a public service and also to sell related advertising space. As the stations and networks became more popular, newspapers published features about various programs and personalities, often generated by the radio industry itself. Now, many publishers felt the stations should pay for that space. In an effort known as the "Louisiana Plan," newspapers in that state agreed to a blackout on unpaid radio publicity. As the newspaper trade publication *Editor & Publisher* reported, "Radio programs were jerked out of the papers overnight. No more 'personality stories' or gossip of the studios found space in the papers." The ban was considered a success, at least initially, because three stations started buying small ads to list their program schedule.[8]

While the newspaper industry heralded the idea of an unfettered press, free of government regulations, many publishers were not above looking for government help to stifle competition. Some publishers pushed or supported legislative efforts to slow down radio's growth. In these instances, publishers found themselves on the same side as broadcast reformers who wanted to change the commercial structure of American radio toward more of a public service model that had been adopted by England with the taxpayer-supported British Broadcasting Company (BBC). Proposed legislation included banning commercials, charging a license tax, and even turning radio news over to newspapers. Commercial broadcasters were able to fight off most of these legislative approaches.[9]

One of the most zealous anti-radio publishers was Ed Harris of the *Richmond (IN) Palladium*. Harris was also chair of the Radio Committee of the American Newspaper Publishers Association (ANPA). He urged his fellow publishers to treat radio as a serious competitor and take whatever means necessary to protect newspaper's economic structure and stature: "There is no doubt that promiscuous broadcasting of news in great quantities at all hours is seriously depreciating the value of news in the minds of listeners."[10]

Gene Howe of the *Amarillo (TX) News and Globe* put it more bluntly: "Publishers are the only persons I know who are engaged in cutting their own throats. There is no such thing as cooperating with radio as the publishers give all and receive nothing in return." The publishers who advocated a tough stand against radio tended to get the most attention, especially in the trade publication *Editor & Publisher*, which advocated "a united fight against radio's invasion of the newspaper's field."[11]

Another group of publishers saw radio as an expansion of their newspaper business model and rejected efforts to reduce its effectiveness. The *Detroit News* and the *Milwaukee Journal* were just two of the newspapers embracing radio's potential. While newspapers accounted for only 7 percent of radio stations in the 1920s, many of those were influential newspapers and stations. When newspaper publishers debated how to confront radio, common ground was hard to find because of the divide, which *Editor and Publisher* described as early as 1932 as "the usual abyss of opinion."[12]

The commercial broadcast industry encouraged the divide among newspaper publishers by publicly supporting newspaper-radio cross ownership. More publishers involved in radio would mean less criticism of the advertiser-supported model put in place by the Radio Act of 1927. By the mid-1930s, newspapers owned a quarter of all radio stations, and that jumped to one-third by the 1940s.[13]

Hot News

Newspaper publishers did have a more specific quarrel with radio stations and networks broadcasting news over an issue that originated with the print medium. In those years, radio stations and networks had few if any people dedicated to covering the news. Instead, local stations were known to just rewrite or even have announcers read stories out of their local paper verbatim. In some cases, the wire services would sell or provide their material for broadcast. The wire services operated mostly as a cooperative, but radio members did little original reporting. The push to protect individual stories, however, started with the wire services well before radio emerged.

For the first two centuries of newspapers in America, printers and publishers shared and repurposed stories quite freely. The news was considered in the public domain and the act of reprinting another publication's work was often considered a form of flattery. The concept of competition and keeping other publications from taking a newspaper's story without permission started to take hold in the mid- to late 1800s with the rise of the telegraph and the Associated Press (AP) wire service. Publishers were paying increasing amounts to cover the news and get it printed as quickly as possible because their readers favored the latest news. With that investment in people and speed, publishers did not like competitors getting credit for their work. Bigger city papers and the AP looked to the US government for copyright protection, at least for what became known as "hot news," the latest news reported by a specific newspaper. The debate became whether or not news was a public service or a commodity.[14]

In the case of radio, at least some publishers realized the broadcast format provided instantaneous communication. If a newspaper would not let a radio station broadcast important information, that paper could be seen as selfish and fighting against the community's interest or safety. Harris of the *Richmond (IN) Palladium* was willing to make exceptions for what he called news "of transcendent importance." George Dealey of the *Dallas (TX) News and Journal* said radio should not broadcast stories from newspapers or the wire services "before publication except in times of great disaster when suffering or loss of life would be prevented by giving warning or issuing appeal for aid."[15]

Cutting Off the News

Newspaper publishers finally acted in unison after the American public learned of Franklin Roosevelt's presidential victory over incumbent Herbert Hoover in 1932 over the radio, hours before any newspaper publications could hit the street. The broadcasters used wire service information to scoop the print press.[16]

After that evening, publishers demanded that the wire services stop providing service to broadcast stations. As William Randolph Hearst put it, "If the radio companies want news, let them get their own news."[17] By the spring of 1933, newspaper publishers had forced the three wire services into cutting off broadcast members. The two top radio networks took Hearst's advice. At NBC, Abe Schechter worked for popular radio commentator Lowell Thomas, and he found he could get most important people to return his calls by mentioning Thomas's name. CBS took a more ambitious approach by setting up its own Columbia News Service, which not only covered news for CBS but was also syndicated to other news outlets.

The wire service ban turned out to be a futile and short-lived effort. The restrictions did not stop radio from broadcasting news; publishers with radio stations did not like the situation; and the wire services missed the broadcast station revenue. A year later, publishers and broadcasters compromised with the "Press-Radio Bureau," a radio-funded operation with wire service stories rewritten in broadcast style and length. This arrangement negated radio's immediacy advantage because publishers demanded the newscasts run after morning and afternoon papers were delivered. In addition, the radio newscasts could not be sponsored.

Given the public's appetite for the latest news, entrepreneurs began setting up alternate news services without the time and sponsorship restrictions. United Press caved by 1936 and set up a special broadcast wire and the Press-Radio Bureau formally closed in 1938. Newspapers had failed in their attempt to control how and when people received the news.[18]

Demonizing Radio

Even though Reuven Frank did not work in radio, he would have recognized the attacks against radio that took places in the decades before he moved into television. Most of the newspaper publishers' arguments against radio news landed squarely on the issues of competition and protecting their product, especially when radio became a major advertising medium.

When the newspaper-radio debate is widened to include both those who ran the newspapers and journalists who worked at those publications, the case against radio took on a more judgmental and paternalistic tone. Instead of the idea of radio as a strong competitor, these arguments were based on demeaning the medium and the people involved. In boundary work, in addition to touting a group's strengths, a common tactic is to marginalize or demonize any people or approaches attempting to threaten that group's perceived professional niche.

In an effort to trivialize the value of radio, S. Howard Evans of the *Ventura (CA) Free Press* compared the medium to the newspaper comic section. Evans was part of an effort to try and take the commercialism out of American radio. While reporters and publishers like to tout their news coverage, newspapers have always been filled with less serious sections to attract readers. In the early twentieth century, comics had become one of those features that newspapers had reluctantly embraced, to increase or stabilize circulation. "Nearly every publisher has been forced to use comic strips, because of their popularity with the readers," said Evans. "He may wake up some day in the not distant future and find himself in the same position with regard to a radio broadcasting service."[19]

One of the common criticisms positioned words on paper as trustworthy, lasting, and solid, contrasting with radio as ephemeral, or "a vibration in the air." Radio, as a platform for delivering information, should not be trusted for disseminating important information for the American public. In a resolution from the radio committee of the ANPA in 1932, publishers made it clear they owned the most important news format: "People hear something over the radio, but it is not definitely fixed in their minds merely by listening to a broadcast. It must be seen in print and be read again before the message is clearly understood and impressed on the mind of the individual."[20]

Newspapers also promoted the idea that the true path to becoming a journalist went through a newsroom, a print newsroom of course. In the 1930s and 1940s, the earliest college journalism programs were only a few decades old, so most training happened on the job. As Gwenyth Jackaway chronicled in her book on newspapers' response to radio, *Media at War,* print journalists chose to align with the publishers and use their standards and codes as a "cloak of professional legitimacy." Aligning with the publishers, Jackaway notes the journalists also inserted the medium into the professional equation, guaranteeing radio would not measure up: "The newsmen invoked standards they had just adopted, claiming these ideals were the true definition of what it meant to be a journalist. The new competition was then measured against this ideal model and found lacking."[21]

The Economics of American Broadcast News

When the advertiser model of funding American radio took hold in the late 1920s, the code word for entertainment versus public affairs programming was "sponsored" versus "sustaining." Advertisers liked the entertainment programs because they were less controversial and brought in larger audiences. In this era, advertisers bought the program time, usually in fifteen- or thirty-minute increments. They could then tell the station what type of programming to offer or their advertising agencies would create the program themselves. The broadcast slots that could not be sold were then used for the less popular public affairs "sustaining" programming. As more advertisers recognized the reach of this new mass medium, stations were tempted to push aside public affairs programming for more sponsored entertainment. As radio advertising took off, the main economic reason stations and networks offered public affairs programs was to fulfill their obligation to serve the "public interest, convenience, and necessity" as mandated by the Federal Communication Commission (FCC).[22]

Public affairs programming on radio took on many forms. First of all, it was mostly live, not recorded. The people talking had to be in the studio or live on location. A common format would be to bring in a politician, an expert, or someone in the news for a speech or an interview. Radio executives said they soon learned to avoid college professors, because they often "treat the radio as though they were in a classroom from which their listeners had no chance to escape."[23]

One of journalism's biggest names in the twentieth century, Edward R. Murrow, started at CBS as the Director of Talks. He did not cover nor broadcast the news. He coordinated guests to appear on CBS airwaves to talk about specific topics. The networks would broadcast speeches from politicians or bring in specific guests to debate an issue. When Franklin Roosevelt took office in 1933, he began speaking directly to the public through radio, later known as fireside chats, partly as a way to get around the newspaper publishers, most of whom did not agree with his policies.

Radio commentators also played a big role in early radio public affairs programming. Networks were able to find sponsors for popular commentators including Lowell Thomas, Boake Carter, Floyd Gibbons, and H. V. Kaltenborn. These commentators were often former newspaper reporters and the programs had a mix of original reporting and a heavy dose of opinion and analysis. During the short-lived wire service ban for broadcast stations, commentators became more important because they were exempt from the "no advertising" clause for radio newscasts.[24]

To provide daily news coverage, stations and networks usually took the cheaper route of paying for a wire service instead of hiring a news staff. A staff announcer or newscaster would read the latest news from Associated Press, United Press, or the International News Service. They often also read directly or rewrote stories from area newspapers, maybe adding a phone call to confirm the information. This common practice of "rip and read" news is why publishers thought they could kill radio news by cutting off wire service access.

Journalism Exclusion

Many publishers and print reporters chose to reject radio from their definition of journalism. Instead of embracing a new way to deliver the news faster, they excluded the formats and the people who worked in broadcasting. Most university journalism programs kept a heavy print emphasis for the rest of the century, with radio, then television, journalism often relegated to other departments, or as an add-on to predominantly print-focused curriculum. Professional organizations limited membership to people who worked in the print press, forcing broadcast journalists to start their own professional groups. To this day, the award that has come to symbolize top American journalism work, the Pulitzer Prize, does not recognize television or radio journalism. That omission caused the National Association of Broadcasters and the University of Georgia to create the George Foster Peabody Awards in 1940 to honor radio achievements, with television added in 1948.[25]

A background in a print newsroom was one of the first ways radio or television journalists could receive a modicum of respect from their print brethren. When Edward R. Murrow arrived in London as CBS's new European Director of Talks in 1937, he was denied membership in the American Foreign Correspondents Association. Murrow had two strikes against him: he worked in radio and had no background in a print newsroom. As late as 1948, a decade after Murrow began to make his mark with coverage of World War II in Europe, a profile in *Editor & Publisher* begins with the writer lamenting that the newspaper industry could not take any credit for Murrow's success because there "isn't a whiff of mailroom paste or printer's ink in the whole reportorial career" of the famous broadcaster.[26]

The journalism community began to accept some radio journalists during World War II because of the work of Murrow and other broadcasters who brought the news of the war home to Americans through their radios much faster than could be accomplished by newspapers. Initially, these newly accepted radio journalists shunned the next new medium, television, and the people who covered the news on that format. When Reuven Frank moved from newspapers into television in 1950, he faced not only the skeptics from his print brethren, but also from news people at his own broadcast network.[27]

Demonizing Television

In September 1962, two of the most powerful men in television news, Don Hewitt and Reuven Frank, sat down together to talk about the state of journalism on their medium. The two men had remarkably similar career paths. Don Hewitt was executive producer of the nightly *CBS Evening News*. He moved from print into television in 1948, two years before Frank. Hewitt quickly became the main producer and director for the CBS nightly television newscast and director on prestige programs including *See It Now* in the 1950s. Hewitt basked in the glow of his position as the brains behind the nightly newscast, while newscaster Douglas Edwards was the familiar face to the viewers. Just months before the interview, Edwards had been replaced on the newscast by Walter Cronkite.

Even though Frank and Hewitt were intense rivals, they agreed to the dual interview for *Television Quarterly*, a new research and practice journal from the National Academy of Television Arts and Sciences (NATAS). Both Hewitt and Frank were considered confident men always willing to speak their mind, but they may have been particularly at ease because the journal took television seriously and did not approach the medium through the critical lens of most print journalists.

Even so, they were first asked to respond to the constant criticisms of the shortcomings of television news. Although they did not use the phrase, both Hewitt and Frank recognized the boundary work involved in positioning print news as superior to television. As Thomas Gieryn and others define the term, boundary work rhetoric doesn't necessarily involve what a profession does, but what it wants to believe it does.[28] While Frank and Hewitt had always understood the strengths and weaknesses of their medium, they felt television news was often compared to what print journalists *wished* they were doing on their format. According to Frank, the "newspaper-versus-television argument has always postulated the *ideal* newspaper against television-as-it-exists."[29]

Don Hewitt focused on television critics working in print publications. He recounted times when media critics admonished television news for covering the same stories that appeared in the critics' own papers. "It's flattering in a way, when they expect more of us than they do of themselves," said Hewitt. "The critics will not excuse us for the daily sins of their publishers." Frank believed the attacks on television news often revealed both an envy of the increasing influence of television and frustrations of the journalism profession's shortcomings: "When they criticize us—and I don't refer only to the critics—they match us against the rosy image they formed as cub reporters or students."[30]

Frank may have been in an especially confident mood at the time of the *Television Quarterly* interview. He had already smuggled the rough cut of *The Tunnel* out of West Berlin and was working on the documentary while only a handful of people at NBC News knew about the project. He already knew he had a powerful story that relied mostly on the moving picture images of the tunnel dig and escape.

The Tunnel cemented Frank's ideas on the strength of television as a news platform through the mix of pictures, words, and sounds. That confidence also led him to write the "transmission of experience" memo the following year. Even though a large percentage of the American public had shown its acceptance of television news through its viewership of newscasts, documentaries, and public affairs programs, Frank knew he was still fighting for the acceptance of the television format, especially the pictures, from the journalism profession, the elites in society that had not accepted the medium, and even broadcast news people in his own news department who continued to favor the printed and broadcast word over the image.

Defining News and Journalism

Two of the most elusive definitions in journalism are the answers to "What is news?" and "Who is a journalist?" Recognizing the slippery contours implied by both queries may help to reduce the confusion of following the disputes between print and broadcast journalists chronicled in the rest of this chapter. The differences in media are easier to explain, but there are also intra-platform boundaries that come into play that take a deeper understanding of actual journalism practice, even if the delineations still may seem unfair and arbitrary.

Using the lens of boundary work, one way to think of journalism is by dividing it into aspirational and actual practice. Aspirational is what journalists wish or like to believe they are doing, and actual is their daily routine. Both of these practices are utilized in the boundary work of journalism.

At the start of the twenty-first century, Bill Kovach and Tom Rosenstiel wrote a foundational text, *The Elements of Journalism*. They took the definition issue head-on, expanding on "what is news" as a bold-text line in the sand: "The primary purpose of journalism is to provide citizens with the information they need to be free and self-governing." This definition firmly aligns journalism with the founding fathers' idea of freedom of the press in the First Amendment. This is aspirational journalism. Journalists will nod their head in approval and people who consume news may roll their eyes considering the crime, entertainment, gossip, sports, and other eye- and ear-catching stories that pass for news. The aspirational versus actual practice, or the range of approaches to journalism, has always included methods either highlighted or shunned in journalism boundary work.[31]

A century before the Kovach and Rosenstiel definition, before radio, television, and the professionalization of journalism, the work of the daily reporter was dramatically different than the lofty proclamations of the famous editors. In most journalism history textbooks, the 1890s is the era when Adolph Ochs rescued the *New York Times* and challenged the sensational papers of William Randolph Hearst and Joseph Pulitzer with his masthead condemnation of yellow journalism, "All the News That's Fit to Print." His original slogan was even more damning: "It Does Not Soil the Breakfast Cloth."[32]

During that same period, struggling reporter Theodore Dreiser of the *St. Louis Globe Democrat* could not figure out how to combine his daily reporting work with the column he had just inherited. Dreiser had taken over a popular feature, "Heard in the Corridors," that involved interviewing famous or intriguing people in hotel lobbies. Dreiser spent hours haunting the St. Louis hotels in a fruitless search for interesting people, while his regular reporting duties suffered. One of his bosses finally told him the stories did not necessarily have to be true. Just make up the profiles. His boss knew

Dreiser wanted to be a novelist and thought it would be a good chance for him to work on his writing.

Dreiser was only exposed and forced to leave the newsroom when a rival paper discovered his fiction. In this case, Dreiser had a time conflict and wrote a review of a traveling acting company production without going to the performance. Because of bad weather, the group never made it to St. Louis, and other newspapers ridiculed the *Globe Democrat* for its phantom review. Dreiser recounted these practices as if they were commonplace in his brief years in journalism in various cities. When he wrote his journalism memoir, *Newspaper Days,* he was already a celebrated author (*Sister Carrie, An American Tragedy*) and had little investment in the reputation of his previous vocation.[33]

The rivalry between the *New York Times* and the newspapers of Pulitzer and Hearst and Dreiser's accepted fabrications are both examples of journalism practice. The former focuses on the aspirational side of newspapers, while the latter shines a light on behavior that journalists, and publishers, were trying to erase by the early twentieth century.

Newsroom Learning

Where do journalists learn what is news and how to be a journalist? That answer has been obvious throughout the twentieth century and up to and including today. They learn in the newsroom. In the *American Journalist* surveys starting in the 1980s, the top two "very influential" factors in learning "newsworthiness" are "journalistic training" from more than 75 percent of respondents and "supervisors" from more than 50 percent of people in the survey.[34]

Since "journalistic training" could include education, another question asked about influential sources for journalism ethics. More than eight out of ten in these surveys listed "newsroom learning," followed by "family upbringing" and "senior editors, reporters, directors."[35]

Back in the 1930s through the 1950s, when radio and television news arrived, newsroom learning was even more important to becoming a journalist as university journalism programs were still relatively new. Before World War II, radio stations and networks rarely had a large news staff, so the obvious place to learn to be a journalist was in a newspaper newsroom. Newspapers had spent the previous hundred years expanding on the system of collecting, checking, and editing information and laying it out in a print format.

Since most newspapers are in the business of both reporting the news and selling papers, the working definition of journalism and journalist is much more complicated than informing the public. In actual journalism, what information readers will pay for (leading directly to what advertisers themselves will pay for) enters the equation. That leads to a much more elusive definition of news than an informed society.

Paul White had a journalism pedigree that was hard to assail in the first half of the twentieth century. He started in small newspapers, graduated from Columbia University's new graduate journalism program funded by Joseph Pulitzer, then worked his way up the ladder at United Press. He later moved to CBS, where he created the Columbia News Service during the wire service ban and proceeded to establish the CBS radio news department in the United States while Edward R. Murrow was building his staff in Europe. When White wrote a journalism how-to book in 1946, *News on the Air*, his chapter on "what is news" is titled "Teaching the Unteachable." His stab at a definition revealed the reality of journalism: "News is the statement of freshly ascertained facts about something of interest that has happened, is happening, is about to happen or that, contrary to expectation hasn't happened, isn't happening, and probably won't happen." As with most definitions of news, he proceeds to explain the flaws in his approach, in this case deciding what "of interest" means. In other words, will people read or listen?[36]

Post–World War II journalism textbooks reveal the emphasis on timeliness and audience interest. *An Introduction to Journalism* lists "the four main reasons for being: to inform, to interpret, to guide, to entertain." In *Exploring Journalism*, journalists "are the men and women who determine what current facts and ideas have the timeliness, scope, and consequence to deserve public attention."[37]

University of Florida journalism professor (and later dean) John Paul Jones reflected the cautious mood of the country after World War II when the Cold War began. Jones clearly felt sloppy journalism could lead to dangerous consequences. He opens his 1949 *Modern Reporter's Handbook* with a section called "Reporters are Important People": "They must have drummed into their minds that news is a powerful weapon, that facts are highly inflammable when used carelessly or with bad intent. They must be told time and again that theirs is a respectable job, a position of trust, a profession with the power to change peace to war, joy to sadness, love to hate, and patriotism to treason." This idea of the need to be responsible would become a common theme of journalism boundary work during the Cold War.[38]

With the absence of a licensing process to clearly determine who is a journalist, add in the dual responsibilities of informing the public and selling papers, competition with other news outlets, a subtle mistrust of learning the craft in a classroom, and the overall agreement on learning on the job, which usually meant a print newsroom, the inclusion or exclusion of a person in the journalism "club" could be quite capricious. Journalist status often involved the camaraderie of working together—bonding, mostly among men—a shared experience that you only received by working in a newsroom. CBS producer Fred Friendly encapsulated this idea when he tried to subtly move Edward R. Murrow's affections away from his World War II radio "Murrow Boys" into the new television *See It Now* group by referring to their television group as a "band of brothers." This mentality resonated for those men (and some women) who either covered or served in World War II.[39]

The nebulous definition works well in boundary work because only a journalist can decide who else is a journalist. (This does not include how the public views journalism or a journalist. That is another matter.) The shared experiences linking journalists could also involve work behavior that would never fit on a Code of Ethics poster or as part of aspirational journalism. Reporter memoirs from the twentieth century are filled with anecdotes of what would be considered unethical in aspirational journalism, but that helped cement a person's newsroom credibility because others would recognize the behavior.

Walter Cronkite proudly recounts these types of stories in his autobiography to explain how he learned to be a journalist. He spends a full page on the art of "picture snatching" during his time on the *Houston Press*. When someone died, his job would be to get a picture of the person. He recounts how he once broke into a house to get a photograph, but after the picture was published, he found out he had the wrong address and wrong picture. Cronkite tempers the theft by wondering why he was not arrested or fired for that stunt, mirroring Theodore Dreiser's case in which the ethical lapse is only a problem if the paper is caught in deceptive behavior. Cronkite laughs it off as youthful ignorance "and a willingness to engage in larceny in the splendid cause of the people's right to know."[40]

With the most experienced journalists and the largest newsrooms largely limited to newspaper and magazine publications in the first half of the twentieth century, coupled with the publisher-journalist alliance to discredit the radio format to retain competitive advantage, the paternalistic criticism from print journalism toward radio news chronicled earlier in the chapter was an obvious reaction.

As the tenets of professionalism strengthened in mid-century, around the time Reuven Frank graduated from school, individuals often felt more allegiance to journalism than to any format or employer. As a result, they would often align with the print supremacy argument even while working in radio or television, partly as a way to maintain their credibility within the journalism community. The television medium also renewed class distinctions that previously surfaced during radio's ascendance, with arguments over the mass media's role to educate or entertain. Finally, this new visual medium arrived saddled with preexisting opinions on motion pictures, newsreels, and even visual learning, which put television journalists on the defensive from the start.

Defining Television

Two years before Reuven Frank began working on *The Tunnel*, his rival network had an idea to start a journal devoted to television. CBS was tired of constant criticisms of the medium and programming from so many directions. The network commissioned people from different occupations to write about television, hopefully with a less negative approach. The journal idea was later scrapped. Instead, the essays were published in a book *The Eighth Art*, a play on the title of Gilbert Seldes's influential 1924 book, *The 7 Lively Arts*.[41]

CBS's *Eighth Art* was an attempt to position television in a more favorable light. In his essay for the book, Gilbert Seldes himself noted how certain groups always denigrated a new media or approach, "likely to denounce a new form for moving into territory already staked out, for degrading whatever it borrows from the past, and for jeopardizing the cultural heritage of mankind."[42]

A few of the entries in the CBS book reflected the negative reaction to television. Anthropologist and race expert Ashley Montagu wrote that the medium does not take itself seriously enough: "The bright speciousness and mindless vulgarity of some of the most popular television programs—programs in which the human experience is neither extended nor enlarged, but impoverished and corrupted—constitute living testimony concerning the depths to which the medium can descend." Two New York Public Library children's book librarians lamented how book adaptations for television do not have "the spirit and integrity" of the original and many programs "deaden instead of kindle the imagination."[43]

Other writers wished the elite would get involved in helping to make television better. Television critic Marya Mannes blamed the nation's intellectuals for acting as if television was beneath them: "He has not only impoverished American culture by depriving the greatest medium of mass communication of his own talents, but he has cut himself off from the common experience of his countrymen." Humorist and scriptwriter Leo Rosten also criticized the elites for unreasonable expectations because "it is foolish to expect television to serve as a magical replacement for a lecture, a seminar, individual analysis, disciplined discussion, or, for that matter, a good magazine."[44]

The print versus radio versus television argument also cut across various academic disciplines in this era in scholarly research. In what came to be known as the "literary thesis," scholars including Eric Havelock, Jack Goody, and Walter Ong positioned the start of critical and logical thought in Greece with the development of an alphabet, superior to the oral cultures since ideas and traditions could now be saved permanently and not altered through retelling. As noted earlier in the chapter, the "permanence" of the printed word was often invoked as the reason for newspaper's superiority over radio and television news.[45]

Journalism Professionalism and Television

The expansion of journalism superiority and judgment from print to include radio happened as soon as television news started to gain an audience. Many journalists got their first personal look at the logistics and impact of television coverage during the presidential conventions in Philadelphia in 1948. Print and radio reporters now had to contend with big cameras, lights, and an instantaneous sight and sound format at an event they used to have to themselves. In addition, their bosses could now watch the conventions in real time and make suggestions or demands on what to cover depending on what they saw on the live television coverage.

New York Herald Tribune media critic John Crosby had long noticed his newspaper colleagues' attitude of "intellectual superiority" toward radio news. When he became a syndicated radio and television critic, Crosby witnessed the same attitude from the radio journalists toward television. He took a subtle jab at how quickly radio news people had moved from outcasts to arbiters of true journalism: "Take it easy, you graybeards in radio. This thing's a new medium and there are bound to be some changes made in the established order."[46]

Murrow on Television

An enlightening look at the complicated criticisms of television and of television news came from an unpublished article by arguably the most famous journalist in any format in this period: Edward R. Murrow. Murrow experienced the rejection from print journalists until his reporting in World War II brought him international fame. CBS had been trying to get him to take on a television news project since his return to the United States after World War II, but he resisted until *See It Now* in 1951. He and his "Murrow Boys" had criticized and dismissed television in the postwar period, and his colleagues would argue that he still enjoyed his nightly radio program much more than television all through the 1950s.

In 1949, when Murrow was still resisting the format, he wrote an article for the *New York Times* that was never published, on his perceptions of television news. Much like his famous RTNDA speech about the deficiencies of television a decade later, Murrow had concerns about the commercial aspects of the medium.

Since Murrow did not start in newspapers, his television views were not tinged with the print superiority approach found among newspaper reporters. In fact, he takes a dig at radio's early exclusion by remarking that television news "has not so far been subjected to the artificial restraints from press associations and newspapers that impeded the development of radio news."[47]

For Murrow, the important question was who would have control over the format: "Is it to be a medium of entertainment or information? Do bathing girls on surf boards get preference over first class but simple chart of the Middle East; or a polar presentation of the areas covered by North Atlantic alliance?" He argued if television news ever wants to be more than just a "picture supplement, it must put the news, not the picture first. It must recognize that much of today's news is made of what goes on in men's minds as reflected in what they say."[48]

Murrow hit on many of the key television news criticisms in the early years (and are often invoked today). The reference to "bathing girls on surf boards" is an obvious reference to the theater newsreels and their avoidance of important topics in favor of staged entertainment film. As discussed in the last chapter, the very format of newsreels forced producers into the use of moving pictures since the narrator is never on camera. The structure of the newsreel made it challenging to include topics that could not be easily filmed.

Another common form of boundary work used to denigrate television news is in his question on whether it wants to be "a medium of entertainment or information." This infers that the format itself is tainted by an appeal to a more frivolous form of communication. It is disingenuous for Murrow to argue the economic structure of American television is "entertainment," since his own preferred format, radio, created the advertiser-supported model that his employer made sure television would follow. The "entertainment" descriptor for the medium or the news presentation is a shorthand way to dismiss television.[49]

Not long after Murrow wrote his essay, *Editor & Publisher* wrote a story on the *New York Times'* classical music radio station, WQXR. When asked if the *Times* would be expanding into television, publisher Arthur Hays Sulzberger said television was not a good substitute for "good music and the prompt dissemination of news by radio." WQXR General Manager Eliot Sanger made the point even clearer, calling television an "entertainment medium" and compared it to a non-news staple of newspapers the *Times* had proudly avoided: "No comics, no television."[50]

The Picture

The other criticism of television that united print and radio journalists happened to be the main advancement of the format over radio: moving pictures, both live and filmed. With traces of the literary thesis of the supremacy of the written word, Murrow delineates between journalism and images by saying the format would have to put "the news, not the picture first."[51] On one level, he is arguing that not all stories can be easily visualized, but those issues should still have value in a newscast. By pitting "news" against "pictures," though, the implication is that logic and ideas need to be written or spoken. With this viewpoint, Murrow was ignoring decades of documentary and other nonfiction films. Even at his own network throughout the 1940s, the CBS television news crew created a complicated cornucopia of approaches to visualize the top stories of the day with little access to timely news film.

Relegating images to supplemental role to written and spoken words, even on a visual medium, brought Murrow closer to print journalists, even with decades of photographs in newspapers. As detailed in the last chapter, the photograph had been a part of print journalism since the mid-1800s when illustrators and artists would use photographs as the basis for their elaborate drawings and illustrations to help explain news events. By the twentieth century, newspapers could more easily print photographs and those images became accepted as a design element for newspaper layouts. Newspapers also added pictorial and rotogravure sections because of their popularity.

Yet the same bias that radio endured over the perceived preeminence of the printed word over the spoken word also applied to the photograph, and the people who took the photographs. They were necessary, but mainly to provide a supplement to the written word. Even with the success of *Life* magazine and its emphasis on photographs to tell a story, print reporters and editors still did not embrace news photographers as equal partners, even when they worked out of the same newsroom.

Finally, in 1946, in an effort to gain more respect, news photographers followed the same path as radio news people at the time and television journalists in the next decade. They formed their own professional organization, The National Press Photographers Association (NPPA). A front-page editorial in NPPA's first magazine issue made the goal clear: "We're no longer going to permit ourselves to be relegated to the position of the unwelcome, but necessary, stepchildren of the Fourth Estate."[52]

With the formation of NPPA, still photographers had their own professional group separate from reporters and editors. Now they could identify both as news photographers and part of the newspaper or magazine platform. With journalism boundary work, newspaper photographers might not like the unequal status in their newsrooms, but they would identify more with their print staff than with radio or even television reporters and photographers.

While reporters and photographers were mostly separate jobs in a print newsroom, in broadcast stations many radio journalists had a forced format transition in the 1950s, as television became the top broadcast medium and radio became a secondary service. At the network level, radio journalists were often expected to work in both formats or leave behind audio. These people often had no or little understanding of images and often felt, like Murrow, that the emphasis on pictures was distracting from the words they were writing and voicing. Those journalists would often side with print journalists on the importance of words over images.

With all these shifting platform and professional allegiances, the definitions of who is a journalist and what is journalism played out throughout the 1950s, all under the auspices of the Cold War and journalism's proper role in covering the serious threats.

Eisenhower Images

An interesting example of journalism boundary work during the rise of television happened when President Dwight Eisenhower suffered a heart attack while golfing in Denver in 1955. Eisenhower was treated at the Fitzsimons Army Hospital and spent a total of six weeks in recovery in Colorado. On one warm sunny October day, the president was wheeled to an outdoor deck of the hospital. An industrious CBS television crew rented a helicopter and flew around the hospital, hoping to capture the first images of Eisenhower since his heart attack. Unfortunately, Eisenhower had already been taken inside when the helicopter got to the hospital. The Secret Service detained the CBS crew briefly when the helicopter landed.

White House press secretary James Hagerty held an emergency press conference to denounce the filming attempt: "The health of the President of the United States is far more important than any sneak photograph, and I believe the people of this nation feel the same way about it." The CBS crew had not broken any laws, but Hagerty attempted to link the attempt to Eisenhower's health, saying the president might be wary of going back outside and he needed the sunshine for his recovery.[53]

Sig Mickelson, the vice president for News at CBS, quickly issued a statement distancing the network from the helicopter incident: "The President's health comes first and we regret that some of our people were overzealous." With the wire services and all the top newspapers covering the president's hospitalization, as Hagerty expected, his press conference gave the story authority. Hagerty's comments were printed in papers across the country, with many versions including Mickelson's apology.[54]

Hagerty's press conference stunt—a public condemnation of a television stunt—stemmed from both his current job and his previous career. As press secretary, he wanted to manage the information, including images, about Eisenhower's health. Previously, Hagerty worked as a reporter at the *New York Times*, so he knew his press conference would generate a story to shame CBS beyond journalism circles. For his part, Mickelson made sure he apologized quickly enough to be included into the original news stories. Mickelson's quick repudiation of his crew showed both the pressure from government on broadcast licenses but also journalism boundary work. Mickelson came from a radio background and echoed Murrow's ideas on the primacy of the word with the pictures playing a secondary role.

Moving beyond journalism, Sol Taishoff, editor of *Broadcasting* trade magazine, complained that if any other medium besides TV tried that helicopter approach, it would not be a news story. Taishoff said television is held up for condemnation because "it is still struggling for recognition as a medium that can be trusted to join company in the living room without making an embarrassing scene." WGN radio and television news director Spencer Allen in Chicago pointed out the hypocrisy of journalism boundary work in a column for the print reporter trade publication, *Quill*. Allen wondered who would have run the film or pictures if the CBS crew had captured the president on the hospital sundeck. "I know what the Chicago television answer would be—because we're used to playing kind of rough here. We learned it from our brethren on the Chicago daily newspapers."[55]

Sneaking pictures of the convalescing president appears to be in the same vein as Cronkite's "picture snatching," accepted as a rite of passage and the importance of competition for a newspaper journalist, but a reckless, immature move for a television photographer. Allen also noted Mickelson's quick apology and wondered if television journalists "are being a bit too instinctively sensitive and on the defensive when an eyebrow is lifted at us now and again." Print journalists had reason to be anxious in the 1950s, with the newspaper business going through major changes as television spread across the country.[56]

The Postwar Newspaper Industry

The strong postwar economy in the United States masked some serious changes in newspaper content and competition that would become painfully evident by the end of the century. Immediately after World War II, and before television took off as a mass medium, American newspapers had some of their strongest years for circulation and revenue. Even as television began to take a larger percentage of the advertising budget, both locally and nationally, the economic growth allowed newspapers, as a whole, to continue to prosper.

Looking at individual communities, however, the trend did not favor those who believed the free market and competition would provide the best product. The number of daily newspapers in the United States had actually been declining since 1919. The United States did not have a truly national, general-interest newspaper until *USA Today* was launched in 1982, so the health of newspaper competition could best be seen in communities across the country. There were seventy cities with competing newspapers in 1950, but less than a quarter century later there were only thirty-seven. Suburban newspapers launched, at the expense of metro newspapers' circulation, but those new outlets rarely had direct competition. By driving out competition, local newspapers became monopolies in their communities, charging higher prices, including more advertising, and not substantially improving the news coverage. Overall, the ratio of news content to advertising flipped shortly after World War II from 60/40 ratio of content to advertising to a 40/60 ratio favoring advertising. Newspaper chains added monopoly newspapers to their group when possible because those properties had the highest potential for revenue.[57]

Newspaper competition became such a contentious topic that the newspaper industry, which normally extolled its independence from government, pushed for Joint Operating Agreements (JOA) in specific cities. Under a JOA, the competing newspapers were able to skirt antitrust laws by combining business and print costs of two papers if their newsrooms remained separate. When individual agreements were found to be illegal, the industry lobbied Congress to pass the Newspaper Preservation Act of 1970, which basically exempted the industry from antitrust laws. In reality, the JOA's allowed the owners to keep up profit margins and charge higher prices since the business side was no longer competitive.[58]

As newspaper chains grew larger and eliminated competition in cities, some chains even made the argument that a daily newspaper was a "natural monopoly," like a public utility, so the lack of competition was the inevitable result. Others argued that if the US government had enforced its antitrust laws more vigorously, more cities could have kept their competing newspapers.[59]

Media historian James Baughman said lack of competition in most cities resulted in "editorial sloth."[60] Reporters tended to avoid stories that might offend their sources in government and law enforcement. Most newspapers relied on wire services for big international stories like the Vietnam War and tended not to make too many local waves in big national subjects such as civil rights and poverty. The lack of competition cut down the amount of investigative reporting but also caused those papers to try to eliminate partisanship from their reporting, even in the area of local editorials. Instead of adding more reporters, the monopoly newspapers could supplement wire service stories or just more advertising.[61]

This view of the newspaper industry, of course, is not how print publications were portrayed in journalism boundary work. As Frank and Hewitt had noted in their 1962 interview, television news was compared to what print reporters wished their employers were doing. Exemplary work from top print publications, such as the *New York Times* or the *New York Herald Tribune,* stood for all print journalism. When television's dominance in total audience and in advertising revenue became even harder to explain, print journalists clung to their professional superiority. Political communication scholar Chad Raphael felt that print commentators "seemed driven by anxious attempts to maintain a higher rung on American journalism's cultural register, if not on its economic ladder."[62]

Printing Their Grievances

The year that Reuven Frank took over NBC's convention and election night coverage must have been some type of tipping point for print news veterans. Two of the most striking and negative assessments of television news came out in May 1956. In a short piece that seemed snatched straight out of late-night bar talk, *Time* magazine chose to let its general audience know about this "interloping Johnny-come-lately" with his "haughty ways." TV men are getting in the way at press conferences. They make too much noise, carry too much equipment, ask stupid questions, and then steal the answers to newspaper reporters' questions and get those quotes on the air before the newspaper can publish. The only source quoted in the short article was, of course, a print reporter, who said the TV interlopers were turning press conferences into "staged nonsense."[63]

The same month, in the print trade publication *Quill, New York Times* Sunday editor Lester Markel tried to calm down his brethren with a piece titled, "Yes, The Printed Word Has a Future, Despite Television and Cinerama." Markel hit most of the key journalism boundary work talking points. In the false equivalency area, he quoted Abraham Lincoln, Benjamin Franklin, Voltaire, and Winston Churchill to prove words are more powerful than pictures. He then sat in judgment by proclaiming television "has not done a good news job." He gave numbered reasons for print's superiority, including its ability to provide more background, television's obsession with interesting pictures, and that "the written word still carries more potential authority because it is set down with deliberation."[64]

Markel was also clearly lecturing other newspapers in his piece, explaining what print publications *should* be doing—in other words, comparing television to the newspaper *ideal*. He dismissed television as an "entertainment medium" while the newspaper "is—or should be—an information medium." Markel then admonished newspapers that seemed too focused on selling papers, an economic reality he chose not to accept: "I insist that there is about every newspaper a public responsibility that must be fulfilled."[65]

Near the end of the piece, Markel moved on from television, as though he had dismissed the medium, and presented an interesting sermon on the importance of the printed word in the Cold War. In this section, beginning with the ominous words "We live in a mine-trapped, fog-bound world," Markel appears to combine American print journalists, US government leaders, and the education system into one monolithic group burdened with informing the public and thereby saving the world from communism, although the evil is not named. He even refers to an undefined collection of the above people as "the custodians of the printed word." According to Markel, this group "must fulfill, wisely and with courage, the role to which history has assigned us. We shall not be able to reach sound judgments that are so urgent unless we have an informed and alert public opinion, unless our information is good."[66]

Most journalism boundary work that reached a general audience was subtler, with the accepted premise that print was the superior information format. *Newsweek* published two cover stories on the American network news battle in the early 1960s, one with Huntley and Brinkley and the other featuring Walter Cronkite. In both cases, the writer focused on the personalities of the main newscasters. We find out about their work habits, their wives (the Huntley-Brinkley profile included almost identically framed photos of each man's wife with her arms around his neck and looking up into his eyes), what they eat for lunch, and what they say during commercial breaks. We get deep details on the sets, salaries, ratings battles, and the celebrity status of these newscasters. We learn almost nothing about what stories are covered on their newscasts, or what type of visualization methods are used to help make issues understandable beyond the print format.

Huntley and Brinkley are compared with Arthur Godfrey, Perry Como, and Ed Sullivan to explain their popularity. The two newscasters had become household names and faces as the newscasters on the top-rated network news programs, so readers may have been somewhat interested in these details. These stories rarely, if ever, talked about the importance of these programs in presenting news in a different format from the printed word.[67]

The Cronkite profile two years later chronicled the start of the network's half-hour newscast in September 1963. This article also gives us deep detail on Cronkite's personality and work routine, his "Cronkite Special" lunch of cottage cheese and a pineapple slice, and his attention to detail. To give Cronkite legitimacy, the writer turns to unnamed print reporters covering the space program who said they "respect" him "particularly for the way he studied his subject."[68]

Cover stories in one of the top news magazines with mostly positive profiles of the men fronting the newscasts were seen as great publicity for the networks. At the same time, the writers rarely used terms such as "journalist" or "reporter" to describe the men. The importance of the wide reach of this format for news are not part of the narrative. Instead, these are celebrities who are popular because of their personalities, and their program just happens to be informational instead of entertainment.

During the same period as the two *Newsweek* cover stories, veteran *New Yorker* magazine reporter Thomas Whiteside wrote a 1962 profile of CBS producer Fred Friendly. The idea that a magazine favored by the literary crowd would assign one of its top reporters to write a long profile of Friendly was a sign of television news' arrival. For most of the article, Whiteside did present a fairly accurate, and fair, look at Friendly and his work. Whiteside included personal information, but he also spent many paragraphs on Friendly's techniques on the documentary series *CBS Reports*.[69]

Whiteside's piece, however, includes bookended disclaimers to make clear how he really felt about the medium. He began with a backhanded compliment, admitting that when television is "used for the purpose of dealing with actualities rather than of passing along the canned daydreams that make up most programs, the results can prove absorbing even to people who normally don't bother with the medium." He concluded his piece by pointing out that one of Friendly's greatest contributions "has been his effort to establish some sort of reasonable ethical and artistic standards in a business that has generally managed to get along without them."[70]

In the complicated world of journalism boundary work, the attacks on television news also came from within the medium, or broadcasting, in the name of competition or loyalty to the journalism profession. As noted, Edward R. Murrow and his "Murrow Boys" made clear their distaste for television when they came home from World War II, and some of them kept up their fealty to radio until the end of their careers. With their allegiance to journalism itself, several in television news continued to tout their print background as evidence of their membership in the true journalism fraternity.

In the 1961 Huntley-Brinkley profile, Frank himself uttered the phrase that had been used against his medium so often. He admitted that the chemistry between Huntley and Brinkley on air was "a phenomenon of show business rather than of the news business." Frank did not shy away from his newscasters' on-camera appeal, but as the producer of the newscast, he knew how much work went into covering and presenting the news in a visual manner.[71]

CBS, and print journalists, began to dismiss the NBC nightly newscast ratings success as somehow the result of, or tainted by, nonjournalistic reasons. Huntley and Brinkley were celebrities and not journalists, others said. Inherent in this argument is that Huntley had no print news experience and that Brinkley had moved from the wire services to NBC in 1943. The two men also did not strongly adhere to the journalism boundary work idea of the importance of learning how to be a journalist at a newspaper. By contrast, Cronkite was proud of his newspaper and wire service career, although he had moved between radio and print multiple times before leaving his print career behind after World War II, just five years after Brinkley.

These subtle distinctions are on display in the 1963 *Newsweek* profile in which CBS president Richard Salant acknowledged the popularity of the NBC newscasters but added that if they worked for him, "for a start, I'd send them out to cover a few stories." It was a bold statement from a corporate lawyer talking about two men who each had decades of reporting experience, and at the time of the writing worked not only on the nightly newscast, but on public affairs programs and documentaries. Later in the piece, the *Newsweek* writer lets the reader know that "Cronkite is a reporter at heart, not a rip-and-read man." Reporter is equated with newspapers and journalism, while "rip-and-read" is a broadcast announcer who never leaves the studio.[72]

To reinforce the wayward priorities of NBC, the article mentions that the network spent $5,000 for three bars of music (the sheet music is shown in the article) to open the newscast, strong evidence that Huntley and Brinkley "lean more toward show business."[73]

Another print-friendly comparison between newspapers and television news that has been repeated over the decades got its public debut in the 1963 *Newsweek* article. When CBS's Salant tried to convince his network and the affiliates to allow the nightly newscast to expand from fifteen to thirty minutes, he superimposed the script from a fifteen-minute CBS newscast over the front page of the *New York Times*. *Newsweek* ran this graphic artwork, showing the newscast script did not even fill three columns of the *Times*' front page. That logic may have helped CBS expand its newscast, but Salant seemed to agree with the idea that the words in a newscast were equated with knowledge. Cronkite also used this logic when he demonstrated the brevity of television news by comparing the 175–350 words in a TV news story with the 1,000 words in a *Times* front-page story. Reuven Frank snidely replied the comparison does not reflect badly on television news but instead highlighted the *New York Times*' "penchant for overwriting and underediting."[74]

Television Critics

While print news reporters mostly relied on sources to criticize broadcast news, much of the serious boundary work concerning appropriate and effective journalism over the decades was left to the broadcast critics of the print press. As Frank and Hewitt had related, people in television news felt the newspaper and magazine television critics held broadcast journalism to a higher standard than their own publications. The television critic of the print press evolved out of the early twentieth-century practice of reviewing books, live theater, vaudeville, and movies for the readers. As radio became a popular mass medium, newspapers and magazines began reviewing broadcast programs as well.

The print publications were not only meeting an interest of their readers, but the extra content allowed room for more radio program and appliances advertisements. Television reviewing became a natural extension of radio or stage criticism. Whether intentionally or not, boundary work came into play in broadcast reviewing and criticism in the print press because the reviewers rarely had any special training in effective audio or visual communication. If they had any journalism training, it was usually in a print format. The reviews often overtly or subtly judged radio or television news and informational programming against a printed word standard.

Television reviews in the top entertainment trade magazines, *Variety* and *The Billboard*, read like a vaudeville or stage play reviews in the 1940s because the reviewers were accustomed to writing about those formats. When it came to television news and informational programming, the reviewers seemed hesitant to judge the journalism or visual communication and instead focused on the person presenting the news, the lighting, or the set. In a *Billboard* review of a 1944 CBS newscast, the critic admonished newscaster Ned Calmer, who "needed to have his suit pressed. Video performers, even newscasters, should learn that wardrobe is important and how." Print critics later used the emphasis on the news anchor personality as an example of the superficial nature of television news, when it was the newspaper and magazine television critics who were often the ones focused on the person presenting the news instead of the content and visualization techniques involved.[75]

As television became a national medium, more newspapers and magazine added television critics to their staff. Most of their efforts focused on the entertainment programs with less emphasis on news and public affairs. The networks would shower these critics with press releases and positive story angles, with the hopes of gaining traction for specific programs or performers. Among the radio and television critics, a small subset of New York and Washington writers had the biggest impact, especially in the area of news and public affairs.

These writers not only reviewed programs but often acted as if they were the conscience of the medium, cajoling the industry into better programming. In the areas of news and public affairs, journalism boundary work played a major role. These critics usually had a print background and often ran in the same circles as the network broadcasters and executives.

Gilbert Seldes was one of these critics, with the added bonus that he had been in charge of CBS television in its early years and had worked hard at creating informational programming. Seldes is remembered as one of the few reviewers who criticized Edward R. Murrow for his famous *See It Now* program on Senator Joseph McCarthy in 1954. While liberals, and most television critics, applauded the takedown of the demagogue, Seldes worried what would happen when a skilled video communicator chose to go after another person or viewpoint and label it as a report. "It was *not* a report. It was an attack, followed by an editorial call to action." That review helped caused a rift between Murrow and Seldes that lasted for years.[76]

The medium-to-medium criticism was mostly a one-way street. Radio and television networks and stations rarely presented regular programs that critiqued newspaper news coverage. In 1947, Don Hollenbeck tried that very format with *CBS Views the Press*, supported by network news president Edward R. Murrow. Each week, Hollenbeck turned the tables and critiqued New York newspaper coverage of major events, calling out bias and unethical reporting. *CBS Views the Press* won major broadcast awards but received mixed reviews among the print press. With the rise of the anticommunism movement, powerful newspaper chains supporting Red Scare tactics, especially Hearst, pressured CBS into muzzling Hollenbeck's systematic critiques. Hollenbeck left the program in 1950, and it was soon canceled. Hearst columnist Jack O'Brian continued to attack Hollenbeck, labeling him as a communist, well after he left *CBS Views the Press*. Those attacks are considered part of the reason Hollenbeck killed himself in 1954.[77]

Gould and Crosby

The two most influential radio and later television critics in New York from the 1940s through the 1960s were Jack Gould of the *New York Times* and John Crosby of the *New York Herald Tribune*. Gould had a high school diploma from the Brown School of Tutoring in New York and started as general assignment reporter for the *New York Herald Tribune* in 1932. He gravitated to reviewing stage plays before the *New York Times* hired him, putting him first on a column called "News and Gossip of the Night Clubs." The paper moved him over to radio, and then added television to his duties.[78]

Crosby attended Yale University but left for a newspaper career before graduating. He was a crime reporter for the *Milwaukee Sentinel* and the *New York Herald Tribune* before joining the National Guard during World War II. When he returned to the *Herald Tribune*, he said the editors did not know what to do with him, so they asked him to write a radio column. In keeping with the boundary work superiority of the print press, Crosby proudly proclaims on the back cover of his 1952 collection of radio and television columns, *Out of the Blue*, that he had "never owned a radio, had listened to it rarely, but took the job until something better showed up."[79]

Crosby was the more entertaining writer and relished the opportunities to take down the programs he did not like. Crosby felt the hardest part of writing a broadcast column was being "forced to be literate about the illiterate, witty about the witless, coherent about the incoherent." Gould had the greater influence, mainly because he worked at the *New York Times*. Gould even received a special Peabody Award in 1956 for his "fairness, objectivity, and authority."[80]

Reuven Frank spent the first two decades of his television career on the receiving end of Jack Gould's opinions, and he had a decidedly different opinion about his work: Gould's "judgments were old-maidish, his writing tortured, and his tastes unsophisticated." Frank did not blame Gould for his influence; instead the fault belonged to network executives who paid close attention to the reviews. Even though by the mid-1950s, programs that Reuven Frank produced were seen by millions of viewers around the country and Gould wrote for a regional New York City audience, among Gould's readers were Frank's bosses at NBC and RCA. Top management at all the networks seemed especially sensitive to both positive and negative reviews in the New York newspapers. "As peddlers of a product that vanishes on sight," wrote Frank, "they are in awe of a medium that survives for an entire day."[81]

Gould, Crosby, Seldes, and others wrote as if they knew the network executives were reading their work. In 1956, Gould presented what he called his "report card on the medium." Quite simply television news programs "are not what they should be; journalistically, video is something of a disappointment." But he does not blame the "backstage laborers in the news vineyard"; instead the bosses are not interested in news because it does not make as much money as "vaudeville."[82]

When it came to news and public affairs, Gould generally favored CBS over NBC, especially the work of Murrow and Friendly. That favoritism might have come from Gould's friendship and regular Saturday breakfast sessions with CBS president Frank Stanton. Gould even quit the *Times* for a short period in 1954 to work for Stanton at CBS, but he quickly returned to his print position.

When *The Tunnel* became a major media controversy in the fall of 1962, Frank could at least take heart that John Crosby had given up his radio/TV column earlier in the year and was now reviewing stage plays in Europe. Unfortunately for Frank, many other print writers and publications were ready to cover and judge NBC's situation. While the writers were focusing on the specific NBC documentary project, their opinions reveal the deep concerns during this critical juncture in journalism history, as the print press was forced to confront a competitor that already was overshadowing their influence in American society.

Journalistic Boundary Work and *The Tunnel*

Much of the boundary work by print journalists and publishers demonizing or dismissing broadcast news took place in person or on the pages of trade magazines and journals. The circumstances surrounding *The Tunnel*'s production and broadcast provided an opportunity for a more public critique of the premise, the program, and the medium in general. First, *The Tunnel* involved a true journalistic scoop, which often draws the ire of competitors. In the next chapter, we see more on how journalistic competition between CBS and NBC played a major role in how the government responded to the NBC project. Journalists look like sore losers if they merely complain about getting beat on a story. In this case, *The Tunnel* production included an important decision that sparked serious journalistic ethical debate, one that Frank tried very hard to justify.

For government officials, both in the United States and Germany, the secret tunnel filming was seen as a problem for international relations, and the network faced intense pressure to cancel the production. The governments' public reaction allowed print reporters to merely cover the press briefings and quote the words of highly placed official sources without any overt journalistic editorializing, the ultimate in high-modern, objective journalism.

One of the most remarkable aspects of *The Tunnel* project was how long NBC was able to keep the production a secret. Even when the escape happened, the news coverage did not include the NBC connection. By choosing to keep the project secret though, NBC lost its public relations advantage when reporters learned, not just of the tunnel production, but the payment to the diggers.

Time magazine was the first to reveal the NBC project in the United States, in its October 5, 1962, issue. The writer focused on the key journalistic ethical question with clear condemnation. Three of the original students who planned the tunnel came to NBC in May 1962 because they were out of money and needed supplies. NBC agreed to pay the students, so they could continue the project in exchange for NBC's exclusive access to film the process.

Reuven Frank, and his boss William McAndrew, knew the payment would be controversial, which is why so few people at NBC or RCA knew about the arrangement. The *Time* article claimed that the students pocketed the NBC money that wasn't spent on supplies and did not tell the other diggers about the payment. The magazine considered the monetary arrangement as a stain on the noble efforts to help people leave East Germany: "Such chicanery tarnishes somewhat the difficult and dangerous work of the idealistic diggers."[83] The *New York Times* repeated the *Time* information in its first article and revealed the length (ninety minutes) and the broadcast date (October 31, 1962) for the first time, scooping NBC on its own documentary.[84]

Once the print press revealed the documentary project and the payment, NBC held a news conference on October 11 to try to tamp down the criticism and promote the broadcast. Frank argued that the tunnel was already sixty feet long when NBC got involved, so it would have been completed with or without the payment. NBC refused to say how much it paid the diggers. Reporters started using the sum of $7,500 in their reporting, which was the original payment, but that did not include the $5,000 NBC paid on completion of the project. Frank's explanation clearly did not convince the *New York Times*; its headline the next day read "N.B.C.-TV Plans Documentary on Berlin Tunnel It Helped Build."[85]

Unfortunately for NBC, the payment controversy then moved to Berlin, where seventeen of the diggers held a press conference demanding NBC cancel the program because they did not know anything about the payment to the three original tunnel organizers. They insinuated that the three men left with the remaining money and that the financial arrangement tarnished their altruistic mission. The West Berlin city government also protested the program, worrying that people identified in the film could be in danger. Both West and East German governments also questioned NBC's program and approach.[86]

The criticisms from Berlin intensified the US government backchannel pressure on NBC (explored in the next chapter) to cancel the broadcast. When that approach did not work, the State Department went public with its concerns, knowing it could keep alive the controversy, and pressure, in the print press. The *Washington Post, New York Times,* and *Chicago Tribune* all published a United Press International story in which State Department spokesman Lincoln White called the NBC tunnel project "risky, irresponsible, undesirable" and "contrary to the best interests of the United States." While behind the scenes the State Department wanted NBC to cancel the program, the public rebukes stopped short of that demand. The only publication to come to NBC's defense, not surprisingly, was the broadcast industry's trade magazine, *Broadcasting*, which said NBC's Berlin crew acted with "discretion and courage," since the network's involvement stayed a secret long after the tunnel escape.[87]

The *New York Times'* Jack Gould jumped into *The Tunnel* controversy with a public scolding for NBC and television news. On Monday, October 22, Gould published what was dubbed an analysis of the NBC payment for the tunnel film. This article ran the week after both the State Department and the diggers condemned the project. In a textbook example of journalism boundary work, Gould positioned NBC, and by default television news, as a reckless interloper in the area of international news reporting, with the implication that print journalists better understood the dangers of the Cold War. In fear-mongering language that was dramatic even by Cold War standards, Gould insinuated that just by filming the tunnel project, NBC could have caused a nuclear war: "With peace hanging by a thread it is not the time for adventurous laymen to show up on the front lines of world tension. No one knows what seemingly small provocation might be grasped as an excuse to press the proverbial button."[88]

In another common approach to criticizing broadcast news, print media critics accused radio or television of being driven by profits and ratings, employing selective amnesia about the for-profit business model of their own employers. Gould explains both the payment to the diggers, and even the act of filming the tunnel project and escape, as examples of "distasteful commercialism" and "video's competitive economics," clearly not the pure journalistic decision-making process of the nation's print press.[89]

Even Gould knew though that criticizing NBC for paying for filming rights would ring a little hollow during this period when *Life* magazine was paying NASA Mercury astronauts roughly $25,000 a year each for exclusive access to their personal stories. Newspapers often bought photographs of events their staff did not cover, a fact that Gould readily admits. In a gymnastic turn of logic, he claims that television's "handicap" and the reason he is holding it to a higher standard is its power and reach: "What the television medium does and the way it does it is news in itself."[90]

The print press quickly dropped the NBC tunnel documentary controversy that Monday evening when President John F. Kennedy went on national television to warn about the construction of missile bases in Cuba. The Cuban Missile Crisis allowed NBC to quietly postpone *The Tunnel* and instead work on a special program about the current crisis for the October 31 broadcast timeslot.[91]

The Tunnel Reviews

As discussed in the next chapter, while the disagreement between the State Department and NBC continued behind the scenes after the resolution of the Cuban Missile Crisis, the tunnel project itself mostly disappeared from newspaper and magazine pages until it was time to review the actual documentary after it finally ran on December 10, 1962.

The Tunnel received mostly strong reviews by television critics of American newspapers and magazines. Frank's initial instincts were confirmed as many of the critics picked up on the very attributes that he had noticed when first looking at the unedited film in Berlin. He knew he had a real-life story that could be as compelling as fiction. The *Boston Globe* and the *Los Angeles Times* felt *The Tunnel* was one of the best programs in American television's short history. *Newsday* and the *Baltimore Sun* noted the documentary was more effective than fiction because it was real, while *Variety* called it "a document full of human courage, dramatic intensity, and suspense."[92]

The writers were not shy with their criticisms of the program. The biggest complaint involved the ninety-minute length and the amount of time devoted to the mundane process of digging the tunnel. A few other reviewers felt Frank had neglected the human element in favor of the tunnel dig process. Some of the reviewers mentioned the payment controversy or the government complaints about the project. For Barbara Delatiner at *Newsday*, the end product "justified the stir it created."[93]

And then there was Jack Gould.

For his October 22 public shaming column, Gould had written as a journalism and Cold War expert. Since his job also included reviewing television programs, he got another crack at *The Tunnel* after it ran. In this case, as a television critic, he zeroed in on the length of the documentary. He felt it would have worked best as an hour-long program, or even just thirty minutes. Reuven Frank isn't just the leader of a group of "adventurous laymen," but also a poor documentary producer: "The extremely slow telling of the story noticeably diminished its expected impact." Even in the short review, Gould still could not resist another scold: "It is well that no serious incident resulted from the adventure."[94]

The Tunnel Reception and Awards

The months following *The Tunnel* controversy and eventual broadcast provided strong vindication for Frank and NBC News for fighting for the right of the public to see the documentary. In addition to the mostly strong reviews, a large audience tuned in to watch the program. *The Tunnel* was one of the rare times a television documentary finished in a virtual tie in the ratings with some of the most popular entertainment programs on network television.

The television industry recognized *The Tunnel* at the Emmy Awards. Not only did *The Tunnel* win for best documentary and Piers Anderton won for best international reporting, Frank's production was chosen as the top overall program of the year. NBC even brought Peter and Klaus Dehmel to the United States, their first visit to the country, to talk with reporters about their experience shooting the documentary. The Dehmels also attended the Emmy Awards. The International Rescue Committee and the Veterans of Foreign Wars (VFW) honored NBC for *The Tunnel*.[95]

And then there was Jack Gould.

Gould chose one more occasion to publish his displeasure about the whole project in an article on the 1963 Emmy Awards. As a parting shot, Gould revived his best hidden Cold War fears and his best journalism boundary work, and he even linked *The Tunnel*'s Emmy Awards to the sad state of American television as a whole.

The strongest line in Gould's diatribe tied together many of his complaints: "The cold war should not be a toy for show business." In one sentence, he sows unnamed fears about communism and compares television to both immature behavior and a decidedly nonjournalistic mission of "show business." Once again, NBC's project was not "responsible conduct," and even though nothing bad happened, it could have: "Had the diggers been apprehended, the injection of the profit motive into the delicate situation involving the trapped East Berliners might have had very grave consequences."

Gould had become so powerful and confident of his opinions that his article on the Emmy Awards is mostly a criticism of the judges for picking the wrong programs: *The Tunnel* should have lost to NBC's *Shakespeare: The Soul of an Age* documentary; Piers Anderton should have lost to CBS's Daniel Schorr; *CBS Reports* is far superior to NBC's *David Brinkley's Journal*. For Gould, *The Tunnel* and other winners represented "the disintegration of the medium" and that unless better programs were chosen, the Emmys "may come to be the hollow crown of TV."[96]

The Government and Journalism Boundary Work

Reuven Frank was a vindicated man with the eventual success of *The Tunnel*. He survived the pressure from the State Department, attacks from print journalists, and questions about his motives in paying the diggers for tunnel access. He was rewarded with awards and congratulations from colleagues and some critics. At this point, Frank was tired of a dozen years of second-guessing and skepticism on the role of television news. He had created a documentary that people compared to the best fiction programming.

When he sat down to write the "transmission of experience" memo during that next year as NBC readied for the expansion of the nightly newscast, he was done apologizing for television news. In addition to some of his key ideas, the memo is remembered for its confidence, its firm message that it was okay to work in television news. There was no reason to be defensive. The *Huntley-Brinkley Report* was the most popular journalistic effort in the nation. He felt the NBC staff members needed to remember the power of television and the importance of their work: "There will be dignity. I do not advocate humility. We have a right to arrogance, and we may need it for sustenance. But it is as true now as seven years ago that if we speak to our equals the others will follow."[97]

Up to this point, most of the criticisms, attacks, and praise for *The Tunnel* presented here have been the public side of this 1962 international controversy. Most of the serious pressure on NBC to cancel or alter the documentary, especially from the US government, was applied in private. The behind-the-scenes negotiations between journalists, government officials, and network executives show the true intertwined relationships between these groups in Cold War America. These groups had their specific reasons to keep the backroom negotiations and counteroffers out of the public eye, because the reality would cast doubt upon the implied separation between government and the press.

The fight over *The Tunnel* also reveals that while journalism boundary work was often used to undercut broadcast news, there was no more churlish behavior than pure competition on an important story, no matter the format. Journalists were quite willing to take sides with the government and cast aspersions on their fellow reporters if it would provide a competitive advantage. The next chapter digs into how one network's government cooperation and a failed tunnel escape led to much of the pressure on NBC to scrap *The Tunnel* documentary. The amount of time and effort the US government spent trying to convince or bully both NBC and CBS into canceling Berlin Wall tunnel projects reveal the growing dominance of television news during this critical juncture in American media history.

CHAPTER SIX

"The Necessary Restraints of National Security"

IN APRIL 1961, roughly a week after the failed Bay of Pigs invasion in Cuba and more than three months before the start of the Berlin Wall, President John F. Kennedy spoke to the American Newspaper Publishers Association (ANPA). In a speech entitled "The President and the Press," Kennedy engaged in the delicate dance popular between the government and journalists during the Cold War. He started by joking that if Horace Greeley had paid his *New York Tribune* London correspondent a little more money back in 1851, Karl Marx might have stayed in the newspaper business and not created this evil known as communism. The president also included several key phrases to signal the importance of an independent press, including that he had no plans "to censor the news, to stifle dissent," or "to cover up our mistakes."[1]

Kennedy then pivoted and compared a loyal communist press to US newspapers readily revealing US national security secrets. He accused journalists of being more devoted to their craft than their country, as people who "recognized only the tests of journalism and not the tests of national security."[2]

Instead of censorship, the president put the pressure on the publishers to employ the "necessary restraints of national security." Kennedy emphasized the danger of the Cold War while reminding the publishers how they cooperated with the government during World War II: "If the press is awaiting a declaration of war before it imposes the self discipline of combat conditions, then I can only say no war ever posed a greater threat to our security."[3]

Kennedy's speech to the American newspaper publishers highlights the contradictory relationship between the American government and the press on full display during the Cold War. Both the government and journalists want the public to see the separation between the two sides. For the American government, freedom of the press is one of the great advantages when touting democracy over communism. For journalists, playing up the adversarial relationship advances the boundary work foundation of the independence of the press, bravely fulfilling the watchdog function of keeping our elected officials honest.

Both partners in this dance have a separate relationship that is just as important yet downplayed for public consumption. The government expects reporters to help the American cause, especially when it comes to international matters. Journalists should put their country's interest first, not the canons of their profession. For journalists, they need government officials as sources for stories. If reporters are cut out of the information loop, they lose their value to their employer. During the Cold War, and many would argue at all times, journalists had a closer relationship with government officials because of the omnipresent threat of a misstep leading to the use of nuclear weapons. Journalists often acted as partners with the government on the premise of keeping the country safe, including holding off publishing stories and even siding with the government in disputes with journalists who dared to go against this unspoken bond. Another important part of the relationship that journalists tend to downplay is the role of the person, company, or shareholders in charge of that news outlet. The owners often had a separate relationship with the government and might come to different conclusions on the value of a journalistic project in relation to the company's interests. This relationship is even more important in the case of American radio and television stations, beholden to the Federal Communication Commission (FCC) for their broadcast licenses.

Both journalists and US government officials knew it was best to keep this second, more cooperative relationship out of the press conferences, off the newspaper pages, or away from the broadcasts. If the world knew the extent of the cooperation, the free press argument would ring less true in the Cold War ideology battle. For journalists, the simpatico relationship would bring them closer to the communist model of a government-approved media.

This critical juncture in American journalism history, as television became a more powerful communication player, reveals the cooperation the government expected on Cold War issues by journalists. Those working in television were still fighting for overall respect and were not always in tune with the unspoken expectations of working quietly and behind the scenes with government leaders on contentious issues.

For journalists, the behind-the-scenes negotiations involved in *The Tunnel* controversy also revealed the ugly side of competition. The last chapter focused mostly on the public face of journalism boundary work, with the print journalists using their newspaper and magazine pages to let their readers know the superiority of the printed word. A side of journalism that might not play as well with the audience also commanded an important role in *The Tunnel* dispute. Journalists were not above trying to gain an advantage for their news outlet through their source relationships. A common practice would involve a source providing an exclusive interview as a reward for previous coverage. In the case of *The Tunnel*, journalists pressured the government to publicly shame NBC, partly because those reporters were jealous of what the network had accomplished. Instead of standing up in solidarity with fellow journalists, these reporters, especially at CBS, sought to alienate NBC through government condemnation.

The first chapter focused on *The Tunnel* story, with a decidedly American (and West German) perspective. The story relied mostly on the public side of the controversy: how the battle between NBC and the government played out if you were following it in the media at the time. This chapter goes through some of the same key events but through the lens of what we now know of what went on behind the scenes. Declassified government documents reveal the quiet meetings, the back-channel pressures, the journalists and government sources using their less public cooperative relationships to gain advantages in the sphere of public opinion.

The Tunnel documentary is a rare case in the reporter-government source relationship because NBC did not need the government on this particular project. Reuven Frank made the decision not to interview American or West German officials for the broadcast. NBC did not have to rely on the government for cooperation to complete the documentary. As we will see, however, the network was very sensitive toward gaining American government approval.

This chapter also digs into one of the most common tactics by government officials to shame reporters during the Cold War: accusing journalists of providing propaganda for the enemy. Under the propaganda accusation approach, any stories that portray the US government or people in a bad light can be criticized as providing ideological ammunition for the other side.

The propaganda threat was used to scare CBS out of its tunnel and then was employed to try to force NBC to cancel its documentary. Did these tunnel projects become a focal point for the communist press? How did the East German and Soviet media cover these journalistic endeavors?

Tunnel Projects as News Stories

In the first months after closing the border between East and West Berlin, the East Germans methodically closed off some of the easier ways to sneak into West Germany. By early 1962, digging a tunnel under the wall became a popular escape method. The stories of successful, failed, and even fatal tunnel projects filled the newspapers and airwaves in the first half of 1962. When the NBC Berlin bureau made the deal with Luigi Spina, Domenico Sesta, and Wolf Schroedter to film their tunnel project, the escape method itself was not particularly novel. What made the NBC agreement such a potentially powerful piece of journalism was the visual side of the project. If successful, NBC could show its viewers what digging a tunnel looked like as it was happening, not just provide words on a page or images after the fact. NBC could also personalize the people who were risking their lives digging under the wall as well as those who wanted to escape. In a way, NBC had the same idea as MGM and director Robert Siodmak, who were in West Berlin at that time filming a fictional account of a tunnel project: make it personal and real. Instead of the safety of a fake wall on a movie set, NBC was filming the real thing, with all the dangers and complications involved.[4]

In the realm of journalistic competition, NBC would only have an advantage if no other film crews had access to the tunnel. If others had the same visuals, NBC would lose its exclusivity, which was why NBC was willing to pay the organizers up to $12,500, even knowing it would be considered a controversial payment. The elaborate lengths Reuven Frank and the Berlin crew went to keep NBC's involvement in the tunnel secret was partly because of the very real safety concerns, but also because they did not want any other news organizations to know what they were doing. They knew journalism competition could sabotage the project if other reporters knew about the Bernauer Strasse tunnel.[5]

While NBC was able to keep its tunnel production quiet, their idea was not exclusive. CBS also was looking for a tunnel project it could film in the summer of 1962, hoping to complete it in time to put together a special program for the anniversary of the border closing in August. CBS correspondent Daniel Schorr got in touch with Rainer Hildebrandt, who was involved in various escape projects. Hildebrandt knew of some students who were close to finishing an ambitious tunnel but had run into problems. They had been digging for a month but were still about five meters away from where the tunnel would terminate in East Berlin.[6]

The planners were looking for some extra funding and a chance at publicizing the escape after it happened. They were hoping to bring more than fifty people through the tunnel. CBS met with the tunnel planners in early August and made a deal for $1,250, a tenth of what NBC invested. The network would be able to bring its camera in the tunnel before it was completed. The organizers also promised to provide film that was shot on the East Berlin side when the border was closed the previous year. Schorr checked with his CBS bosses in New York and the deal was made.

CBS was able to film in the tunnel at least once before the scheduled escape in the afternoon of Tuesday, August 7, less than week after it first found out about the project. This timeline would give Schorr six days to put together a documentary for the Berlin Wall anniversary.[7]

Government Intervention in Network Television Tunnel Projects

In early August 1962, NBC and CBS were involved in two separate tunnel projects under the Berlin Wall. The journalists did not contact US government officials about their plans due to secrecy concerns, journalism competition, and not needing information from government officials. Over the next four months, the interactions between the government officials, the journalists, and the media companies' leaders in New York revealed the complicated and contested relationship between government and journalists during the Cold War. While a tunnel escape was a good Cold War story for journalists, for the US government in Washington, tunnels were another reminder of the lack of a stronger response to the building of the wall.

There is one obvious reason why Daniel Schorr and his camera crew were not in Berlin when the tunnel project they paid to cover was thwarted by the East German police: US government intervention. In his haste to find a story that he could run in time for the Berlin Wall anniversary, Schorr chose a sloppy tunnel project. Fritz Wagner, well known in Berlin escape circles, and his group started digging the short tunnel under the wall in the Treptow section of Berlin in April 1962 but ran out of money. The project restarted in June with the hopes of completion within a month. The West German secret police, Landesamt für Verfassungsschutz (LfV), learned about the tunnel in July and knew immediately when CBS paid for film rights. The LfV first tried to convince the tunnel group not to let more people know about the project. When that did not work, it contacted the US officials in Bonn and Berlin. At that time, the West German secret police told the US officials that it appeared the Treptow tunnel was still a secret from East Germany: "Groups concerned have excellent record successful escapes and no concrete indications compromise noted."[8]

Even with these assurances, Secretary of State Dean Rusk told his German staff to convince Schorr to drop the project. Officials in both Berlin and Bonn met with him, downplaying the publicity concerns and emphasizing the chance the East Germans could find out about the tunnel: "a situation in which other side would have the documentary evidence and possibly in the end some of his people in their hands."[9] When Schorr dismissed efforts from State Department officials in West Germany to get him to drop the project, they pushed for Washington to work on his bosses at CBS.

Rusk met with CBS News general manager Blair Clark, who had been friends with President Kennedy since their days at Harvard. Rusk convinced Clark to call his reporter to scrap the project from the Secretary's office on a secure line. While Schorr had ignored the pleas from State Department officials in Berlin, when his boss called from the secretary of state's office, Schorr begrudgingly agreed to leave Berlin with his cameraman so he could not be implicated if the East Germans found out about the escape. Schorr did make tentative plans to have a freelance film crew on site for the escape footage.[10]

On August 7, word about the tunnel escape had spread to other journalists who then positioned themselves near the West Berlin terminus of the tunnel. Piers Anderton and his NBC crew were among the group of reporters and photographers waiting to see what would happen.

Unfortunately, the East Germans had also learned about the escape plan and the location in East Berlin where the diggers planned to surface. East German police arrested several people as they made their way to the escape spot. Police were waiting in the house when the diggers broke through the floorboards. The diggers and rescuers were warned just in time, and they made it safely back through the tunnel. No one from East Germany escaped.

From the West side of the wall, reporters could see East German police swarming the area where the escape was supposed to happen. According to later intelligence reports, at least two people were arrested and as many as fifteen more involved on the Eastern side could be in custody.

State Department officials in Germany felt by removing Schorr they had avoided "the worst aspect of what could have been politically very embarrassing." They reported to Secretary Rusk that Schorr was upset at the government interference, saying the State Department was good at preventing action but not very good at initiating action, apparently in reference to the tepid response to the closing of the border and the building of the Berlin Wall.[11]

Rusk demanded his West German staff have another talk with Schorr, treating him more like an insubordinate staff member than an independent journalist. The secretary of state wanted the CBS correspondent to know he had "proceeded amateurishly in a matter filled with greatest danger for all concerned. As we anticipated, other side turned out to be fully aware of entire matter and laid a trap which could have resulted in massacre [of] those involved." They also attempted to scare Schorr by hinting CBS could be implicated by the East Germans in a public trial involving the people who were arrested. Even with these scoldings, the US diplomatic staff in Germany felt Schorr was not "contrite" for his involvement: "Whether discussion made any impression on him can only be determined by his future actions and statements."[12]

The government pressure now switched from CBS to NBC and from Berlin to the United States. The inside tunnel knowledge also changed sides, with NBC knowing more than the State Department, and the network using that knowledge differential to keep its project alive.

NBC Tunnel Surprise

Since NBC's Piers Anderton had been at the scene of the aborted CBS tunnel escape, and because of a tipoff from CBS, the State Department mistakenly thought NBC also had a role in the compromised tunnel. The State Department decided Anderton needed a personal scolding and warning as well. The NBC correspondent was considered no less obstinate than Schorr on following government orders, a "generally uncooperative attitude," so the Berlin staff suggested "high level intervention" in the United States, since it had been effective in the CBS situation.[13]

In the United States, Assistant Secretary of State for Public Affairs Robert J. Manning became the point person in dealing with the network Berlin tunnel controversies. Manning had spent years in print journalism, including at the *New York Herald Tribune* and *Time* magazine, before coming to the State Department. Manning sent an assistant to meet with NBC News president William McAndrew to express strong concerns about American companies becoming involved in tunnel escape projects. When McAndrew realized the State Department was referring to the compromised CBS tunnel and apparently did not know about the NBC project, he chose not to mention it. NBC had already shot roughly three hours of film in its tunnel and was waiting for the diggers to finish the final two meters.[14]

On September 14, 1962, the NBC Berlin bureau film crew, brothers Peter and Klaus Dehmel, waited in the basement of a building on Bernauer Strasse in West Berlin looking down a ladder into a dark hole. Twenty-nine people, adults and children, came up that ladder on that Friday and Saturday, the largest escape by tunnel at that time since the wall separated Berlin. By Sunday, the tunnel filled with water. West German government officials, who knew about the escape, shut it down and warned East Germans to stay away from the dangerous passage. West German officials asked journalists to embargo stories of the historic escape until they were sure no more East Germans would try to risk the flooded tunnel.[15]

At this point in the story, as recounted in chapters 1 and 5, NBC came under intense criticism and scrutiny both from government sources, in the United States and West Germany, and also from journalists who disagreed with the exclusivity payment or questioned the network's journalistic credibility. A major reason for the government and media pressure on NBC stemmed from less noble motivations: journalistic competition and jealousy. Analyzing declassified government documents and other archive material from this period reveals the extent to which the State Department and journalists, especially at rival CBS, crafted their public responses and coverage to paint NBC, often unfairly, as unprofessional or even un-American, in taking on and not canceling the tunnel project.

Journalism Competition and Government Pressure

In the first of two embarrassing intelligence lapses for the US mission in Berlin, the State Department apparently first learned of the tunnel escape when the *New York Times* ran a story on September 19, five days after the initial escape. The Berlin staff's weak excuse was "exceptionally tight control by German authorities and unusual press discipline." The staff was still not sure of the exact location.¹⁶

Two weeks later, the importance of journalism competition and jealousy became intertwined in the government response to the tunnel project when *Time* magazine first revealed NBC's involvement in the tunnel escape. The story referred to the film rights payment as "chicanery" and suggested the tunnel organizers pocketed much of the money and disappeared. CBS News' Blair Clark called the State Department and, as related in a memo to the German diplomatic staff, "has justifiably asked whether his excellent cooperation in suppressing CBS effort on earlier tunnel project has in effect left CBS out in the cold." The State Department official said he felt "obliged" to let CBS know what happened. "Was [NBC's Piers] Anderton's enterprise carried out with US knowledge and approval? Was he asked to desist or was this enterprise unknown to us?"¹⁷

The Berlin Mission admitted it did not know about NBC's involvement in a tunnel that itself had been a surprise to the staff. The Berlin Mission's main excuse was that it did not seek out knowledge about escape projects so there could be no way to link the State Department with these tunnels, regarded as aggressive military moves by East Germans. Concerning the implication that, as with CBS, NBC could have been stopped if the diplomatic staff had known about the project, the Berlin staff once again urged for pressure to be applied at the level of media upper management: "In final analysis most effective contact with US news media is that of Dept with their respective headquarters in US. Must be recognized each time we intervene with correspondents here to persuade him to drop refugee enterprise, we antagonize him and risk loosing [*sic*] his cooperation on manners in which he handles reporting on other important developments." The US mission in Berlin needed the reporters to cover other stories and did not want to have an adversarial relationship with the Berlin journalists. Manning followed that advice and called NBC News president William McAndrew to voice displeasure with the project.¹⁸

NBC Defends Tunnel Escape Project

NBC tried to turn the criticisms into promotion by holding a press conference formally announcing the ninety-minute documentary, *The Tunnel*, scheduled for October 31, 1962. Reporters instead continued to frame the project as a question of journalism ethics, with the emphasis on NBC paying for the film rights. CBS was still upset that its tunnel project had been a failure and NBC looked to have a powerful documentary.[19]

CBS News president Richard Salant issued a press release that correspondent David Schoenbrun read over the phone to Robert Manning at the State Department. The carefully worded statement leaves the impression that the two networks had been working on the same tunnel project: "CBS News in early August this summer had in preparation a report on the refugee tunneling operation under the Berlin Wall. After receiving from the U.S. State Department certain intelligence information on the U.S. national interest aspect of the Berlin Wall tunneling operation CBS stopped the preparation of its report and has not resumed it." To further ingratiate the network with the State Department, Schoenbrun reportedly told Manning that CBS still agreed with "the correctness of the Department's interference in their tunnel activity and the correctness of their decision in withdrawing from the project." Even though CBS's response was misleading and never mentioned the failed tunnel escape, the *New York Times* chose to print Salant's full statement as the final paragraph of its critical coverage of the NBC press conference. The State Department, CBS, and print journalists conspired to paint CBS as the responsible Cold War partner and NBC as the reckless outlier.[20]

As a former journalist, Manning could see the complications of the State Department favoring one network over the other. When he related these details to Secretary Rusk, he said he said he intended "to play it carefully by ear, discreetly giving some of the background but avoiding any recriminatory comparison of the two networks." The State Department did attempt to clarify the tunnel controversy the next day by providing spokesman Lincoln White with new talking points for the department press briefing. In his guide, White had separate paragraphs for the two network tunnel projects, clearly showing NBC and CBS were not covering the same tunnel dig. The memo still does not make clear the CBS tunnel was a failure while NBC's had been successful. Newspaper coverage also ignored the distinction.[21]

If NBC had any hopes that the documentary controversy would dissipate as Reuven Frank worked toward the October 31 broadcast, those aspirations disappeared in the next few days when the negative response to the project moved to Germany and appeared to strengthen the argument the network was tangled up in a questionable endeavor.

International Condemnation

In West Berlin, many of the people working on the Bernauer Strasse tunnel apparently did not know about the money arrangement NBC made with the tunnel organizers until the payment controversy hit the papers. Those diggers held a press conference on October 13 to pressure NBC to cancel the documentary because they believed the money arrangement tainted their altruistic work. Reporters Don Cook of the *New York Herald Tribune* and George Bailey of ABC were quick to let the Berlin Mission know about this new development, which was then cabled to the State Department.[22]

The next day, both the West German Embassy and the West Berlin Senat told the US government the project should be canceled, mainly because of the danger to any diggers or escapees identifiable in the film. From the other side of the wall, the East German government sent an official protest, demanding that the US government "inflict severe penalty" on NBC because the company had "financed and filmed the construction of a tunnel for secret agents." These criticisms were dutifully covered by major US newspapers and wire services.[23]

The exclusive tunnel escape broadcast that was meant to show the power of freedom over communism was turning into a diplomatic disaster for the network. On Wednesday, October 17, McAndrew and Frank traveled to the State Department to meet first with Manning, then with Rusk. While reiterating the West German calls for canceling the documentary, Manning said the State Department's main concern was NBC's involvement in the tunnel project, now completed, and "it must leave to you the question of whether the film should be televised." Rusk also emphasized the network needed to "give every consideration" to the objections of the West Berlin government. While they were at the State Department, Frank and McAndrews also spoke with a representative from the West Berlin Senat, who was asking NBC to cancel the documentary because of the propaganda advantage it would give East Germany. The State Department made clear it had "strong reservations" about the NBC project, but it was ultimately up to the network whether it should broadcast the documentary.[24]

While McAndrew and Frank were encouraged after their private meetings, the State Department public response took a more critical turn after the pressure from the West German embassy, West Berlin, the diggers, and East Germany. Two days later, spokesman Lincoln White had a new page of talking points for the State Department press briefing. Now, CBS was thanked for "promptly and wisely" withdrawing from its tunnel project, while NBC ignored the US government's warning. Instead, NBC continued on a project that the State Department now called "risky, irresponsible, undesirable, and not in the best interests of the United States." Versions of that damning phrase ran in newspapers and magazines over the next few days. Mirroring Kennedy's speech to newspaper publishers, the revised State Department "guidance" memo for its spokesman both acknowledged press freedom while also piling on government and possible public pressure: "The remaining question—of whether the resultant film is to be telecast by NBC in the face of protests from West Berlin, including that City's Senate and representations from the Federal German Republic Embassy in Washington—is for NBC to decide. I think our view of the question is quite clear."[25]

Network International Diplomacy

With the secretary of state pointedly urging NBC to deal with the criticism in West Germany, the tunnel broadcast controversy moved into the highest levels of the network. NBC president Robert Kintner related later that "the pressure was unremitting" for a month. He dispatched NBC lawyer Lester Bernstein to West Germany to try to reverse government opposition there. In his media career memoir, Frank claimed to have been unaware at the time of the efforts by Kintner and Bernstein to work with West German officials.[26]

In response to the identification concerns, NBC agreed to edit out or obscure the faces of anyone in the documentary who did not sign a release form. In Berlin, Bernstein reminded West German and West Berlin officials that if they really wanted more world attention on the wall, the NBC documentary would provide that publicity. According to NBC, *The Tunnel* would be "one of the most compelling human documents ever produced for television, celebrating, as it does, man's unconquerable drive to be free." The West Berlin Senat removed its objections to *The Tunnel*, noting the network was "guided by the wish to bring by an authentic report to the public of the United States a direct impression, which is in the interest of Berlin," a comment Kintner later passed along to Rusk.[27]

Cuban Missile Crisis

While NBC journalists and managers attempted to placate State Department leaders critical of the tunnel escape broadcast, some of those same officials were also dealing with a more serious and pressing Cold War crisis. On October 16, 1962, the day before Secretary Rusk met with NBC about *The Tunnel*, President Kennedy first learned the Soviet missile sites being constructed in Cuba were in fact designed for offensive nuclear weapons that could hit major North American cities. That development might play into to the reason the State Department ratcheted up its complaints about the NBC project.

On Monday, October 22, Kennedy told the American public about the Soviet missiles in Cuba. He warned of military consequences if Russian leader Nikita Khrushchev did not remove the missiles: "He has an opportunity now to move the world back from the abyss of destruction." The next day, NBC quietly postponed *The Tunnel*, stating "this is not an appropriate time" to broadcast the documentary. By Sunday, October 28, the Soviets had agreed to remove the missiles in Cuba and the international tensions diffused.[28]

The Tunnel Negotiations

After the Cuban Missile Crisis dissipated, Reuven Frank was busy producing the network's November election night coverage. The Kennedy administration was able to avoid a midterm loss in Democratic congressional seats partly because of the international incident. Republicans had targeted the Cuba situation as a key election issue well before the confrontation, painting Kennedy as weak on foreign policy. His handling of the volatile situation helped his standing with those voters.

Still no word on the fate of *The Tunnel*. Away from public view, and even hidden from the newsroom, the top levels of NBC and the Kennedy administration engaged in the type of negotiations neither side wanted to be made public. In aspirational journalism, NBC would take into account the government's concerns and make an independent decision on whether or not to run *The Tunnel*, balancing any foreign policy risk with the importance of the subject for the audience. In reality, NBC president Robert Kintner wanted, and maybe needed, Secretary of State Rusk's concerns turned into blessings before he would schedule *The Tunnel*.

Kintner compiled a lengthy document to persuade Rusk to remove his objections. Frank claimed no knowledge of this correspondence at the time. The five-page single-spaced letter sent to Rusk on November 20, 1962, also included an eight-page memorandum with the timeline of the NBC tunnel project. While Kintner starts the correspondence by insisting NBC would be running *The Tunnel*, the tone of the letter made clear he was trying to convince Rusk that NBC had approached the tunnel project "honorably and responsibly." Kintner listed all the safety precautions followed by the Berlin crew while filming in the tunnel and the steps taken to get permission to show the faces of some of the diggers and escapees. He then outlined how the West German and West Berlin government removed most of their objections after hearing from NBC on those security precautions.[29]

The NBC president, who was a former journalist, also made sure to meticulously disparage his main television rival in the letter. NBC was still smarting over the State Department's stronger tone in the October 19 briefing in which CBS was praised while NBC's project was painted as risky and irresponsible. Kintner spelled out the differences in the two tunnel projects: the CBS tunnel was organized by an "unsavory West Berlin character" who dug tunnels for profit. The CBS tunnel was only thirty yards long and was "bungled both in the digging and with respect to its security." CBS abandoned the project only when it was clear the tunnel had been compromised, a fact that had not been mentioned in any State Department briefings.[30]

By contrast, the NBC tunnel was a "model of engineering and secrecy," running 140 yards underground, well beyond the wall on both sides, taking four months to dig, and not discovered by the East Germans until after it was flooded and abandoned: "By any standard, the tunnel proved the most successful operation of its kind yet conducted to bring East German refugees across the Wall." Kintner would not admit to producing a program to please the US government, but he did believe *The Tunnel* would be in the national interest by giving "millions of Americans a keener awareness of their stake in Berlin and a deeper insight into the nature of the struggle between Communism and freedom."[31]

Kintner ended his letter with an oblique plea for approval, hoping "our intention of presenting the program will meet with your sympathetic understanding." More to the point, Robert Manning told Rusk that Kintner wanted a letter from the secretary of state "to appease some members of the Board of Directors."[32]

A week later, Rusk gave Kintner the requested written response. The secretary of state referred to tunnel projects as "adventurous journalism" and once again warned NBC about "the question of risks, personal and political, surrounding the covert involvement of American television or other unofficial personnel in affairs so delicate and explosive as the Berlin wall escape problem." Rusk thanked NBC for addressing security concerns and reiterated it was ultimately NBC's decision on whether or not to run the documentary. The secretary of state ended the letter on a positive note, apparently aimed at Kintner's bosses, offering that from the description, *The Tunnel* must be "a moving human document." Two days after receiving that letter, NBC wrote a press release announcing *The Tunnel* would be broadcast on December 10, 1962.[33]

In one section of Kintner's lengthy missive to Rusk, the NBC president touches on one of the key Cold War arguments against both the CBS and NBC tunnel projects: propaganda. The point is usually couched in vague language, but the insinuation is obvious: these projects might provide informational ammunition the Soviets could turn back on the West. Kintner admits he postponed *The Tunnel* during the Cuban Missile Crisis "to remove any possible pretext for propaganda points" for the Russians. He then refutes the propaganda argument by saying the Soviets follow their own course "so that no decision of this kind by NBC, one way or the other, could have a tangible effect upon Soviet actions."[34]

The propaganda points argument was usually used just as a scare tactic, to try to shame the journalists into promoting the government viewpoint and encourage the public to question the loyalty of the organization. *The Tunnel* controversy provides an opportunity during this critical juncture in journalism history to dig into an actual incident to see how the communist press used information labeled by the West as propaganda ammunition. For the communists, the NBC project was just another example of the mendacity of America's touted free press.

East German Media and the Cold War

In the German Democratic Republic (GDR), the first head of the Office of Information had intimate knowledge of America's journalistic Cold War contradictions. Gerhart Eisler grew up in Germany and joined the Communist Party before the Nazis came to power. He promoted communism in the United States in the 1930s and 1940s but was sentenced to prison for refusing to talk to the House Un-American Activities Committee (HUAC) and including false information on his immigration papers. Eisler jumped bail and left the United States. After returning to East Germany, he was put in charge of the Office of Information. With his background in the United States, Eisler helped East German reporters emphasize the plight of American journalists critical of McCarthy-era trials. He encouraged American journalists with socialist or communist sympathies to write for GDR newspapers about US press censorship. Military censorship by US authorities also came under fire. Such cases were held up as evidence of American hypocrisy in conjunction with freedom of expression and independent journalism and appeared in the pages of primary newspapers in the GDR.[35]

The most prominent East German newspaper, *Neues Deutschland*, was the central organ of the SED (Communist) party. The *Berliner Zeitung* was also controlled by the SED, with a more popular tone. The *Neue Zeit* was smaller in reach and was the central party organ of the East German branch of the CDU (Christian Democratic Union).[36]

Throughout the 1950s, the United States seemed to preoccupy the GDR regime. GDR leaders saw the United States as a threat to their existence on the world stage and constructed a systematic propaganda campaign depicting US soldiers as "crude fellows, resembl[ing] cartoon stereotypes." Western journalists were portrayed as spies for the CIA. By the end of the 1950s, an image of the United States as lacking culture, but posing a threat to East Germany, had been firmly established in GDR media. The US involvement in the war in Korea provided fodder for such characterizations.[37]

At the same time the GDR was sending out media messages dismissive of Americans, East German officials seemed to want to work with American journalists to advance the country's agenda. East German leader Walter Ulbricht had begun a publicity campaign of sorts to push the Western powers to agree to sign a separate peace treaty with the GDR. Ulbricht wanted to make his case directly to the American public, granting his first interview with a Western journalist, Betty Adams of WBZ-TV Boston, in late 1959. Several other Westinghouse stations broadcast the interview as well. One GDR newspaper noted that five million Americans saw the broadcast, and a transcript of the interview took up a full page of the paper. This was the same publicity campaign in which Ulbricht walked out on an interview with CBS's Daniel Schorr.[38]

When Soviet premier Nikita Khrushchev visited the United States, the State Department refused to grant three East German journalists visas to participate in coverage of the visit. That prompted one GDR article to declare, "Are three journalists dangerous?" The article derided one of the reasons a State Department official provided for the refusal, that the United States had no formal diplomatic relations with the GDR: "But the GDR also has no diplomatic relations with the U.S. That hasn't prevented us from giving almost 100 American journalists since 1958 the possibility to get to know our country and to travel in it."[39]

Throughout the early 1960s, as Walter Ulbricht and the GDR fought for acceptance on the world stage, they also engaged in a protracted public relations struggle against Western media outlets over the decision to erect a barrier through the heart of Berlin. As Western journalists reported on escapes, attempted escapes, and arrests and shootings of escapees and linked those events to a cruel government menacing its own citizens, GDR officials and journalists formulated counter-narratives depicting the wall as protection from Western threats. Western journalists emerged in the counternarratives not merely as documenters of tensions along the wall, but as a driving force behind the threats.

In the first few years of the Berlin Wall, the GDR press connected at least two tunnel escapes to West German media propaganda. In June 1962, as related in chapter 1, East German Pvt. Reinhold Huhn became an early martyr for the country when he was shot and killed as a family escaped through a tunnel near Checkpoint Charlie. The tunnel opened up on the West side of the wall on the property of Axel Springer, publisher of the tabloid *Bild* and other German publications. Springer had given permission for the digging, despite the misgivings of the *Bild* editor.[40]

East Germany's primary daily newspaper, *Neues Deutschland*, addressed the incident under the headline "*Springer organisiert den Mord*" ("Springer organizes murder"). The article claimed the Springer press had created a "Wall psychosis," and that the escape tunnel's location directly adjacent to the Springer building was no coincidence. As the GDR border guard was shot and killed, photographers for the *Bild* newspaper, along with other Western journalists, documented the scene from the roof of the Springer headquarters. According to the article, "the murder was planned and prepared in cold blood by employees of the Springer organization."[41]

GDR newspapers displayed large portraits of the dead guard on front pages the next day, and quickly drew connections between the incident and Western journalists. "Everything about this provocation was set up to be propagandistically exploited," accused one writer after describing how reporters from a West Berlin television station had set up large-scale technical equipment "directly at the place of the murder."[42]

West German media reappeared as threats to the GDR border in subsequent years, after *The Tunnel* controversy, notably in the autumn of 1964. Escape helpers shot and killed a GDR border guard in the process of leading fifty-seven people via a tunnel to West Berlin. Photos of the escape appeared in the West German magazine *Stern*, apparently via freelance West Berlin reporters who had paid the escape helpers. The GDR government saw this incident as evidence of direct involvement of Western journalists in the killing of a GDR border guard, and quickly moved to expel *Stern* correspondents based in East Berlin. East German news items included dramatic headlines, including " 'Stern' finances murderers."[43]

As East Germany's larger Cold War nemesis, the United States was regularly implicated in the background of many West German threats. The two 1962 tunnels involving CBS and NBC provided new ammunition for GDR press coverage painting Western media as a danger to the GDR's existence. When the US mission in Berlin tried to scare Schorr away from the CBS tunnel by saying it would be a big story in East Germany and CBS would be implicated, they were half-right. The compromised tunnel in August 1962 did become a major news story in East Germany, a "large-scale terrorist campaign," but CBS was never identified in the coverage, most likely because Schorr had been sent away, removing CBS from the tunnel itself the day it was discovered.[44]

Under the headline "Deaths were planned for," one article included confessional statements from two "agents" who testified about their roles in interviews aired on East German television. As further evidence of Western involvement in the tunnel, the article points to "numerous police officers, photojournalists and cameramen, doctors and ambulances standing by" on the Western end of the tunnel. "That it didn't result in a blood bath is only thanks to our security forces," the piece concluded.[45]

Trials for the accused individuals garnered prominent coverage in the GDR press in late August. The men were sentenced to lengthy prison terms and were declared to be spies and "Western agents." One article proclaimed that the "U.S. is complicit" and suggested that along with the West German government, the CIA "sits in the dock [alongside the accused] . . . as they enriched themselves from these degenerate and greedy subjects."[46]

Communist Press Response to NBC

The East German press did not report on the successful tunnel escape in September but did pick up the story once the Western press had connected NBC to the project. A short article in *Neue Zeit* summarized a recent *Times* of London exposé on how profit motives may have been driving some tunnel rescue activity. The article then notes NBC's admission that it had paid those involved in a tunnel project. The students were described as "agents" who attempted an "armed breakthrough" into the GDR. The following day, *Neues Deutschland* reported further detail on the payment under the headline "2500 dollars per agent." Tunnel supporter Eberhard Weyrauch is quoted as saying that a "lucrative profit" had been made from the NBC payment.[47]

The subsequent GDR press coverage of the tunnel activity and NBC's involvement continued these themes. The articles focused on a profit motive for all those involved, suggesting monetary greed as pervasive in Western capitalist society. The coverage depicted participants (both students and journalists) as "agents," implying close connections to Western governments. The stories characterized the tunnel as an "attack" on the GDR, driven by "revengist" elements in the West who could not come to terms with the GDR's existence, particularly its border measures embodied by the Berlin Wall. NBC is cast in the role approximating that of a state-level entity on the international stage, executing a geopolitical agenda set out by a colluding capitalist force and the US government.

"They still cannot overcome the fact that our protective wall has presented them with an insurmountable border," argued one East German columnist. The writer goes on to note that the "human traffickers" are driven by profit motives, as even the *Times* of London had recently reported.[48]

This commentary piece is particularly interesting not only for its "revengist" and profiteering accusations, but for the manner in which it links the NBC tunnel project with the MGM fictional account of the "Tunnel 28" escape directed by Robert Siodmak, retitled *Escape from East Berlin*, which had been filmed that summer in West Berlin. "The American movie studio

MGM wants to add one more to its innumerable exports of crime movies," the writer maintained. "The authors: America's television station NBC." Such rhetoric seems to play off stereotypes of America created in the GDR media, including Hollywood culture as well as painting escape tunnels as criminal aggressive acts against East Germany.⁴⁹

The East German coverage of the NBC tunnel controversy also revealed a parallel feeling that both Soviet and American government officials had about the other country's leader, an impression that became clearer when the behind-the-scenes negotiations during the Cuban Missile Crisis were revealed years later. Both Kennedy and Khrushchev felt the other leader might be willing to negotiate, but that each was being pressured by hardliners in his government to take a stronger stance, both on situations in Cuba and in Berlin.

Under the headline "USA monopolist circles organized border penetration," *Neues Deutschland* again attempted to establish links between the journalists' activities and broader capitalist interests. The article draws connections between the NBC network and both big business as well as government factions: "the broadcaster, which is dominated by representatives of the American arms industry" and "American monopolist interests who are dissatisfied with the allegedly 'soft Kennedy course.'"⁵⁰

The latter remark refers to frustration in some circles in the United States that President Kennedy had not confronted the GDR militarily in order to prevent construction of the wall in 1961. The article offered NBC's intransigence in not acceding to State Department demands right away as evidence of a "large-scale campaign against Kennedy," in contrast to CBS's earlier decision not to pursue a tunnel film. The article concluded with a listing of a handful of "monopolist representatives on the NBC board."⁵¹

On October 18, the GDR formally protested the NBC tunnel project, the letter delivered via Czechoslovakia since the United States did not recognize East Germany. As State Department officials had warned, the GDR predicted the incident would affect East-West relations because the project would "increase tension and impede a peaceful solution of the West Berlin problem." The East German government demanded the people involved be punished because the US government "bears full responsibility for the act perpetrated by the National Broadcasting Company and members of its staff in defiance of international law.⁵²

Neue Zeit carried the announcement under the headline "Protest against border attack by NBC," implying a sort of militaristic activity on the part of the network.⁵³ An article in *Neues Deutschland* carried similar text but added a segment at the end under the subhead "Hit the Mark." This last segment argues that State Department spokesman Lincoln White's public remarks cautioning NBC were spurred by the GDR official complaint, and that White would have remained silent without the GDR complaint. The article prefaced White's remark that the decision was ultimately NBC's to make by noting the "contradictory" nature of his comments.⁵⁴

Several days later, the paper reported that NBC had withdrawn plans to air its tunnel program "evidently in response to the U.S. State Department." The article pointed out that this had occurred after the GDR government had delivered its note of protest, and that State Department spokesman White had "practically confirmed [the facts contained in the protest note] and had declared that NBC had been warned that the action was 'risky, irresponsible, and not in the interests of the U.S.' "⁵⁵ In this case, while the government was accusing journalists of providing propaganda for East Germany, the State Department's own criticism of NBC provided an angle for the East German press. In this manner, the article weaves White's remarks and the series of events into a narrative that meshes with the official East German perspective.

In the Soviet Union, the main news outlet, *Pravda*, published considerably fewer articles about Berlin Wall tunnels, but the overall framing of the projects reflects the East German coverage. In February 1962, *Pravda* ran an article and photograph of a GDR press conference in an East Berlin train station where a tunnel had been discovered. The tunnel is described as a "provocative sortie" by the West German government and the discovery by East German police "irrefutably proves this underground loophole is intended to transport spies to the GDR." In a story the next month on another discovered tunnel, the Berlin Wall border is referred to as the "anti-fascist shaft" that has caused a "powerless rage" among West Germans who want to sneak "spies and saboteurs" into "democratic Berlin."⁵⁶

During the NBC tunnel controversy in October 1962, *Pravda* ran a story that quoted both the *New York Times* coverage and CBS president Richard Salant's comments on how his network had walked away from a tunnel project. The article paints the NBC tunnel as a work of fiction, with the headline "Provocation Manufacturers." *Pravda* compared it to the famous, although probably fictional, comment attributed to American newspaper publisher William Randolph Hearst at the time of the Spanish-American War: "You furnish the pictures and I'll provide the war." The article accuses NBC of passing off its fake tunnel as real, "one of the many in a long and growing list of provocative actions of the American ruling circles."[57] The Americans and West Germans were digging these tunnels not only to sneak spies into East Germany, but also to mask the growing crisis in West Berlin after being cut off from the east side of the city.

Press Freedom and Cold War Threats

The negotiations between the US government and two powerful American television networks, as well as reaction in the Eastern Bloc press, highlight the complicated and often heated relationship between the US government and journalists during the Cold War. Both journalists and government officials trumpeted two seemingly contradictory messages, press freedom and Cold War cooperation. During the height of the debate and negotiations over the tunnel documentaries, the US government accused the networks of providing propaganda talking points for the Soviet Union and its allies, when in reality the structure of the US media system and the government's efforts to manage American journalism furnished communists with arguments that were used in their coverage of the tunnel projects.

The Tunnel broadcast signals a triumphant moment for American television news and coverage of the Berlin Wall. Just as important, though, is an understanding of all of the behind-the-scenes threats and negotiations that transpired between the first idea of the tunnel documentary and the broadcast. The communication between the State Department and the American television networks over the tunnel escape broadcasts reveals the pressures, compromises, and attempts to seek approval involved in Cold War journalism. The negotiations played out in newspaper headlines and in secret government telegrams and private letters from media executives, with the declassified documents providing a rare glimpse at the tactics debated and employed that neither side ever expected to be made public.

Unlike the usual government source and journalist relationship, in the case of the tunnel projects, the journalists did not think they needed information from their government sources, so they were not at an information disadvantage. Even so, the networks went to great lengths to curry favor with their government sources, attempting to gain approval for the projects they were producing. Government officials at times seemed to treat the journalists as wayward employees who needed to be brought into line and at other times showing an understanding of journalistic norms and especially, journalistic competition.

The negotiations in part mirror President Kennedy's speech to newspaper publishers in 1961, with both the government and the networks acknowledging the twin concepts of freedom of the press and Cold War cooperation. The disagreements revolved around different interpretations of Kennedy's "necessary restraints of national security." State Department officials at times tried to demand cooperation from journalists in Berlin, while their best success came from putting pressure on media executives in the United States.[58]

Journalists and network executives, including Reuven Frank, did not see these projects as adversarial journalism. They believed broadcasting a successful Berlin Wall tunnel escape would highlight the importance of freedom over communism. Journalists also did not consider these programs American propaganda since they independently tracked down these stories. As Robert Kintner wrote in his letter to the secretary of state, "NBC News is not, of course, in the propaganda business; our interest is in accurate, authentic reporting of the facts."[59]

The negotiations also highlight the divergent needs and expectations involved at different levels in network television and the government's strategies to capitalize on those differences. For network journalists, the motivations involved producing important stories and beating the competition. An exclusive report on a Berlin tunnel escape represented a journalistic coup, especially for journalists living in Berlin, who were more sympathetic to West Germany's anger over the lack of a strong response to the Berlin Wall. After talking to Daniel Schorr, a US diplomatic official in Germany said the reporter hoped a tunnel escape documentary would be "his greatest television achievement" and he could not be easily convinced to drop the project. NBC's Piers Anderton is described as being just as uncooperative in listening to government directives.[60]

In both cases, the German diplomatic staff urged the State Department to apply the pressure in the United States. Dean Rusk convinced CBS News general manager Blair Clark to call Schorr directly to cancel the CBS tunnel project, possibly in part because of Clark's long friendship with President Kennedy. NBC News president William McAndrew traveled to Washington to meet with Rusk concerning the NBC tunnel project. When the criticism escalated, Kintner, the person in charge of the entire NBC television and radio operation, took over and worked behind the scenes, even sending a top network attorney to Berlin, to get approval for the project from both the West German government and Secretary of State Rusk.

Even though Clark, McAndrew, and Kintner all had journalism backgrounds, in their roles as managers for American television networks they were more attuned than journalists to the pressures involved in broadcast regulation. In the case of NBC, parent company RCA had important defense contracts that had to be taken into consideration.

The mixed signals from the government also put network executives in a contradictory position. The tunnel escape projects happened in the year after FCC chairman Newton Minow's famous "vast wasteland" television speech, during a period when Congress seemed interested in heavier regulation of broadcasters to encourage more news and public affairs programming. The networks had responded by beefing up their news programming to avoid more regulation. The scheduling of *The Tunnel* in a coveted primetime slot is partly in response to government pressure, but the government had issues with the topic chosen and methods employed.

Another important aspect in the networks' attempts to gain government approval is public opinion. During this period of the Cold War, the American public considered communism to be a real threat and generally supported the government efforts to fight communism, both at home and around the world. The networks did not want to appear to be complicating the government's efforts to control the strength of the Soviet Union.[61]

The negotiations between the State Department and network television also highlight the unseemly pressure of journalism competition and the government's understanding of that aspect of managing the news. When NBC's involvement in the successful tunnel escape became public, CBS management felt the network had been hurt competitively by complying with the government's request to cancel its tunnel project. Robert Manning at the State Department felt obligated to publicly thank CBS and criticize NBC, even though the tunnel projects were vastly different. The unexpected ratcheting up of a criticism of the NBC project ("risky, irresponsible, undesirable, and not in the best interests of the United States") may have been a case of rewarding CBS for compliance, or it may have been the result of Dean Rusk suddenly dealing with the very real pressures of the Cuban Missile Crisis. The behind-the-scenes communication includes both NBC and CBS disparaging the other network's tunnel projects, hinting at ethical lapses and bad decision making in veiled attempts to gain an upper hand with government officials.[62]

The fact that the CBS tunnel was discovered by the East Germans, and that people were arrested and put on trial, was never disclosed in the United States during the controversy. Even in his autobiography almost four decades later, Schorr does not mention what happened to his tunnel but paints the incident as an example of his network caving to government pressure: "Our rivals had been less squeamish than CBS about the State Department concerns."[63]

One of the criticisms that runs throughout the negotiations over the tunnel projects is the idea of providing propaganda for the communists, which is a very serious charge for an American business in an era when the public generally supported government efforts to promote democracy around the world. The US mission staff in Berlin attempted to scare Schorr with threats that CBS would be implicated in the compromised tunnel in public trials in East Berlin. In reality, the trials did receive heavy press attention, but CBS was not directly mentioned, mainly because Schorr had been ordered out of the city under government pressure.

In the case of NBC's payment for filming rights of the successful tunnel, the East German and Russian press did use the opportunity to connect the US television network to government policy. The coverage emphasized the financial payments as evidence of the greed inherent in capitalism. The GDR press also highlighted the business side of NBC, and its parent company RCA, focusing on the members of the board of directors who had strong ties to the military establishment. While the NBC project provided a new example, the communist press mostly relied on its existing views on the convergence of American media, government, and the military. While US journalists would rarely acknowledge the importance of their company's board of directors, Robert Kintner's private letter to Rusk, and his request for a private letter in response for the Board of Directors, indicates a stronger than acknowledged role for the top levels of media ownership.

West German television network ARD ran an edited version of *The Tunnel* on June 11, 1963, under the name *Ein Tunnel*. A review published in *Der Spiegel* was critical of German producers who had replaced the original NBC "sober description" of the tunnel digging process with "false emotionalism" in the German narration.[64] Searches of GDR newspapers did not turn up any mention of that broadcast east of the wall. Two weeks after *Ein Tunnel* ran on West German television, President Kennedy came to Berlin to give a speech in which he ad-libbed the phrase that forever connected him to the divided city: "Ich bin ein Berliner," roughly translated as "I am a Berliner."[65]

In a final vindication for Reuven Frank and NBC, one of the most prominent examples of *The Tunnel* as a propaganda tool did not happen on the communist side of the wall. Instead, it was the US Information Agency, the public diplomacy division of the US government, which bought a hundred copies of *The Tunnel* to show around the world as an example of the benefits of freedom over communism.[66]

Epilogue

ONCE AGAIN, REUVEN Frank wanted out of daily news production. He had marshaled the *Huntley-Brinkley Report* through its transition to thirty minutes in 1963 and also continued his role as producer of political convention and election night coverage during the 1964 presidential campaign. The *Huntley-Brinkley Report* won its sixth Emmy Award in a row as best network television newscast. Frank's convention coverage productions with Chet Huntley and David Brinkley brought in such large audiences that CBS made the dramatic move of replacing Walter Cronkite with Robert Trout and Roger Mudd between the Republican and Democratic conventions.[1]

Frank toyed with an offer from the *Saturday Evening Post* to take over as its editor until NBC agreed in a four-year contract to let him focus on longer-form productions. One of his first documentaries under the new agreement, *The Big Ear,* concentrated on FBI director J. Edgar Hoover's secret program to eavesdrop on American citizens, including putting a recording device in the former first lady Eleanor Roosevelt's hotel room.[2]

While he enjoyed the hour-long programs, the networks were cutting back on documentaries. Frank felt NBC needed a program that could handle stories that were not worth a full hour but were too long for the nightly newscast. In a 1965 interview with the *New York Times,* Frank envisioned a "flexible, weekly hour show with three news correspondents," in which a topic could take up the whole hour or the time could be split among the reporters.[3]

Frank's magazine format idea would have to wait. Once again, NBC pulled him away from long-form productions. In 1966, NBC News president William McAndrew asked Frank to join news management after the network fired Robert Kintner as its president. Two years later, McAndrew died unexpectedly. NBC picked Frank for the top position at NBC News.

NBC News President

Reuven Frank's five years as president of NBC News, 1968–1973, coincided with some of the most tumultuous times in the United States in the twentieth century. Frank ran the network news division during the anger and rioting caused by the stalling of civil rights advancements, the growing disenchantment with the Vietnam War, and a heightening distrust in government and media. Conservatives and others who supported the Vietnam War, as well as those who were against forced busing to integrate schools, felt newspapers and television journalists were promoting a liberal viewpoint. The networks came under attack, both literally and figuratively, at the 1968 Democratic Convention when Mayor Richard J. Daley had his police department beat up Vietnam War protestors on the streets of Chicago while security inside the convention roughed up delegates and reporters.

When Richard Nixon became president in 1969, he tapped into the idea of journalism's liberal bias by tasking Vice President Spiro Agnew with the job of telling the American people that network news did not reflect the views of the majority of Americans. In November 1969, Agnew gave a speech in Des Moines, Iowa, covered live by all three networks, in which he said it was time to start questioning the motives of a small group of men in the "intellectual confines" of Washington and New York City. At that time, forty million Americans watched the network evening newscasts. Agnew wondered why the country should trust the news chosen by "a handful of men responsible only to their corporate employers and is filtered through a handful of commentators who admit to their own set of biases."[4]

The nightly newscast on the three main networks became such an important and popular source of news for Americans that the process of covering and presenting the news came under increased scrutiny. Scholars, many of whom had shunned the medium until the Kennedy assassination in 1963 made it impossible to ignore, also started questioning what ended up on the newscast and in what form. The "high modern" era of objectivity in which the journalists considered themselves uniquely qualified to decide what is news, as a mirror on society, seemed outdated. Researchers began studying what other factors determined what Americans would see on the screen each night.[5]

For Frank, the short honeymoon that the public had shown toward network news in the 1950s and early 1960s ended in the late 1960s, when critics from all sides questioned motives and editorial decisions. Politicians accused the networks of stirring up war hysteria or turning the public against the Vietnam War. Frank said in hindsight that network news officials complained too much about the criticism: "They missed the point; the public rarely likes news or its mongers. It is the years when they are popular that are the exception."[6]

The late 1960s also signaled the end of the *Huntley-Brinkley Report*'s run as the most popular nightly newscast. The *CBS Evening News with Walter Cronkite* had caught up in the ratings and began to beat the NBC newscast. CBS supporters chalked it up to Cronkite's stronger journalism background and his ability to spend hours on the air live, especially covering the NASA rocket launches. One theory is that a 1967 union strike showed viewers that the two NBC newscasters might not be as close as once thought. Both Cronkite and Brinkley honored the strike and stayed home, but Huntley broke the picket line and said that he never felt comfortable in the union. Frank also blames himself for his decision to send only reporters to Vietnam who wanted to cover the war. Several of NBC's best-known correspondents chose not to go, while CBS featured both veteran and up-and-coming correspondents covering the conflict over the years.

Huntley retired in 1970, and NBC News spent the next decade trying both dual and single-anchor formats, with David Brinkley and John Chancellor, under the new title of *NBC Nightly News*. The *CBS Evening News with Walter Cronkite* was the top-rated network newscast throughout the 1970s.[7]

60 Minutes and *First Tuesday*

As NBC News president, Reuven Frank did not have the power of his predecessor in scheduling news and public affairs programming in prime time. After NBC fired Robert Kintner, his successors were less inclined to cancel entertainment programming for news. Frank's push for a magazine-style news program was ignored until 1968, when NBC entertainment programmers had a two-hour hole to fill once a month in a weekly movie timeslot. Frank took his idea and the monthly opportunity and created *First Tuesday*.

Over at CBS, Don Hewitt had a similar idea for a magazine program. Fred Friendly had removed him as director of the *CBS Evening News* in 1965, and

Hewitt had been looking for new opportunities at the network. His idea was to combine hard news with softer features in an hour-long program. After years of pitching this idea, Hewitt convinced both Mike Wallace and Harry Reasoner to help him with a pilot he could show to the network. Neither man thought it would ever get on the air. Reluctantly, CBS let Hewitt go forward with his program. *60 Minutes* debuted in September 1968, running twice a month for an hour on Tuesday nights. Over at NBC, *First Tuesday* debuted in January 1969, running monthly for two hours.

At first, *First Tuesday* brought in a larger audience than *60 Minutes*. Then NBC started moving around the program on the schedule and reducing the length. Moved to Friday nights, the title was changed to *Chronolog*. Eventually the program regained its original name when moved back to Tuesdays, but now only running one hour a month. Meanwhile, CBS changed *60 Minutes'* schedule a few times in the early years, then settled on the Sunday 7:00 p.m. weekly timeslot, after NFL football games. *60 Minutes* went on to become the most popular news program in the history of American television.[8]

First Tuesday eventually died a quiet death, as Frank put it, "strangled in its crib." Even though the two programs covered similar issues and had roughly the same format, Frank insisted they took decidedly different approaches. He considered *60 Minutes* as "star journalism," putting the emphasis on Mike Wallace and the others. For *First Tuesday*, Frank used his ideas from the "transmission of experience" memo, emphasizing "picture reporting with a heavy emphasis on style and writing."[9]

Weekend

By 1973, Frank had enough of management and stepped down to once again produce documentaries and other news programs. Ironically, NBC turned to Frank when the affiliated stations asked for a program like *60 Minutes*. The only timeslot available in the fall of 1974 was ninety minutes once a month on Saturday nights after the late news, replacing reruns of the *Tonight Show*. Frank's venture was called *Weekend* with correspondent Lloyd Dobyns. Because of the late-night broadcast, Frank and his crew were able to cover the stories they wanted, produced in the way they wanted, with limited oversight. Frank made sure the pictures and sounds would be edited first, and only then would Dobyns and the correspondents write a script to complement the pictures. In its first year on the air, *Weekend* won a Peabody Award. The judges chose the program for both the stories presented and "how the language can be employed with grace and precision."[10]

Weekend also attracted more viewers in that monthly late-night period than NBC expected, which proved to be the show's undoing. The next year, NBC decided to try an experimental live comedy show the other three weeks of the month at 11:30 p.m. The program, eventually known as *Saturday Night Live*, became so popular, viewers began complaining about the news program that preempted it once a month. In a reversal from previous decades, newspaper television writers liked what Frank was doing with *Weekend*, giving the program needed publicity. Frank even made it a point to travel to different cities and meet with television critics so they would write about *Weekend*.[11]

The 1970s were years of turmoil for NBC. Both entertainment and news programming fell into third place. ABC had finally emerged as a true competitor and dominated network entertainment programming. NBC programmers had little good news to report, so the small weekend monthly news program became a rare sign of success, especially because of the positive newspaper coverage.

NBC asked Frank to move *Weekend* into a weekly primetime spot. He was skeptical because he was not sure the understated, quirky program that downplayed the correspondents and focused on the stories would fit in with a primetime entertainment lineup. Frank also knew his program would be under more management scrutiny. He said he would only take *Weekend* to primetime if management promised the program would be given time to find an audience, just as CBS had done with *60 Minutes*. NBC agreed. Frank hired more producers and added Linda Ellerbee to co-host the program with Lloyd Dobyns when it moved to the Sunday 10:00 p.m. timeslot.

As Frank suspected, the NBC management soon had ideas on how to make *Weekend* more popular. They asked him to replace Lloyd Dobyns with a flashy, up-and-coming interviewer named Tom Snyder. Frank said no. Eight months later, NBC canceled *Weekend*. Meanwhile, *60 Minutes*, still in its 7:00 p.m. Sunday timeslot, became the first news program in American television history to top the Nielsen ratings, during the 1979–1980 season.[12]

Frank settled back into producing documentaries for NBC. He worked with his small team and stayed far away from management issues. As one television critic put it, "He had been largely forgotten, a ghostly presence, a half-remembered vision of past grandeur." When the president of the National Press Photographers Association, Larry Hatteberg, himself a well-respected television storyteller, invited Frank to the annual NPPA conference, he politely declined. "My message is usually the same and it has begun to sink in that very few are listening," wrote Frank. "It is time for someone else to preach the text."[13]

One More Time

In 1982, NBC pulled Frank away from his editing room for the final time. Ratings and morale at NBC News had fallen so dramatically that management decided the guy who had been around for more than three decades might be able to get the staff back to previous glory. Sixty-year-old Reuven Frank reluctantly started his second stint as NBC News president. Network television news had experienced dramatic changes in the decade since he last ran the news division. Much of his time was spent in wooing, hiring, and placating the highly paid news anchors who were now considered the main factor in ratings success or failure. The network evening newscasts had been eclipsed in importance by the morning news programs and the local stations owned by the network.

Frank did facilitate one short-lived news program that had a cult following among television journalists. Cable News Network (CNN) was launched in 1980 and the broadcast networks were under pressure from affiliates to offer more news. In 1982, Frank once again paired up Linda Ellerbee and Lloyd Dobyns for an hour-long program that started at 1:30 a.m., *NBC News Overnight*. With a minuscule budget and a small audience, *NBC News Overnight* became known for its great writing, inventive approach to the news, and the complete rejection of the growing culture of the self-important news anchor.[14]

Restoring morale to the NBC News staff was one matter. Placating angry NBC affiliated stations because of low ratings was a bigger challenge. They were not shy in asking why a guy who started his television career in the 1950s was tasked with reviving and updating the look of NBC News. Frank quietly let his bosses know that he was not interested in extending his contract as president. *NBC News Overnight* was canceled at the end of 1983 and by March 1984, he was once again producing news programs, in this case, the 1984 political convention coverage. Two years later, NBC management tried to quietly fire Frank, but the reaction in the trade press forced the network to keep him on to do a few more documentaries.[15]

Reuven Frank left NBC News in 1988, more than a quarter-century after *The Tunnel* broadcast and close to four decades after joining the network. The year after he left, the Berlin Wall came down.

Reuven Frank's Impact

In August 2003, I interviewed both Reuven Frank and Don Hewitt. Frank was long retired, living with his wife, Bernice, in New Jersey. Hewitt was still firmly in charge of *60 Minutes* at age eighty, although he would be forced to retire the next year.

Two of the most important men in American television news history, who filled many of the same roles over the decades at their respective networks, still strongly disagreed on the most effective use of television for covering the news. Hewitt insisted the script and interviews were most important. When a reporter and producer had a *60 Minutes* story for Hewitt to review and approve, he purposely turned his back to the screen so he could only hear the story. "I realized a long time ago," said Hewitt, sitting in his corner office at *60 Minutes* on West 57th street in Manhattan, "that it's your ear much more than your eye that keeps you to a television set. It's what you hear."[16]

Frank, fifteen miles away in Tenafly, New Jersey, believed the emphasis should be on the stories, not on the reporters or news anchors. Strong visuals are one part of television news, and the viewers needed to watch the news to get the full impact. He said his approach was more than just focusing on the visuals, however. "It's a storytelling medium. It's a beginning, middle, and end, medium," said Frank. "Aristotle laid down the rules twenty-five hundred years ago. How do you tell a story?"[17]

At eighty-two years of age, Frank insisted television was at its best when the emphasis on the images and sounds transports the viewer to the scene, to "experience" the story. While news managers had wholeheartedly embraced the outsized role of the news anchor and reporter over the decades, Frank considered that approach lazy and short-sighted. He did have a rare moment of doubt after his retirement when he compared the fortunes of his news magazine ventures to *60 Minutes:* "History has shown that Hewitt was right and I was wrong."[18]

As a journalist, Reuven Frank felt he had to acknowledge the success of his long-time rival Don Hewitt's program, *60 Minutes*. The comparison of their magazine programs' fortunes as a referendum on the most effective use of television for news and public affairs is far too simple and plays into the common tropes surrounding the format.

On a specific level, if NBC had shown the patience with either *First Tuesday* or *Weekend* that CBS did with *60 Minutes*, those programs might have shown similar growth, much as Frank's *Huntley-Brinkley Report* weathered some rough early years in the 1950s before the large audience found the program.

The different approaches to news magazine programs in the 1970s and 1980s do not define the importance of Frank's vision for television news. The "transmission of experience" model found its outlet in large and small ways, in both network and local television news. The NPPA News Video Workshop in Oklahoma is still a yearly chance for photographers, editors, and reporters to share ideas, challenge each other, and then take their ideas back to their respective newsrooms.

One of the most passionate advocates of Reuven Frank's ideas and the use of television as a storytelling medium is former NBC correspondent Bob Dotson. Dotson spent more than thirty years at NBC, overlapping with Reuven Frank for more than a decade, and later became known for his "American Story" features on the *Today Show*. Dotson is often a featured speaker at the NPPA News Video Workshop and travels the country promoting the storytelling approach to television news.

Dotson learned documentary film techniques in a graduate program at Syracuse University and then put those skills to use at one of the top visual local news departments in the country in the 1970s, WKY in Oklahoma City. NBC hired Dotson after one of his WKY documentaries won national awards.[19]

At NBC, Reuven Frank gave Dotson a chance to try the type of stories he was producing for *Weekend*. Just as he advocated in the "transmission of experience" memo and in *The Tunnel*, Frank wanted the film and interviews edited first, then Dotson would write the words needed to enhance the images. Dotson had already used the pictures-first method. He connected with Frank's idea of making the news understandable and relatable and carried it through his career. "The more you can humanize a story or a concept and bring it in to everybody's backyard the better they're going to understand, the better they're going to experience it, the better they're going to actually learn," said Dotson. "Isn't that the definition of news?"[20]

Dotson also said Frank had more respect for news photographers and editors than most news managers and tried to hire photographers and editors who had won NPPA awards at local stations around the country.

The emphasis on the visuals and story structure were just a few of Frank's legacies. Robert MacNeil, who worked at NBC News during the early 1960s, described the journalistic style of the *Huntley-Brinkley Report* as "a little irreverence, a distaste for overearnestness," while at the same time "never underestimating or undervaluing the true gravity of the events." MacNeil said during his later years, at PBS, the *MacNeil/Lehrer NewsHour* specifically hired a former *Huntley-Brinkley Report* producer to re-create the "editorial atmosphere" created by Frank at NBC.[21]

The Absence of Television News in Academic Scholarship

Much as the events earlier in the twentieth century influenced how the different groups responded to *The Tunnel* in 1962, disruptions in media and journalism in the twenty-first century should be a time for media professionals and scholars to look back for guidance. The subsequent introduction of cable, satellite, the internet, blogs, mobile, social media, and other offshoots of the transition to digital communication find journalists constantly on the defensive about their expertise, invoking boundary work tactics of extolling their own practices and criticizing other efforts.

Unfortunately, the dismissive attitude directed at *The Tunnel* specifically, and television news in general, has continued over the decades, especially among media scholars, leaving us with a dearth of meaningful scholarship to help us better understand the current media transition. In a review of thirty years of scholarship in the two top American journalism history journals, television news accounts for less than 10 percent of the articles, during a span when the format was the most popular in the United States. The numbers were even lower for *Journalism & Mass Communication Quarterly* in the 1990s, a period when that publication was considered the leading American mass communication journal and usually focused on current media. The problems of television did become more important in the social sciences during periods when the US government and foundations funded research into potential effects of television violence on viewers.[22]

The absence of serious scholarship and the very real problem of nonexistent or inaccessible historic broadcasts has allowed personal accounts and reminisces to fill the void as television and television news history, oftentimes buttressed by dismissive print media critics accounts from the period under investigation. Since a key component of boundary work involves invoking historic events or people as icons or cautionary tales, the lack of dispassionate research has allowed boundary work to serve as accepted history.

Since television news has been the most popular medium for journalism for more than half a century, shouldn't we want to know more about its appeal and approach? Shouldn't we be able to rely on serious research instead of personal reminisces and anecdotes that often, consciously or unconsciously, invoke boundary work notions of acceptable journalistic practices?

Reuven Frank's multiple approaches to journalism and nonfiction communication over his career (newspapers, television newscasts, magazine programs, documentaries, political convention and election night coverage) also reveal a shortcoming in the silo approach to academic scholarship. Focusing on just print journalism, film documentaries, television news, or television documentaries misses the true work environment and influences, since many media professionals, including Frank, worked across platforms often at the same time. What he learned on a documentary influenced how he approached the nightly newscast.

The Tunnel and the "Transmission of Experience" Memo during a Critical Juncture in Journalism History

The early 1960s witnessed a critical juncture in American journalism and media history. As television emerged as the most popular mass medium, television news topped newspapers, magazines, and radio as the preeminent format for Americans to learn about their communities, the nation, and the rest of the world. As this shift in how Americans kept up with events and issues was taking place, the United States and the Soviet Union entered one of the most dangerous periods of the Cold War.

In the midst of the geopolitical tensions and the upheaval in the media landscape, NBC's Reuven Frank was producing both the most popular journalism platform in the country, the nightly *Huntley-Brinkley Report* as well as the internationally controversial documentary *The Tunnel* about a dramatic escape under the Berlin Wall. Frank's experiences on both *The Tunnel* and a dozen years in television news provided him the insight and confidence to write the influential "transmission of experience," or "bible," memo on the strengths, and weaknesses, of television news as a journalistic platform. The production and reception of *The Tunnel* and Frank's views on television news, as well as the obvious connections between the documentary and nightly newscast formats, provide insights, details, and context to help understand this critical juncture in media history.

While nine out of ten homes in the United States already had televisions by the early 1960s, the concept of television news as an important part of our society was still new and contested among print journalists, scholars, government officials, and the elite. Analyzing the differing approaches to television news, including documentaries, and reactions to those efforts allows us, as media historian Lisa Gitelman puts it, to view "the contested relations of force that determine the pathways by which new media may eventually become old hat."[23]

The growing popularity and power of television news in this period also sparked very specific examples of boundary work; as journalists, documentarians, government officials, and other groups attempted to define what role the new medium was allowed to serve through their reactions to *The Tunnel* and television news in general. Each group wanted to protect its professional identity and push back against any encroachment by the new communication platform.

The production of *The Tunnel* and the *Huntley-Brinkley Report* reveals how one television news leader used the power and unique characteristics of the medium while the reception reveals the contested ground, with differing opinions on the proper role and use of television news and documentaries. The controversy surrounding and the polarized reactions to *The Tunnel* at the time of its initial broadcast and in subsequent scholarship appears contradictory, mainly because the program is usually examined in a single context: as a Cold War broadcast, as a documentary film, or as a journalistic piece. With Frank's experience in both print and television journalism, as well as daily news and documentary film work, coupled with his enlightened views on television's unique capability in presenting issues, *The Tunnel* broadcast and the "transmission of experience" memo are best understood as key insights into the emergence of television news as the United States' most popular format for journalism from the 1960s well into the twenty-first century.

Postscript

Reuven Frank died on February 5, 2006, just under nine months shy of the fiftieth anniversary of the launch of the *Huntley-Brinkley Report* and forty-three years after *The Tunnel* broadcast.[24]

NBC decided to honor the half-century anniversary of the *Huntley-Brinkley Report* in memory of the three men most responsible for its success. Chet Huntley had died in 1974 and David Brinkley in 2003. The network held the celebration in Rockefeller Center's legendary NBC Studio 8H, originally built for Arturo Toscanini's NBC Symphony Orchestra. Studio 8H has been best known during the television era as home for *Saturday Night Live*. The guest list included NBC News people from the past and present, with an emphasis on those who worked on the *Huntley-Brinkley Report*. The crowd included family and friends of Frank, Huntley, and Brinkley, members of the NBC Page program, and even Columbia University sociologist Herbert Gans, who wrote one of the first serious looks at the process of producing the evening newscast, *Deciding What's News*.

The event was filled with laudatory speeches about Huntley, Brinkley, and Frank and stories of behind-the-scenes events over the decades. Finally, Tom Brokaw stepped to the microphone. Brokaw had served as the host of the *Today Show* in the 1970s and moved to *NBC Nightly News* in 1982. Reuven Frank had chosen Brokaw to be the sole anchor of the newscast, a position Brokaw held for twenty-two years, six years longer than the run of the *Huntley-Brinkley Report*. The NBC nightly newscast during Brokaw's era returned to the top of the ratings, where it stayed through the transition in 2004 to the next anchor, Brian Williams.

After talking about the importance of the *Huntley-Brinkley Report* and the three men, Brokaw pulled out a well-worn document and held it out in his hand. Brokaw told the crowd he had come across a copy of the Reuven Frank "transmission of experience" memo when he was beginning his television career in Omaha, Nebraska, well before he ever joined NBC News. Brokaw said Frank's words on those pages had been a guiding force throughout his entire career. "I remember receiving this and thinking, my God, it is the lodestone," said Brokaw. "It will show me the way. And it has."[25]

Notes

ABBREVIATIONS
ARCHIVES

CCOH   Columbia Center for Oral History, Columbia University, New York City

ERM-T   Edward R. Murrow Papers, Tufts University Digital Collections and Archives, Medford, MA

FF-C   Fred Friendly Papers, 1917–2004, Rare Book and Manuscript Library, Columbia University Library, New York City

FSP-DS   Records of the Foreign Service Posts of the Department of State, 1788—ca. 1991, Record Group 84, National Archives at College Park

MMC   Mass Media & Culture Archive, University of Maryland, College Park

NBC-WHS   National Broadcasting Company Archives, Wisconsin Historical Society, Madison

P-MMC   Pamphlets, Mass Media and Culture Archives, University of Maryland, College Park

RB-MMC   Rudy Bretz Papers, Mass Media and Culture Archive, University of Maryland, College Park

RFT   Reuven Frank Papers, 1940–2008, Tufts University Digital Collections and Archives, Medford, MA

RMA   Robert Manning Papers 1938–1993, Houghton Library, Harvard University, Cambridge, MA

SM-CAH   Sig Mickelson Papers 1930–2005, Briscoe Center for American History, University of Texas at Austin

ORAL HISTORY INTERVIEWS

BD-OH   Bob Dotson, interview with author, October 7, 2013, Bloomington, IN, videotape recording

CB-OH2   Chester Burger, interview by author, August 11, 2003, New York City, videotape recording, Briscoe Center for American History, University of Texas at Austin

DH-OH2   Don Hewitt, interview with author, August 13, 2003, New York City, videotape recording, Briscoe Center for American History, University of Texas at Austin

LR-OH2   Larry Racies, interview with author, August 12, 2003, New York City, videotape recording, Briscoe Center for American History, University of Texas at Austin

RB-OH2   Robert Bendick, interview by author, August 18, 2003, Guilford, CT, videotape recording, Briscoe Center for American History, University of Texas at Austin

RF-OH1   Reuven Frank, interview by author, June 18, 2003, audiotape recording of telephone conversation

RF-OH2   Reuven Frank, interview by author, August 14, 2003, Tenafly, NJ, videotape recording, Briscoe Center for American History, University of Texas at Austin

WC-OH   Walter Cronkite, interview by author, November 11, 2005, New York City, videotape recording

INTRODUCTION

1. The Roper Organization, *Public Perceptions of Television and Other Mass Media: A Twenty-Year Review 1959–1978* (New York: Television Information Office, 1979).
2. Giovanni Capoccia and R. Daniel Keleman, "The Study of Critical Junctures: Theory, Narrative, and Counterfactuals in Historical Institutionalism," *World Politics* 59 (April 2007): 341; James Mahoney, "Path Dependent Explanations of Regime Change: Central America in Comparative Perspective," *Studies in Comparative International Development* 36, no. 1 (Spring 2001): 111–41; John Hogan, "Remoulding the Critical Junctures Approach," *Canadian Journal of Political Science* 39, no. 3 (September 2006): 657–79.
3. Thomas Doherty, *Cold War, Cool Medium: Television, McCarthyism, and American Culture* (New York: Columbia University Press, 2003), 18.
4. George H. Gallup, *The Gallup Poll: Public Opinion 1935–1971*, vol. 3, 1959–1971 (New York: Random House, 1972), 1741.
5. Thomas F. Gieryn, "Boundary-Work and the Demarcation of Science from Non-Science Strains and Interests in Professional Ideologies of Scientists," *American Sociological Review* 48, no. 6 (December 1983): 781–95; Thomas F. Gieryn,

NOTES TO PAGES 7–22   237

George M. Bevins, and Stephen C. Zehr, "Professionalization of American Scientists: Public Science in the Creation/Evolution Trials," *American Sociological Review* 50, no. 3 (June 1985): 392–409.
6. Gieryn, "Boundary-Work," 791.
7. Jane B. Singer, "Out of Bounds: Professional Norms as Boundary Markers," in *Boundaries in Journalism: Professionalism, Practices, and Participation*, ed. Matt Carlson and Seth C. Lewis (New York: Routledge, 2015), 23.
8. Paul N. Edwards, Lisa Gitelman, Gabrielle Hecht, Adrian Johns, Brian Larkin, and Neil Safier, "AHR Conversation: Historical Perspectives on the Circulation of Information," *American Historical Review* 116, no. 5 (December 2011): 1396; Mike Conway, "The Ghost of Television News in Media History Scholarship," *American Journalism* 34, no. 2 (2017): 229–39.

CHAPTER ONE: CAPTURED ON FILM

1. John P. Shanley, "Reuven Frank—Roving Producer," *New York Times*, March 12, 1961, X19.
2. John Bainbridge, "Die Mauer: The Early Days of the Berlin Wall," *New Yorker*, October 27, 1962, https://www.newyorker.com/magazine/1962/10/27/die-mauer (accessed March 6, 2019).
3. Reuven Frank, *Out of Thin Air: The Brief Wonderful Life of Network News* (New York: Simon and Schuster, 1991).
4. Reuven Frank, "The Making of *The Tunnel*," *Television Quarterly* 2 (Fall 1963): 9.
5. Frederick Taylor, *The Berlin Wall: 13 August 1961–9 November 1989* (London: Bloomsbury, 2006), 103.
6. Chris Tudda, *Cold War Summits: A History, From Potsdam to Malta* (London: Bloomsbury, 2015).
7. Taylor, *The Berlin Wall*.
8. George H. Gallup, *The Gallup Poll: Public Opinion 1935–1971*, vol. 2, 1949–1958 (New York: Random House, 1972), 1534; Lawrence Freedman, *Kennedy's Wars: Berlin, Cuba, Laos, and Vietnam* (New York: Oxford University Press, 2000), 47; David Halberstam, *The Fifties* (New York: Villard Books, 1993).
9. Aleksandr Fursenko and Timothy Naftali, *"One Hell of a Gamble": Khrushchev, Castro, and Kennedy, 1958–1962* (New York: W. W. Norton, 1997); Vladislav M. Zubok, "Khrushchev and the Berlin Crisis, 1958–1962" (Working Paper no. 6, Cold War International History Project, Woodrow Wilson International Center for Scholars, Washington, DC, 1993).
10. "Section B: The Destruction of the City," *Berlin Wall Memorial Orientation Map* (Berlin: Berlin Wall Foundation).
11. Edward R. Murrow to Don Wilson, "DOS Discusses Need for Providing People of Berlin with the Reassurance of U.S. Support in Light of Ulbricht Closing the Borders," Department of State, August 16, 1961, *U.S. Declassified Documents Online*, http://tinyurl.galegroup.com/tinyurl/65J705 (accessed March 6, 2019).
12. Taylor, *The Berlin Wall*.
13. Daniel Schorr, *Staying Tuned: A Life in Journalism* (New York: Pocket Books, 2001); Frank, *Out of Thin Air*.

14. W. R. Smyser, *Kennedy and the Berlin Wall: "A Hell of a Lot Better than a War"* (Lanham, MD: Rowman & Littlefield, 2009).
15. Fursenko and Naftali, *"One Hell of a Gamble"*; Smyzer, *Kennedy and the Berlin Wall*; Zubok, "Khrushchev and the Berlin Crisis."
16. Taylor, *The Berlin Wall*.
17. Frank, *Out of Thin Air*; Frank, "The Making of *The Tunnel*."
18. "Berlin Reds Shut Escapers' Tunnel," *New York Times*, January 26, 1962, 6; "Berlin Reds Tell of New Tunnel," *New York Times*, February 2, 1962, 1; "2 Groups Escape From East Berlin," *New York Times*, June 13, 1962, 1; "Red Guard Killed At Berlin's Wall," *New York Times*, June 19, 1962, 1; "Rusk Says Wall Dividing Berlin Will Come Down," *New York Times*, June 22, 1962, 1.
19. *Escape from East Berlin*, DVD, directed by Robert Siodmak (1962, Burbank, CA: Warner Home Video, 2015); "Escape from East Berlin," Film Review, *Variety*, October 24, 1962, 6.
20. *The Tunnel* script, File 00014: manuscripts, correspondence, journals and clippings, 1940s–1960s, Box 13107551 (RFT); Ellen Sesta, *Der Tunnel in die Freiheit: Berlin, Bernauer Straße*, 2nd ed. (Berlin: Ullstein, 2001); Frank, "The Making of *The Tunnel*."
21. Sesta, *Der Tunnel in die Freiheit*.
22. Robert Kintner to Dean Rusk, November 20, 1962, Correspondence 1962, NBC documentary film "The Tunnel" (RMA); Frank, *Out of Thin Air*.
23. Kintner to Rusk; Frank, "The Making of *The Tunnel*."
24. Taylor, *The Berlin Wall*.
25. "Red Guard Killed at Berlin's Wall"; Taylor, *The Berlin Wall*.
26. *The Tunnel* script.
27. "Rusk Says Wall Dividing Berlin Will Come Down," 1; Frank, *Out of Thin Air*.
28. Ralph A. Brown "For the Record" memo, August 3, 1962, Hulick to Hillenbrand, n.d., Gerald Sabatino, "Possible Refugee Influx," August 7, 1962; all from Eyes Only Telegrams 1963 + S/S—L.D., box 36 (FSP-DS); Schorr, *Staying Tuned*.
29. "Compromised Escape Tunnel," memorandum, August 8, 1962 (FSP-DS).
30. Taylor, *The Berlin Wall*.
31. Taylor, *The Berlin Wall*, 320; Fursenko and Naftali, *"One Hell of a Gamble"*; Freedman, *Kennedy's Wars*.
32. The total number of people who came through the tunnel is still debated. At the time, it was believed thirty people escaped on Sunday in the flooded tunnel, for a total of fifty-nine. Anderton even uses this number in *The Tunnel*. Reuven Frank later wondered if US intelligence agencies used the tunnel to secretly get their people out. Another explanation is West German escape groups used the inflated number to draw attention away from other escape methods. Frank, *Out of Thin Air*; Greg Mitchell, *The Tunnels: Escapes under the Berlin Wall and the Historic Films the JFK White House Tried to Kill* (New York: Crown, 2016); Frank, "The Making of *The Tunnel*."
33. "29 East Berliners Flee Through 400-Foot Tunnel," *New York Times*, September 19, 1962, 2.

34. Harry Castleman and Walter J. Podrazik, *The TV Schedule Book: Four Decades of Network Programming from Sign-On to Sign-Off* (New York: McGraw-Hill, 1984); Frank, "The Making of *The Tunnel*."
35. "Tunnels, Inc.," *Time*, October 5, 1962, 47; Val Adams, "TV Film Records Refugees' Flight," *New York Times*, October 5, 1962, 49.
36. "Tunnelers Fight Berlin TV Show," *New York Times*, October 14, 1962, 10.
37. "West Berlin 'Regrets' TV Escape Film," *Washington Post*, October 17, 1962, 14.
38. Richard K. Doan, "Berlin Tunnel Film is Opposed," *New York Herald Tribune*, October 17, 1962, 25; "Berlin Tunnel Film Irks East Germans," *New York Times*, October 21, 1962, 20.
39. "State Brands NBC 'Irresponsible,'" *Washington Post*, October 20, 1962, 13; "U.S. Criticizes NBC Filming of Berlin Tunnel," *Chicago Tribune*, October 20, 1962, 8; "U.S. Criticizes N.B.C. on Film in Berlin," *New York Times*, October 20, 1962, 2.
40. Richard K. Doan, "Now CBS Will Air Berlin Escapes," *New York Herald Tribune*, October 16, 1962, 23; Richard K. Doan, "Tunnel Documentary Shelves," *New York Herald Tribune*, October 24, 1962, 23.
41. Jack Gould, "TV: N.B.C. and Berlin Wall Tunnel," *New York Times*, October 22, 1962, 46.
42. Kintner to Rusk (RMA); Frank, *Out of Thin Air*; Richard K. Doan, "The Berlin Tunnel," *New York Herald Tribune*, October 23, 1962, 21.
43. Elie Abel, *The Missile Crisis* (Philadelphia: J. B. Lippincott, 1966), 121.
44. Richard F. Shepard, "N.B.C. Postpones Tunnel Telecast," *New York Times*, October 24, 1962, 62.
45. Robert A. Caro, *The Passage of Power: The Years of Lyndon Johnson* (New York: Knopf, 2012), 212.
46. The agreement also included the provision that the United States would remove missiles in Turkey, but Kennedy convinced Khrushchev to keep that out of the formal exchange and committed to having the missiles removed at a later date so their removal would not look like part of the Cuban missile deal.
47. Fursenko and Naftali, *"One Hell of a Gamble,"* 285.
48. Frank, "The Making of *The Tunnel*"; Frank, *Out of Thin Air*.
49. "The New Nielsens: Top 15," *Variety*, January 16, 1963, 25.
50. Castleman and Podrazik, *The TV Schedule Book*, 133.
51. "The New Nielsens," *Variety*; "TV Ratings, 1962," *ClassicTVHits.com*, http://www.classictvhits.com (accessed March 6, 2019).
52. "Awards Search," *Television Academy*, https://www.emmys.com (accessed March 6, 2019).
53. Doan, "Now CBS Will Air Berlin Escapes"; "Escape From East Berlin," *Variety*.
54. Frank, "The Making of *The Tunnel*"; Frank, *Out of Thin Air*; Greg Mitchell, *The Tunnels*; Alex Ritman, "Paul Greengrass Cold War Thriller 'The Tunnels' Finds Writer," *The Hollywood Reporter*, September 22, 2015, https://www.hollywoodreporter.com/news/paul-greengrass-cold-war-thriller-826120 (accessed March 6, 2019).

CHAPTER TWO: PARALLEL PATHS

1. "No Tears for 'Professor': Tavern Folk Say He and Battered Piano are Safe Despite Television," *Newark Evening News*, September 2, 1947, 13, Scrapbook 1940s, Box 13107551 (RFT).
2. "No Tears for 'Professor.'"
3. "No Tears for 'Professor.'"
4. Joe Csida, "3,962,336 Saw Series On TV," *The Billboard*, October 17, 1947, 4, 15; Joe Csida, "Home TV's Series Score," *The Billboard*, October 11, 1947, 3, 16, 18; "Radio-TV Draw Huge Series Audience," *Broadcasting-Telecasting*, October 6, 1947, 83, 85.
5. "Reuven Frank," *Current Biography*, June 1973, 8–11, History-Personal '71–86, Box 13107537; "Reuven Frank," NBC News Press Release, May 1984, Magazine Press Excess 82–84, Box 13107538; Reuven Frank, oral history interview with Mary C. O'Connell, NBC 60th Anniversary project, June 19, 1986, History & Personal, '71–86, Box 13107537; Marvin Kitman, "Reuven Frank," *Washington Journalism Review*, July/August 1982, 39–45, Magazine Press Excess, '82–85, Box 13107538 (all RFT).
6. After his time at NBC, Green became a celebrated author and screenwriter. His novel *The Last Angry Man* was made into a popular movie. Later in his career, he wrote the novel and screenplay for the 1978 television mini-series *Holocaust*, which won multiple Emmy Awards. Margalit Fox, "Gerald Green, 84, Author and Screenwriter, Is Dead," *New York Times*, August 31, 2006, 22; Jeff Kisseloff, *The Box: An Oral History of Television 1920–1961* (New York: Penguin Books, 1995).
7. Reuven Frank, interview by author (RF-OH2); Reuven Frank, interview by author (RF-OH1).
8. Frank, interview (RF-OH1).
9. Reuven Frank, *Out of Thin Air: The Brief Wonderful Life of Network News* (New York: Simon and Schuster, 1991).
10. Don Hewitt, interview with author (DH-OH2); Walter Cronkite, interview by author (WC-OH); Fred W. Friendly, *Due to Circumstances Beyond Our Control . . .* (New York: Random House, 1967); Walter Cronkite, *A Reporter's Life* (New York: Alfred A. Knopf, 1996).
11. O. B. Hanson to John H. MacDonald, NBC Memo, March 25, 1948, Kinescope Recordings '47–48, Box 585 Kersta, Noran (NBC-WHS); John Crosby, *Out of the Blue: A Book about Radio and Television* (New York: Simon and Schuster, 1952); Andrew F. Inglis, *Behind the Tube: A History of Broadcasting Technology and Business* (Boston: Focal Press, 1990); Stanley Cloud and Lynne Olson, *The Murrow Boys: Pioneers on the Front Lines of Broadcast Journalism* (Boston: Mariner, 1996); Mike Conway, *The Origins of Television News in America: The Visualizers of CBS in the 1940s* (New York: Peter Lang, 2009).
12. Frank, *Out of Thin Air*.
13. Davidson Taylor to Charles R. Denny, NBC Memo, September 14, 1951, Ad Schneider to Stan Rotkewicz, NBC Memo, September 6, 1951, both Peace Conference, Box 310 McCall, Francis (NBC-WHS).

14. Thomas H. Hutchinson, *Here Is Television: Your Window on the World* (New York: Hastings House, 1946); Capt. William C. Eddy, *Television: The Eyes of Tomorrow* (New York: Prentice-Hall, 1945); David E. Fisher and Marshall Jon Fisher, *Tube: The Invention of Television* (San Diego: Harvest, 1996); James Von Schilling, *The Magic Window: American Television 1939–1953* (New York: Haworth Press, 2003).

15. Joseph H. Udelson, *The Great Television Race: A History of the American Television Industry* (Tuscaloosa: University of Alabama Press, 1982); Donald G. Godfrey, *C. Francis Jenkins: Pioneer of Film and Television* (Urbana: University of Illinois Press, 2014); Rudy Bretz, *Techniques of Television Production* (New York: McGraw-Hill, 1953).

16. Edward Bliss Jr., *Now the News: The Story of Broadcast Journalism* (New York: Columbia University Press, 1991); Conway, *The Origins of Television News*.

17. "Television II: 'Fade In Camera One!,'" *Fortune*, May 1939, 69–74, 154–64.

18. Richard W. Hubbell, *4000 Years of Television: The Story of Seeing at a Distance* (New York: G. P. Putnam's Sons, 1942).

19. Conway, *The Origins of Television News in America*.

20. This location became a part of pop culture a half-century later when Black Entertainment Television (BET) had its studios in the building and named a popular music program after cross streets 106 & Park.

21. William F. Brooks to Niles Trammel, "Monthly Summary of Operations," September 1948, Reports, NBC Brooks, Box 284 Brooks, William F. (NBC-WHS); Frank, *Out of Thin Air*.

22. Frank, interview (RF-OH2).

23. Frank, interview (RF-OH2).

24. Frank, interview (RF-OH2); "Television Personnel: News & Special Events," Television, Box 288 William Brooks (NBC-WHS).

25. Will Baltin, "TV's Progress in 1950," *The 1951 Radio Annual* (New York: Radio Daily, 1951), 45.

26. Ralph A. Renick, "News on Television," Miami, FL, May 1950, Pamphlet 3637 (P-MMC); Charles A. Siepmann, *Radio, Television, and Society* (New York: Oxford University Press, 1950).

27. "TV Stations 1950–1951," *1951 Radio Annual*, 1090–1117; Mike Conway, "'See It Now': Television News," in *Getting the Picture: The Visual Culture of the News*, ed. Jason E. Hill and Vanessa R. Schwartz (London: Bloomsbury, 2015), 168–75.

28. Conway, *The Origins of Television News*.

29. Frank, *Out of Thin Air*; Douglas Brinkley, *Cronkite* (New York: Harper, 2012).

30. David Halberstam, *The Coldest Winter: America and the Korean War* (New York: Hyperion, 2007); Frank, *Out of Thin Air*.

31. Thomas Doherty, *Cold War, Cool Medium: Television, McCarthyism, and American Culture* (New York: Columbia University Press, 2003), 1.

32. Edwin R. Bayley, *Joe McCarthy and the Press* (New York: Pantheon, 1981).

33. Douglass Cater, *The Fourth Branch of Government* (Boston: Houghton Mifflin, 1959), 7; David Halberstam, *The Fifties* (New York: Villard: 1993), 55.

34. Dinah Zeiger, "'Things Will Never Be the Same Around Here': How *See It Now*

Shaped Television News Reporting," in *A Moment of Danger,* ed. Janice Peck and Inger L. Stole (Milwaukee: Marquette University Press, 2011), 84.
35. "The McCarthy Years," *Edward R. Murrow Television Collection,* DVD, produced and edited by Edward R. Murrow and Fred W. Friendly (1991, New York: CBS News, 2005); Thomas Rosteck, *See It Now Confronts McCarthyism: Television Documentary and the Politics of Representation* (Tuscaloosa: University of Alabama Press, 1994); Edward R. Murrow and Fred W. Friendly, eds., *See It Now* (New York: Simon and Schuster: 1955).
36. Jack Gould, "Television in Review: Murrow vs. McCarthy," *New York Times,* March 11, 1954, 38.
37. Gary Edgerton, "The Murrow Legend as Metaphor: The Creation, Appropriation, and Usefulness of Edward R. Murrow's Life Story," *Journal of American Culture* 15, no. 1 (Spring 1992): 88; "A Study of Reactions To The 'See It Now' Programs on Senator McCarthy," *Elmo Roper,* April 1954, See It Now McCarthy Program, Related, Box 172 (FF-C); Brian Thornton, "Published Reaction When Murrow Battled McCarthy," *Journalism History* 29, no. 3 (Fall 2003): 133–46.
38. Crosby, *Out of the Blue,* 251; James L. Baughman, *Same Time, Same Station: Creating American Television, 1948–1961* (Baltimore: Johns Hopkins University Press, 2007); Doherty, *Cold War, Cool Medium.*
39. Richard D. Heldenfels, *Television's Greatest Year: 1954* (New York: Continuum, 1994), 131.
40. David Baird, "An Emerging Emphasis on Image: Early Press Coverage of Politics and Television," *American Journalism* 20, no. 4 (Fall 2003): 13–31.
41. Daniel Talbott, "Historic Hearings: From TV to Screen," in *The Documentary Tradition: From Nanook to Woodstock,* ed. Lewis Jacobs (New York: Hopkinson and Blake, 1971), 392–94; Jack C. Ellis and Betsy A. McLane, *A New History of Documentary Film* (New York: Continuum, 2005).
42. Doherty, *Cold War, Cool Medium.*
43. Herbert J. Gans, *Deciding What's News: A Study of CBS Evening News, NBC Nightly News, Newsweek, and Time* (New York: Pantheon Books, 1979) 39; Gans, *Deciding What's News,* 42.
44. James Aronson, *The Press and the Cold War* (New York: Monthly Review, 1970), 78; J. Fred MacDonald, *Television and the Red Menace: The Video Road to Vietnam* (New York: Praeger, 1985), 10.
45. Edward S. Herman and Noam Chomsky, *Manufacturing Consent: The Political Economy of the Mass Media* (New York: Pantheon, 1988), 30–31.
46. Doherty, *Cold War, Cool Medium,* 2, 1, 2.
47. "Duck and Cover," film, YouTube, https://youtu.be/IKqXu-5jw60 (accessed March 6, 2019); George H. Gallup, *The Gallup Poll: Public Opinion 1935–1971,* vol. 2, 1949–1958 (New York: Random House, 1972),1535.
48. Castleman and Podrazik, *The TV Schedule Book.*
49. "Road to Spandau" script, June 27, 1954, TV Guide Circa '68 Spandau/Harpers, Box 13107537 (RFT); "Sigma Delta Chi Honors Year's Best in American Journalism," *The Quill,* June 1955, 11–14.
50. Mike Conway, "Before the Bloggers: The Upstart News Technology of Television

at the 1948 Political Conventions," *American Journalism* 24, no. 1 (Winter 2007): 33–58; Conway, *The Origins of Television News*.
51. Barbara Matusow, *The Evening Stars: The Making of the Network News Anchor* (Boston: Houghton Mifflin, 1983).
52. Pat Weaver with Thomas M. Coffey, *The Best Seat in the House: The Golden Years of Radio and Television* (New York: Alfred A. Knopf, 1994); Mike Mashon, "NBC, J. Walter Thompson, and the Struggle for Control of Television Programming, 1946–1958," in *NBC: America's Network,* ed. Michele Hilmes (Berkeley: University of California Press, 2007), 135–52; Matusow, *The Evening Stars.*
53. The term "anchor man" was not used to describe a newscaster until the 1960s. Mike Conway, "The Origins of Television's 'Anchor Man': Cronkite, Swayze, and Journalism Boundary Work," *American Journalism* 31, no. 4 (Winter 2014): 445–67; Patsy G. Watkins, "John Cameron Swayze," in *Encyclopedia of Television News,* ed. Michael D. Murray (Phoenix: Oryx Press, 1999), 250–51.
54. Frank, interview (RF-OH2); Frank, *Out of Thin Air;* Matusow, *The Evening Stars.*
55. Frank, *Out of Thin Air,* 113; On the script for the first newscast, Huntley's final line reads, "Goodnight for NBC News and the Studebaker Packard dealers of America," Folder 1, Box 527 (NBC-WHS).
56. Frank, *Out of Thin Air,* 113; Motivation Analysis, Inc., "Viewers' Attitudes to Edwards and Huntley-Brinkley TV News Show," January 1961, 1961 Viewers Attitudes Towards Edwards & Huntley-Brinkley, Box 4ZD488 (SM-CAH).
57. Frank, *Out of Thin Air,* 112.
58. Tommy V. Smith, "Frank McGee," in *Encyclopedia of Television News,* 141–42.
59. Aniko Bodroghkozy, *Equal Time: Television and the Civil Rights Movement* (Urbana: University of Illinois Press, 2012); Kay Mills, *Changing Channels: The Civil Rights Case That Transformed Television* (Jackson: University of Mississippi Press, 2004); Bliss, *Now the News.*
60. Bodroghkozy, *Equal Time,* 68.
61. Gary Paul Gates, *Air Time: The Inside Story of CBS News* (New York: Berkley, 1978), 40; Bliss, *Now the News;* Bodroghkozy, *Equal Time.*
62. Bodroghkozy, *Equal Time,* 3.
63. Frank, *Out of Thin Air;* Castleman and Podrazik, *The TV Schedule Book.*
64. The American Broadcasting Company was created in 1943 when the government forced NBC to sell off one of its two radio networks. Erik Barnouw, *The Golden Web: A History of Broadcasting in the United States, Volume II, 1933–1953* (New York: Oxford University Press, 1968).
65. David Weinstein, *The Forgotten Network: DuMont and the Birth of American Television* (Philadelphia: Temple University Press, 2004); Robert E. Kintner, *Broadcasting and the News* (New York: Harper & Row, 1965).
66. Frank, *Out of Thin Air,* 133.
67. Christopher Sterling, *Electronic Media: A Guide to Trends in Broadcasting and Newer Technologies 1920–1983* (New York: Praeger, 1984); Bonnie Brennen, "Quiz Show Scandals," in *Encyclopedia of Television News,* 200–201; Erik Barnouw, *Tube of Plenty: The Evolution of American Television,* 2nd rev. ed. (New York: Oxford University Press, 1990).

68. Victor Pickard, *America's Battle for Democracy: The Triumph of Corporate Libertarianism and the Future of Media Reform* (New York: Cambridge University Press, 2015); Robert W. McChesney, *Telecommunications, Mass Media, & Democracy: The Battle for the Control of U.S. Broadcasting, 1928–1935* (New York: Oxford University Press, 1993).
69. Newton Minow, "Television and the Public Interest" speech, May 9, 1961, *AmericanRhetoric.com*, http://www.americanrhetoric.com/speeches/newtonminow.htm (accessed March 6, 2019); Mary Ann Watson, *The Expanding Vista: American Television in the Kennedy Years* (New York: Oxford University Press, 1990).
70. Richard Cawston, "Television—A World Picture," in *The Eighth Art: Twenty-Three Views of Television Today* (New York: Holt, Rinehart and Winston, 1962), 1.
71. Cawston, "Television—A World Picture," 13.
72. Rowland Evans Jr., "A New Tool for Politics," in *The Eighth Art*, 53; Edward W. Chester, *Radio, Television and American Politics* (New York: Sheed and Ward, 1969); Sterling, *The Electronic Media*.
73. "The Texaco Huntley-Brinkley Report," *The Peabody Awards*, 1960, http://www.peabodyawards.com/award-profile/the-texaco-huntley-brinkley-report (accessed March 6, 2019).
74. Bill Ewald, "First Team," *Newsweek*, March 13, 1961, 53.
75. "No Tears for 'Professor,' " 13.

CHAPTER THREE: THE TRANSMISSION OF EXPERIENCE

1. Tom Wolfe, "Preface," in *The New Journalism*, ed. Tom Wolfe and E. W. Johnson (New York: Harper and Row, 1973).
2. Tom Wolfe, "Like a Novel," in Wolfe and Johnson, eds., *The New Journalism*, 15.
3. Reuven Frank, untitled "transmission of experience" memo, n.d., 3, Personal Speeches-Written Works, '63–'71, Box 13107551 (RFT).
4. Reuven Frank, *Out of Thin Air: The Brief Wonderful Life of Network News* (New York: Simon and Schuster, 1991), 181; Frank, "transmission" memo.
5. Donald Fraser, "Newsreel: Reality or Entertainment?," *Sight and Sound* 2, no. 7 (Autumn 1933): 89–90; Gilbert Seldes, "The Unreal Newsreel," *Today*, April 13, 1935, 6–7, 18.
6. Scott L. Althaus, "The Forgotten Role of the Global Newsreel Industry in the Long Transition from Text to Television," *International Journal of Press/Politics* 15, no. 2 (2015): 193–218.
7. Joseph E. J. Clark, "'Canned History': American Newsreels and the Commodification of Reality, 1927–1945" (PhD diss., Brown University, 2011); Stephen McCreery and Brian Creech, "The Journalistic Value of Emerging Technologies: American Press Reaction to Newsreels During WWII," *Journalism History* 40, no. 3 (Fall 2014): 177–86; Raymond Fielding, *The American Newsreel 1911–1967* (Norman: University of Oklahoma Press, 1972); Althaus, "Global Newsreel Industry."
8. Joseph Clark, "'Public Forum of the Screen': Modernity, Mobility, and Debate at the Newsreel Cinema," in *Getting the Picture: The Visual Culture of the News*, ed. Jason E. Hill and Vanessa R. Schwartz (London: Bloomsbury, 2015), 161–67.

9. Reuven Frank, interview by author (RF-OH2).
10. Reuven Frank, interview by author (RF-OH1).
11. Harry E. Heath Jr., "News by Television; A Review of Practices and Possibilities," *Journalism Quarterly* 27, no. 4 (Fall 1950): 409–17.
12. "1950 Television News Study," *University of Missouri School of Journalism*, March 29, 1951, Pamphlet 2614 (P-MMC).
13. Heath, "News by Television," 411.
14. Heath, "News by Television," 413; Craig M. Allen, *News Is People: The Rise of Local TV News and the Fall of News from New York* (Ames: Iowa State University Press, 2001); Mike Conway, *The Origins of Television News in America: The Visualizers of CBS in the 1940s* (New York: Peter Lang, 2009).
15. Heath, "News by Television"; Ralph A. Renick, "News on Television," Miami, FL, May 1950, Pamphlet 3637 (P-MMC).
16. Heath, "News by Television."
17. "1950 Television News Study."
18. Heath, "News by Television," 417.
19. "1950 Television News Study," 417; Heath, "News by Television," 416.
20. Michael Stamm, *Sound Business: Newspapers, Radio, and the Politics of New Media* (Philadelphia: University of Pennsylvania Press, 2011).
21. "1950 Television News Study," 6.
22. Reuven Frank to William R. McAndrew, NBC Memo, January 9, 1963, 1, Address Lists 1973, Box 13107538 (RFT).
23. While the network news at this time usually ran at 6:45 p.m., CBS did not broadcast its network newscast until 7:15 p.m. in New York City. Jack Gould, "2 TV Networks Vie in Newscasts," *New York Times*, January 31, 1963, 4.
24. Wolfe, "Like a Novel," 15.
25. Wolfe, "Like a Novel," 21. Emphasis in original.
26. Michael J. Arlen, "Notes on the New Journalism," *The Atlantic*, May 1972; Kevin Kerrane and Ben Yagoda, eds., *The Art of Fact: A Historical Anthology of Literary Journalism* (New York: Touchstone, 1997).
27. Walter Cronkite and Don Carleton, *Conversations with Cronkite* (Austin, TX: Dolph Briscoe Center for American History, 2010); Edward W. Chester, *Radio, Television and American Politics* (New York: Sheed and Ward, 1969); Susan and Bill Buzenberg, eds., *Salant, CBS, and the Battle for the Soul of Broadcast Journalism: The Memoirs of Richard S. Salant* (Boulder, CO: Westview Press, 1999); Doug James, *Walter Cronkite: His Life and Times* (Brentwood, TN: JM Press, 1991).
28. Frank, "transmission" memo, 3.
29. Frank, "transmission" memo, 6.
30. Frank, "transmission" memo, 20.
31. Linda Ellerbee, in *"The Huntley-Brinkley Report" and Remembering Reuven Frank*, DVD (New York: NBC News, 2006).
32. Frank, *Out of Thin Air*, 121; Frank, "transmission" memo, 3.
33. Frank, "transmission" memo, 3.
34. Frank, "transmission" memo, 3.
35. Frank, "transmission" memo, 24.

36. Frank, "transmission" memo, 20.
37. Frank, "transmission" memo, 19.
38. Frank, "transmission" memo, 18.
39. Frank, "transmission" memo, 24.
40. Kiku Adatto, "Sound Bite Democracy: Network Evening News Presidential Campaign Coverage, 1968 and 1988," June 1990 (Research paper R-2, Shorenstein Center for Media, Politics, and Public Policy, Harvard University); Daniel C. Hallin, "Sound Bite News: Television Coverage of Elections, 1968–1988," *Journal of Communication* 42, no. 2 (Spring 1992): 5–24.
41. Adatto, "Sound Bite Democracy," 4; Hallin, "Sound Bite News," 23.
42. Geoffrey Baym, *From Cronkite to Colbert: The Evolution of Broadcast News* (New York: Oxford University Press, 2009); Thomas E. Patterson, *Out of Order: How the Political Parties and the Growing Power of the News Media Undermine the American Way of Electing Presidents* (New York: Alfred A. Knopf, 1993); Wolfgang Donsbach and Olaf Jandura, "Chances and Effects of Authenticity: Candidates of the German Federal Election in TV News," *Harvard International Journal of Press/Politics* 8, no. 1 (Winter 2003): 49–65; Dennis T. Lowry and Jon A. Shidler, "The Sound Bites, The Biters and the Bitten: An Analysis of Network TV News in Campaign '92," *Journalism & Mass Communication Quarterly* 72, no. 1 (Spring 1995): 33–44.
43. The term "sound bite" was not in use when Frank wrote the memo.
44. Frank, "transmission" memo, 7.
45. Frank, "transmission" memo, 7.
46. Frank to McAndrew, memo, 3; Madeleine Liseblad, "'Clearing a Path for Television News': The First Extended Newscast at Sacramento's KCRA," *Journalism History* 42, no. 4 (Winter 2017): 182–90.
47. Conway, *Origins of Television News*.
48. Frank, "transmission" memo, 17.
49. Edward Bliss Jr., *Now the News: The Story of Broadcast Journalism* (New York: Columbia University Press, 1991).
50. Edward Jay Epstein, *News from Nowhere: Television and the News* (New York: Random House, 1973); Paul C. Simpson, *Network Television News: Conviction, Controversy, and a Point of View* (Franklin, TN: Legacy Communication, 1995).
51. Daniel C. Hallin, *The 'Uncensored War': The Media and Vietnam* (Berkeley: University of California Press, 1986).
52. Reuven Frank, "The Making of *The Tunnel*," *Television Quarterly* 2 (Fall 1963): 16.
53. Frank, "The Making of *The Tunnel*," 16.
54. Frank, "The Making of *The Tunnel*," 20.
55. Frank, "The Making of *The Tunnel*."
56. Frank, "transmission" memo, 20.
57. *The Tunnel* script, December 10, 1962, 17, Manuscripts, Correspondence, Journals & Clippings '40s–'60s, Box 13107551 (RFT).
58. Donald Kirkley, "Look and Listen," *The [New York] Sun*, December 14, 1962, 12; Jack Gould, "TV: Tunnel Under Wall," *New York Times*, December 12, 1962, 4; Frank, "Making of *The Tunnel*," 19.
59. *The Tunnel* script, 24.

60. *The Tunnel* script, 8.
61. Frank, "Making of *The Tunnel*," 20.
62. *The Tunnel* script, 2, 11, 9.
63. Frank, "Making of *The Tunnel*," 20.
64. *The Tunnel* script, 24.
65. *The Tunnel* script, 1, 2, 24.
66. Frank, "Making of *The Tunnel*," 21.
67. Frank, "Making of *The Tunnel*," 21.
68. *The Tunnel* script, 20.
69. A. William Bluem, *Documentary in American Television: Form, Function, Method* (New York: Hastings House, 1965).
70. Epstein, *News From Nowhere*, 152.
71. Rose, "The Tunnel," *Variety*, December 12, 1962, 31; Cecil Smith, "'Tunnel'—450 ft. of Pure Excitement," *Los Angeles Times*, December 12, 1962, D18; Cynthia Lowry, "'The Tunnel' Called TV at Its Best," *Hartford Courant*, December 11, 1962, 23C.
72. Charles Kuralt, *A Life on the Road* (New York: Ivy Books, 1990); Bob Dotson, *American Story: A Lifetime Search for Ordinary People Doing Extraordinary Things* (New York: Viking, 2013).

CHAPTER FOUR: JOURNALIST VS. FILMMAKER

1. Reuven Frank, Tokyo Documentary speech transcript, May 1971, Writing and Tokyo, 40, Box 13107537 (RFT).
2. Frank, Tokyo speech, 18–19.
3. Frank, Tokyo speech, 15.
4. Michael Curtin, *Redeeming the Wasteland: Television Documentary and Cold War Politics* (New Brunswick, NJ: Rutgers University Press, 1995); Mary Ann Watson, *The Expanding Vista: American Television in the Kennedy Years* (New York: Oxford University Press, 1990); A. William Bluem, *Documentary in American Television: Form, Function, Method* (New York: Hastings House, 1965).
5. Erik Barnouw, *Tube of Plenty: The Evolution of American Television*, 2nd rev. ed. (New York: Oxford University Press, 1990); Erik Barnouw, "Reminiscences of Erik Barnouw," 1977 (CCOH).
6. Erik Barnouw, *Documentary: A History of Non-Fiction Film*, 2nd rev. ed. (New York: Oxford University Press, 1993).
7. Matt Carlson and Seth C. Lewis, eds., *Boundaries in Journalism: Professionalism, Practices, and Participation* (New York: Routledge, 2015).
8. Paul Spehr, *The Man Who Made Movies: W.K.L. Dickson* (New Barnet, UK: John Libbey, 2008); W. K. L. Dickson and Antonia Dickson, *History of the Kinetograph, Kinetoscope, and Kineto-Phonograph* (New York: Museum of Modern Art, 2000); Bill Nichols, *Introduction to Documentary*, 2nd ed. (Bloomington: Indiana University Press, 2010); Brian Winston, ed., *The Documentary Film Book* (London: British Film Institute, 2013); Barnouw, *Documentary*.

9. Raymond Fielding, *The American Newsreel 1911–1967* (Norman: University of Oklahoma Press, 1972).
10. W. K. L. Dickson, *The Biograph in Battle* (Trowbridge, UK: Flicks Books, 1995); Fielding, *The American Newsreel*.
11. Fielding, *The American Newsreel*, 45.
12. Fielding, *The American Newsreel*, 66; Nichols, *Documentary Film*.
13. Barnouw, *Documentary*; Fielding, *The American Newsreel*; Joseph E. J. Clark, "'Canned History': American Newsreels and the Commodification of Reality, 1927–1945" (PhD diss., Brown University, 2011).
14. Fielding, *The American Newsreel*, 72.
15. *Nanook of the North* promotional poster, 1922, IMDb Database, http://www.imdb.com/title/tt0013427 (accessed March 6, 2019).
16. Nichols, *Introduction to Documentary*; Paul Henley, "Anthropology: The Evolution of Ethnographic Film," in *The Documentary Film Book*, 309–19; Barnouw, *Documentary*; Robert Sherwood, "Robert Flaherty's *Nanook of the North*," in *The Documentary Tradition: From Nanook to Woodstock*, ed. Lewis Jacobs (New York: Hopkinson and Blake, 1971), 15–19.
17. Lewis Jacobs, "Precursors and Prototypes (1894–1922)," in *The Documentary Tradition*, 8.
18. John Grierson, *Grierson on Documentary*, ed. Forsyth Hardy (London: Faber & Faber, 1979).
19. Barnouw, *Documentary*, 58.
20. Richard Barsam, *Non-Fiction Film* (Bloomington: Indiana University Press, 1973), 57; John Grierson, "Flaherty's Poetic *Moana*," in *The Documentary Tradition*, 25–26.
21. Barsam, *Non-Fiction Film*; Grierson, *Grierson on Documentary*.
22. Federal Communications Commission, *The Communications Act of 1934* (Washington, DC: United States Government Printing Office, 1961), 41. In the 1927 Act, "or" was used in place of "and." Erik Barnouw, *The Golden Web: A History of Broadcasting in the United States, Volume II, 1933–1953* (New York: Oxford University Press, 1968).
23. Edward Bliss Jr., *Now the News: The Story of Broadcast Journalism* (New York: Columbia University Press, 1991).
24. R. LeRoy Bannerman, *On a Note of Triumph: Norman Corwin and the Golden Years of Radio* (New York: Lyle Stuart, 1986), 3; Bliss, *Now the News*.
25. Bliss, *Now the News*, 68, 67; Robert T. Elson, *Time Inc.: The Intimate History of a Publishing Empire, 1923–1941* (New York: Antheneum, 1968); "Fred Smith, Radio Pioneer, Dies: Helped Create 'March of Time,'" *New York Times*, August 15, 1976, 53.
26. Michael Emery and Edwin Emery, *The Press and America: An Interpretive History of the Mass Media*, 6th ed. (Englewood Cliffs, NJ: Prentice Hall, 1988); Kevin G. Barnhurst and John Nerone, *The Form of News: A History* (New York: Guilford Press, 2001).
27. Barnhurst and Nerone, *Form of News*, 176.
28. Richard Meyer, "Public Execution, Sing Sing Prison, 1928," in *Getting the Picture:*

The Visual Culture of the News, ed. Jason E. Hill and Vanessa R. Schwartz (London: Bloomsbury, 2015), 48–51.
29. Elson, *Time Inc.;* David E. Sumner and Janice Hume, "Modern Magazines, 1900–Present," in *The Age of Mass Communication,* 2nd ed., ed. Wm. David Sloan (Northport, AL: Vision Press, 2008), 391–407.
30. Jacob A. Riis, *How the Other Half Lives: Studies Among the Tenements of New York* (New York: Charles Scribner's Sons, 1890).
31. Lisa Soccio, "Clarence H. White," *International Center of Photography* website, https://www.icp.org/browse/archive/constituents/clarence-h-white?all/all/all/all/0 (accessed March 6, 2019).
32. James Agee and Walker Evans, *Let Us Now Praise Famous Men,* in James Agee, *Let Us Now Praise Famous Men, A Death in the Family, & Shorter Fiction* (New York: Library of America, 2005); James R. Mellow, *Walker Evans* (New York: Basic Books, 1999); Robert Hariman and John Louis Lucaites, *No Caption Needed: Iconic Photographs, Public Culture, and Liberal Democracy* (Chicago: University of Chicago Press, 2007).
33. Leo Hurwitz, "One Man's Voyage: Ideas and Films in the 1930's," *Cinema Journal* 15, no. 1 (Autumn 1975): 3, 9.
34. They had dropped "Workers" from their Film and Photo League title.
35. "George Stoney on *The Plow* and *The River,*" special feature, *The Plow That Broke the Plains* and *The River,* DVD, Executive Producer Joseph Horowitz (Naxos, 2007); Barnouw, *Documentary,* 118.
36. Gilbert Seldes, "Pare Lorentz's *The River,*" in *The Documentary Tradition,* 123–25.
37. Elson, *Time Inc.;* Bluem, *Documentary in American Television,* 38.
38. Gilbert Seldes, 'The 'Errors' of Television," *Atlantic Monthly,* May 1937, 531–41; Gilbert Seldes, *The 7 Lively Arts* (New York: Sagamore Press, 1924).
39. Worthington Miner, *Worthington Miner,* interviewed by Franklin J. Schaffner (New York: Directors Guild of America Oral History Series, 1985); Richard W. Hubbell, *Television Programming and Production* (New York: Murray Hill, 1945).
40. Robert Bendick, interview by author (RB-OH2); Mike Conway, *The Origins of Television News in America: The Visualizers of CBS in the 1940s* (New York: Peter Lang, 2009).
41. Hurwitz, "One Man's Voyage," Chester Burger, interview by author (CB-OH2).
42. Rudy Bretz to Gilbert Seldes, "Documentary Films Shown at the World's Fair," October 1939, Documentary Film-Review Notes, Box 6 (RB-MMC).
43. William K. Everson, "*The Triumph of the Will,*" in *The Documentary Tradition,* 138–40; Parker Tyler, "Leni Riefenstahl's *Olympia,*" in *The Documentary Tradition,* 136–37; Kathleen M. German, "Frank Capra's *Why We Fight* Series and the American Audience," *Western Journal of Speech Communication* 54 (Spring 1990): 237–48; Nichols, *Introduction to Documentary;* Barnouw, *Documentary.*
44. Frank S. Nugent, "Film Men of the Air Force," *New York Times,* April 30, 1944, SM14; Larry Racies, interview by author (LR-OH2); Bendick, interview with author (RB-OH2).
45. André Bazin, "On *Why We Fight:* History, Documentation and the Newsreel (1946)," *Film & History* 31, no. 1 (2001): 61.

46. Bosley Crowther, "Documentary Evidence," *New York Times*, March 22, 1953, X1; Paul Rotha, "Television and the Future of Documentary," *Quarterly of Film, Radio, and Television* 9, no. 4 (Summer 1955): 366–73; Winifred Holmes, "What's Wrong With Documentary?," *Sight and Sound* 17, no. 65 (Spring 1948): 44–45; John Grierson, "Prospect for Documentary," *Sight and Sound* 17, no. 66 (Summer 1948): 55–59.
47. Victor Pickard, *America's Battle for Democracy: The Triumph of Corporate Libertarianism and the Future of Media Reform* (New York: Cambridge University Press, 2015).
48. Matthew C. Ehrlich, *Radio Utopia: Postwar Audio Documentary in the Public Interest* (Urbana: University of Illinois Press, 2011), 2.
49. Ehrlich, *Radio Utopia*.
50. Ralph Engelman, *Friendlyvision: Fred Friendly & the Rise and Fall of Television Journalism* (New York; Columbia University Press, 2009); Mike Conway, "The Origins of Television's 'Anchor Man': Cronkite, Swayze and Journalism Boundary Work," *American Journalism* 31, no. 4 (Winter 2014): 445–67.
51. Mike Conway, "Murrow and Friendly's Multimedia Maturation: How Two Non-Visual Communicators Created a Groundbreaking Television Program" (paper presented at Association for Education in Journalism and Mass Communication annual conference, Washington, DC, 2013).
52. "DOCUMENTARIES: WMAR-TV Pioneers New Series," *Broadcasting*, March 8, 1948, 38B; Conway, *The Origins of Television News*.
53. Fred Friendly CBS Contract, October 30, 1950, I Can Hear It Now Contract, Box 168 (FF-C); Murrow Television Show Ideas, 1950, Murrow Television Show, Box 131, MS025-004.003 (ERM-T).
54. Palmer Williams, oral history interview with Joe Persico, November 29, 1984, audiocassettes, Box 107 Person to Person (ERM-T); Edward R. Murrow and Fred W. Friendly, eds., *See It Now* (New York: Simon and Schuster: 1955); Fred W. Friendly, *Due to Circumstances Beyond Our Control . . .* (New York: Random House, 1967); Joeseph E. Persico, *Edward R. Murrow: An American Original* (New York: Da Capo, 1997); A. M. Sperber, *Murrow: His Life and Times* (New York: Freundlich Books, 1986).
55. Peter C. Rollins, "*Nightmare in Red:* A Cold War View of the Communist Revolution," in *American History, America Television: Interpreting the Video Past*, ed. John E. O'Connor (New York: Frederick Ungar, 1983), 135.
56. Douglas Brinkley, *Cronkite* (New York: Harper: 2012), 173.
57. Tom Mascaro, *Into the Fray: How NBC's Washington Documentary Unit Reinvented the News* (Washington, DC: Potomac Books, 2012).
58. Edward R. Murrow, "RTNDA Speech," October 15, 1958, *Radio Television Digital News Association* website, https://www.rtdna.org/content/edward_r_murrow_s_1958_wires_lights_in_a_box_speech (accessed March 6, 2019).
59. Edward Jay Epstein, *News from Nowhere: Television and the News* (New York: Random House, 1973).
60. Who's Who in NBC News," NBC Press Release, July 17, 1963 (MMC); Raymond Carroll, "Economic Influences on Commercial Network Television Documentary Scheduling," *Journal of Broadcasting* 23 (Fall 1979): 411–25.

61. Stephen Mamber, *Cinema Verite in America: Studies in Uncontrolled Documentary* (Cambridge, MA: MIT Press, 1974); Robert C. Allen and Douglas Gomery, *Film History: Theory and Practice* (New York: McGraw-Hill, 1985); Kevin Macdonald and Mark Cousins, *Imagining Reality: The Faber Book of Documentary* (London: Faber and Faber, 1996); Bill Nichols, *Representing Reality* (Bloomington: Indiana University Press, 1991); Nichols, *Introduction to Documentary*; Barnouw, *Documentary*; Winston, *The Documentary Film Book*; Jacobs, *The Documentary Tradition*.
62. P. J. O'Connell, *Robert Drew and the Development of Cinema Verite in America* (Carbondale: Southern Illinois University Press, 1992).
63. There is debate on whether or not these documentaries should be called *cinéma vérité* or "direct cinema." That debate is beyond the scope of this project. I mostly use the term *cinéma vérité*.
64. Mamber, *Cinema Verite*, 2.
65. Bluem, *Documentary in American Television*, 258.
66. Daniel C. Hallin, "The Passing of the 'High Modernism' of American Journalism," *Journal of Communication* 42, no. 3 (Summer 1992): 14.
67. Jack Gould, "Hagerty to Succeed John Daly as Head of A.B.C. News Service," *New York Times*, November 18, 1960, 1.
68. Reuven Frank, untitled "transmission of experience" memo, n.d., 15, Personal Speeches-Written Works, '63–'71, Box 13107551 (RFT).
69. Barsam, *Non-Fiction Film*, 1.
70. Thomas Whiteside, "The One-Ton Pencil," *New Yorker*, February 17, 1962, 70.
71. *The Tunnel* script, December 10, 1962, 2, Manuscripts, Correspondence, Journals & Clippings, 1940s-60s, Box 13107551 (RF-T); *The Tunnel* script, 5.
72. Reuven Frank, "The Making of *The Tunnel*," *Television Quarterly* 2 (Fall 1963): 16.
73. Reuven Frank, *Out of Thin Air: The Brief Wonderful Life of Network News* (New York: Simon and Schuster, 1991), 200–201.
74. Frank, *Out of Thin Air*, 201.
75. *The Tunnel*, NBC News, December 10, 1962, videocassette, MS137/003-005 #00009, ARMS 13107552 (RF-T).
76. This section is based on, and the quotes are taken from, an abridged transcript of the NATAS event included in Bluem, *Documentary in American Television*, 255–66.
77. Bluem, *Documentary in American Television*, 256; Curtin, *Redeeming the Wasteland*, 5.
78. Bluem, *Documentary in American Television*, 258; Don Hewitt, interview by author (DH-OH2); Don Hewitt, *Tell Me a Story: Fifty Years and 60 Minutes in Television* (New York: Public Affairs, 2001); Whiteside, "The One-Ton Pencil."
79. Bluem, *Documentary in American Television*, 267.
80. Bluem, *Documentary in American Television*, 144.
81. Chad Raphael, *Investigated Reporting: Muckrakers, Regulators, and the Struggle over Television Documentary* (Urbana: University of Illinois Press, 2005), 105; Dean Rusk to Robert E. Kintner, letter, November 28, 1962, NBC Documentary Film "The Tunnel" Correspondence 1962 (RM-H).

CHAPTER FIVE: ADVENTUROUS LAYMEN

1. Jack Gould, "TV: N.B.C. and Berlin Wall Tunnel," *New York Times*, October 22, 1962, 46.
2. David T. Z. Mindich, *Just the Facts: How "Objectivity" Came to Define American Journalism* (New York: New York University Press, 1998); Kevin G. Barnhurst, "The Rise of the Professional Communicator," in *The International Encyclopedia of Media Studies: Media History and the Foundations of Media Studies*, ed. John Nerone (Malden, MA: Wiley-Blackwell, 2013): 463–76; Mark Deuze, "What Is Journalism?," *Journalism* 6, no. 4 (2005): 442–64; Michael Schudson, *Discovering the News: A Social History of Newspapers* (New York: Basic Books, 1978).
3. David H. Weaver, Randal A. Beam, Bonnie J. Brownlee, Paul S. Voakes, and G. Cleveland Wilhoit, *The American Journalist in the 21st Century: U.S. News People at the Dawn of the New Millennium* (Mahwah, NJ: Lawrence Erlbaum, 2007).
4. Adolph Och's famous pledge for the *New York Times*. Susan E. Tifft and Alex S. Jones, *The Trust: The Private and Powerful Family Behind the New York Times* (Boston: Little, Brown and Co., 1999), xix.
5. Lisa Mullikin Parcell, "The Modern Newspaper 1900–1945," in *The Age of Mass Communication*, 2nd ed., ed. Wm. David Sloan (Northport, AL: Vision Press, 2008), 299–316; Mitchell Stephens, *A History of News*, 3rd ed. (New York: Oxford University Press, 2007).
6. Christopher H. Sterling, *Electronic Media: A Guide to Trends in Broadcasting and Newer Technologies 1920–1983* (New York: Praeger, 1984); Michael Stamm, *Sound Business: Newspapers, Radio, and the Politics of New Media* (Philadelphia: University of Pennsylvania Press, 2011).
7. George A. Brandenburg, "Inland Awaits National Action on Radio, Tabling Attack on 'Newscasting,'" *Editor & Publisher*, February 25, 1933, 5–6, 39.
8. "Ban Radio from News Columns to End Problem, Ewing Says," *Editor & Publisher*, December 17, 1932, 6; Arthur Robb, "Keep News from Radio, S.N.P.A. Urges," *Editor & Publisher*, July 23, 1932, 7–8, 20.
9. Robert W. McChesney, *Telecommunications, Mass Media, and Democracy: The Battle for the Control of U.S. Broadcasting, 1928–1935* (New York: Oxford University Press, 1993).
10. Brandenburg, "Inland Awaits," 5.
11. Brandenburg, "Inland Awaits," 5; John W. Perry, "Showdown on Radio Problem Expected as A.N.P.A., A.P. Act on Protests," *Editor & Publisher*, December 10, 1932, 5.
12. Robb, "Keep News from Radio," 8.
13. Stamm, *Sound Business*.
14. Victoria Smith Ekstrand, *News Piracy and the Hot News Doctrine: Origins in Law and Implications for the Digital Age* (New York: LFB Scholarly Publishing, 2005); Barbara Cloud, "News: Public Service or Profitable Property?," *American Journalism* 13, no. 2 (Spring 1996): 141–56.
15. Brandenburg, "Inland Awaits," 5; Perry, "Showdown on Radio Problem," 6.
16. Paul W. White, *News on the Air* (New York: Harcourt, Brace and Company, 1947);

Edward Bliss Jr., *Now the News: The Story of Broadcast Journalism* (New York: Columbia University Press, 1991); Mike Conway, *The Origins of Television News in America: The Visualizers of CBS in the 1940s* (New York: Peter Lang, 2009).

17. Perry, "Showdown on Radio Problem," 5.
18. White, *News on the Air*; Bliss, *Now the News*.
19. George H. Manning, "U.S. Senators Hear Charges That Radio Endangers Newspapers," *Editor & Publisher*, January 21, 1933, 10; McChesney, *Telecommunications*.
20. "'News' by Radio," *New York Times*, April 19, 1929, 18; Perry, "Showdown on Radio Problem," 6.
21. Gwenyth L. Jackaway, *Media at War: Radio's Challenge to the Newspapers, 1924–1939* (Westport, CT: Praeger, 1995), 48.
22. The Federal Radio Commission (FRC) became the Federal Communication Commission (FCC) with the passage of the Communications Act of 1934. Federal Communication Commission, *The Communications Act of 1934* (Washington, DC: United States Government Printing Office, 1961), 41.
23. "Education Programs on Radio Relegated to Daytime Hours," *Editor & Publisher*, March 5, 1932, 10.
24. White, *News on the Air*; Irving E. Fang, *Those Radio Commentators!* (Ames: Iowa State University Press, 1977).
25. Gerry Lanosga, "The Power of the Prize: How an Emerging Prize Culture Helped Shape Journalistic Practice and Professionalism," *Journalism: Theory, Practice and Criticism* 16, no. 7 (October 2015): 953–67; "Origin of the Award," *Peabody Awards* website, http://www.peabodyawards.com/about#originawards (accessed March 7, 2019).
26. Jerry Walker, "Campbell Soups Air Biggest News Package," *Editor & Publisher*, January 17, 1948, 48.
27. Stanley Cloud and Lynne Olson, *The Murrow Boys: Pioneers on the Front Lines of Broadcast Journalism* (Boston: A Mariner Book, 1996); Conway, *The Origins of Television News*.
28. Thomas F. Gieryn, "Boundary-Work and the Demarcation of Science from Non-Science Strains and Interests in Professional Ideologies of Scientists," *American Sociological Review* 48, no. 6 (December 1983): 781–95; Thomas F. Gieryn, George M. Bevins, and Stephen C. Zehr, "Professionalization of American Scientists: Public Science in the Creation/Evolution Trials," *American Sociological Review* 50, no. 3 (June 1985): 392–409; Matt Carlson, "Introduction: The Many Boundaries of Journalism," in *Boundaries in Journalism: Professionalism, Practices, and Participation*, ed. Matt Carlson and Seth C. Lewis (New York: Routledge, 2015), 1–18.
29. Reuven Frank and Don Hewitt, "Dialogue," *Television Quarterly* 1 (November 1962): 7.
30. Frank and Hewitt, "Dialogue," 9, 8.
31. Bill Kovach and Tom Rosenstiel, *The Elements of Journalism: What Newspeople Should Know and the Public Should Expect* (New York: Three Rivers, 2007), 12.
32. Michael Emery and Edwin Emery, *The Press and America: An Interpretive History of the Mass Media*, 6th ed. (Englewood Cliffs, NJ: Prentice Hall, 1988), 274.

33. Theodore Dreiser, *Newspaper Days*, ed. T. D. Nostwich (Philadelphia: University of Pennsylvania Press, 1991); Richard Lingeman, *Theodore Dreiser: An American Journey* (New York: John Wiley and Sons, 1993); Theodore Dreiser, *Journalism, Volume 1: Newspaper Writings, 1892–1895*, ed. T. D. Nostwich (Philadelphia: University of Pennsylvania Press, 1988).
34. Weaver et al., *American Journalist*, 154.
35. Weaver et al., *American Journalist*, 159.
36. White, *News on the Air*, 170, 171.
37. F. Fraser Bond, *An Introduction to Journalism: A Survey of the Fourth Estate in All Its Forms* (New York: Macmillan, 1954), 5; R. E. Wolseley and Laurence R. Campbell, *Exploring Journalism: With Special Emphasis on Its Social and Vocational Aspects* (New York: Prentice-Hall, 1946), 3.
38. John Paul Jones, *The Modern Reporter's Handbook* (New York: Rinehart and Co, 1949), 2.
39. Cloud and Olson, *The Murrow Boys*, 293.
40. Walter Cronkite, *A Reporter's Life* (New York: Alfred A Knopf, 1996), 50; Cronkite, *Reporter's Life*, 51.
41. Gilbert Seldes, *The 7 Lively Arts* (New York: Sagamore Press, 1924); *The Eighth Art: Twenty-three Views of Television Today* (New York: Holt, Rinehart and Winston, 1962).
42. Gilbert Seldes, "Beg, Borrow—or Annex," in *The Eighth Art*, 101.
43. Ashley Montagu, "Television and the New Image of Man," in *The Eighth Art*, 129; Frances Lander Spain and Margaret C. Scoggin, "They Still Read Books," in *The Eighth Art*, 177.
44. Marya Mannes, "The Lost Tribe of Television," in *The Eighth Art*, 24; Leo Rosten, "A Disenchanted Look at the Audience," in *The Eighth Art*, 32.
45. James Collins and Richard K. Blot, *Literacy and Literacies: Texts, Power, and Identity* (New York: Cambridge University Press, 2003); David R. Olson and Nancy Torrance, eds., *Literacy and Orality* (New York: Cambridge University Press, 1991).
46. John Crosby, "A Short Trip from Video into the Past," *Washington Post*, February 27, 1949, L4.
47. Edward R. Murrow, "Television News," April 1949, 1, File 49: 286–Admin; Davidson Taylor, Box 049 (ERM-T).
48. Murrow, "Television News," 1, 3.
49. Neil Postman, *Amusing Ourselves to Death: Public Discourse in the Age of Show Business* (New York: Penguin Books, 1985).
50. Jerry Walker, "Radio—But No Video—in N. Y. Times Plant," *Editor & Publisher*, April 15, 1950, 46.
51. Murrow, "Television News," 3.
52. "Legacy," *National Press Photographers Association* website, https://www.nppa.org/about (accessed March 7, 2019).
53. "'Copter Spies on Sunning Ike," *Baltimore Sun*, October 11, 1955, 5; Edward T. Folliard, "Nixon Trip to Near East Is Cancelled," *Washington Post*, October 11, 1955, 1.

54. "'Sneak' Photographers of President Rebuked," *New York Herald Tribune*, October 11, 1955, 6.
55. "No Help to Progress," *Broadcasting-Telecasting*, October 17, 1955, 130; Spencer Allen, "It's Time TV Developed News to Fit Its Maturity," *The Quill*, February 1956, 7.
56. Allen, "It's Time TV," 7.
57. David R. Davies, *The Postwar Decline of American Newspapers, 1945–1965* (Westport, CT: Praeger, 2006), 135.
58. James L. Baughman, *The Republic of Mass Culture: Journalism, Filmmaking and Broadcasting in America since 1941*, 3rd ed. (Baltimore: Johns Hopkins University Press, 2006); Davies, *The Postwar Decline*.
59. John C. Busterna, "Daily Newspaper Chains and the Antitrust Laws," *Journalism Monographs* 110 (March 1989): 1–37.
60. Baughman, *Republic of Mass Culture*, 120; Davies, *The Postwar Decline*.
61. Baughman, *Republic of Mass Culture*; David R. Davies, "The Contemporary Newspaper, 1945–Present," in *The Age of Mass Communication*, 423–38.
62. Chad Raphael, *Investigated Reporting: Muckrakers, Regulators, and the Struggle over Television Documentary* (Urbana: University of Illinois Press, 2005), 169.
63. "Evil Eye," *Time*, May 21, 1956, 68, 69.
64. Lester Markel, "Yes, the Printed Word Has a Future Despite Television and Cinerama," *The Quill*, September 1956, 20.
65. Markel, "Yes, the Printed Word Has a Future," 20.
66. Markel, "Yes, the Printed Word Has a Future," 20.
67. Bill Ewald, "First Team," *Newsweek*, March 13, 1961, 53–57.
68. "CBS and NBC: Walter vs. Chet and Dave," *Newsweek*, September 23, 1963, 63.
69. Thomas Whiteside, "The One-Ton Pencil," *New Yorker*, February 17, 1962, 41–88.
70. Whiteside, "One-Ton Pencil," 41, 88.
71. Ewald, "First Team," 56.
72. "CBS and NBC," 65.
73. "CBS and NBC," 65.
74. Walter Cronkite, "Television and the News," in *The Eighth Art*, 227–40; Reuven Frank, *Out of Thin Air: The Brief Wonderful Life of Network News* (New York: Simon and Schuster, 1991), 175.
75. Marty Schrader, "CBS Television," *The Billboard*, June 3, 1944, 7.
76. Gilbert Seldes, "Murrow, McCarthy and the Empty Formula," *Saturday Review*, April 24, 1954, 26; Michael Kammen, *The Lively Arts: Gilbert Seldes and the Transformation of Cultural Criticism in the United States* (New York: Oxford University Press, 1996).
77. Loren Ghiglione, *CBS's Don Hollenbeck: An Honest Reporter in the Age of McCarthyism* (New York: Columbia University Press, 2008).
78. Lewis L. Gould, "Portrait of a Television Critic," in *Watching Television Come of Age: The New York Times Reviews by Jack Gould*, ed. Lewis L. Gould (Austin: University of Texas Press, 2002), 1–31.
79. John Crosby, *Out of the Blue: A Book about Radio and Television* (New York: Simon and Schuster, 1952).

80. Crosby, *Out of the Blue*, x; "Personal Award: Jack Gould," 1956, *Peabody Awards* website, http://www.peabodyawards.com/award-profile/personal-award-jack-gould-for-outstanding-contribution-to-radio-and-televis (accessed March 7, 2019).
81. Frank, *Out of Thin Air*, 78, 92.
82. Jack Gould, "Television Today: A Critic's Appraisal," *Watching Television Come of Age*, 224–25.
83. "Tunnels, Inc.," *Time*, October 5, 1962, 26.
84. Val Adams, "TV Film Records Refugees' Flight," *New York Times*, October 5, 1962, 49.
85. Val Adams, "N.B.C.-TV Plans Documentary on Berlin Tunnel It Helped Build," *New York Times*, October 12, 1962, 50; Robert E. Kintner, *Broadcasting and the News* (New York: Harper and Row, 1965).
86. "West Berlin 'Regrets' TV Escape Film," *Washington Post*, October 17, 1962, 14; "Tunnelers Fight Berlin TV Show," *New York Times*, October 13, 1962, 10.
87. "U.S. Criticizes N.B.C. On Film in Berlin," *New York Times*, October 20, 1962, 2; "U.S. Criticizes N.B.C on Filming of Berlin Tunnel," *Chicago Daily Tribune*, October 19, 1962, 2; "State Brands NBC 'Irresponsible,'" *Washington Post*, October 20, 1962, A13; "Enterprising Journalism," *Broadcasting*, October 22, 1962, 114.
88. Gould, "N.B.C. and Berlin Wall Tunnel," 46.
89. Gould, "N.B.C. and Berlin Wall Tunnel," 46.
90. Gould, "N.B.C. and Berlin Wall Tunnel," 46; Harlan Makemson, *Media, NASA, and America's Quest for the Moon* (New York: Peter Lang, 2009); Robert Sherrod, "The Selling of Astronauts," *Columbia Journalism Review* (May/June 1973): 16–25.
91. Richard F. Shepard, "N.B.C. Postpones Tunnel Telecast," *New York Times*, October 24, 1962, 62.
92. Rose, "The Tunnel," *Variety*, December 12, 1962, 31; Percy Shain, "Wait for 'Tunnel' Well Worth It," *Boston Globe*, December 11, 1962, 43; Cecil Smith, "'Tunnel'—450 ft. of Pure Excitement," *Los Angeles Times*, December 12, 1962, D18; Donald Kirkley, "Look and Listen," *Baltimore Sun*, December 14, 1962, 12.
93. Barbara Delatiner, "NBC's 'The Tunnel' Justifies Stir It Caused," *Newsday*, December 11, 1962, 2C.
94. Jack Gould, "TV: Tunnel under Wall," *New York Times*, December 12, 1962, 4.
95. Lawrence Laurent, "Institute Praises 'Tunnel' Producer," *Los Angeles Times*, June 17, 1963, D15.
96. Jack Gould, "A Prize Package?," *New York Times*, June 2, 1963, 121.
97. Reuven Frank, untitled "transmission of experience" memo, n.d., 32, Personal Speeches-Written Works, '63–'71, Box 13107551 (RFT).

CHAPTER SIX: "THE NECESSARY RESTRAINTS OF NATIONAL SECURITY"

1. John F. Kennedy, "The President and the Press," address before the American Newspaper Publishers Association, New York City, April 27, 1961, John F. Kennedy Presidential Library and Museum, https://www.jfklibrary.org/archives/other-resources/john-f-kennedy-speeches/american-newspaper-publishers-association-19610427 (accessed March 7, 2019).

2. Kennedy, "The President and the Press."
3. Kennedy, "The President and the Press."
4. *Escape from East Berlin*, directed by Robert Siodmak (1962, Burbank, CA: Warner Home Video, 2015), DVD.
5. Reuven Frank, "The Making of *The Tunnel*," *Television Quarterly* 2 (Fall 1963): 8–23; Reuven Frank, *Out of Thin Air: The Brief, Wonderful Life of Network News* (New York: Simon & Schuster, 1991).
6. Rainer Hildebrandt was an anticommunism resistance fighter in Germany. He started the Mauer Museum, located next to Checkpoint Charlie in Berlin.
7. Ralph A. Brown, memo, August 3, 1962, Eyes Only Telegrams 1963 + S/S—L.D., box 36; Classified Central Subject Files, 1963–1975 (FSP-DS); Daniel Schorr, *Staying Tuned: A Life in Journalism* (New York: Pocket Books, 2001).
8. Lightner to Secretary of State, "Eyes Only for Secretary," August 7, 1962, More Tunnel, Box 13107536 (RF-T).
9. Hulick to Hillenbrand & Williamson, "Secret," n.d. (FSP-DS).
10. Rusk to Hulick, "Eyes Only," August 7, 1962, and Hulick to Hillenbrand and Williamson, "Secret," n.d. (FSP-DS); Schorr, *Staying Tuned;* Eric Pace, "Blair Clark, 82, CBS Executive Who Led McCarthy's '68 Race," *New York Times*, June 8, 2000.
11. Hulick to Secretary, "Eyes Only for Secretary," August 8, 1962 (FSP-DS).
12. Rusk to Morris and Williamson, Telegram, August 10, 1962 (FSP-DS); Morris to Rusk, "Eyes Only for Secretary," August 10, 1962 (FSP-DS).
13. Lightner to Secretary, "Eyes Only for Secretary," August 12, 1962, More Tunnel, Box 13107536 (RF-T); Robert Kintner to Dean Rusk, letter and memorandum, November 20, 1962, Tunnel, Box 13107536 (RF-T).
14. Robert Kintner to Dean Rusk, November 20, 1962, Correspondence 1962, NBC documentary film 'The Tunnel' (RMA); Mark Feeney, "Robert Manning, a Writer and Innovative Editor at The Atlantic," September 29, 2012, Boston.com, https://www.boston.com/news/local-news/2012/09/29/robert-manning-a-writer-and-innovative-editor-of-the-atlantic (accessed March 7, 2019); William Yardley, "Robert J. Manning, Former Editor of the Atlantic, Dies at 92," *New York Times*, October 2, 2012.
15. "29 East Berliners Flee through 400-Foot Tunnel," *New York Times*, September 19, 1962, 2; Frank, "The Making of *The Tunnel*"; Frank, *Out of Thin Air*.
16. Hulick to Secretary of State, "Confidential," September 19, 1962, Tunnel, Box 13107536 (RF-T).
17. Ball to Berlin, Outgoing Telegram, Department of State, October 5, 1962, Tunnel, Box 13107536 (RF-T); "Tunnels, Inc.," *Time*, October 5, 1962, 25–26.
18. Hulick to Secretary of State, "Secret," October 6, 1962, Tunnel, Box 13107536 (RF-T).
19. Val Adams, "N.B.C.-TV Plans Documentary on Berlin Tunnel It Helped Build," *New York Times*, October 12, 1962, 50.
20. CBS Tunnel Press Release, October 11, 1962, Tunnel, Box 13107536 (RF-T); Manning to The Secretary, CBS Statement, October 11, 1962, Tunnel, Box 13107536 (RF-T); Adams, "N.B.C.-TV Plans Documentary."
21. Manning to The Secretary, October 11, 1962.
22. Lightner to Secretary of State, "Limited Official Use," October 15, 1962, Tunnel,

Box 13107536 (RF-T); "Tunnelers Fight Berlin TV Show," *New York Times,* October 14, 1962, 10.
23. German Democratic Republic to Government of the United States of America, "Unofficial Translation," October 18, 1962, Tunnel, Box 13107536 (RF-T); Robert J. Manning to William McAndrew, letter, October 17, 1962, Tunnel, Box 13107536 (RF-T); "West Berlin 'Regrets' TV Escape Film," *Washington Post,* October 17, 1962, 14.
24. Manning to McAndrew, letter; Jim Greenfield to Mr. Manning, NBC Tunnel memo, October 17, 1962, Tunnel, Box 13107536 (RF-T).
25. "Guidance for Link on Berlin Tunnel," October 18, 1962, Tunnel, Box 13107536 (RF-T); "NBC's 'Tunnel' Officially Rebuked," *Broadcasting,* October 22, 1962, 62; "U.S. Criticizes NBC Filming of Berlin Tunnel," *Chicago Tribune,* October 20, 1962, 8; "U.S. Criticizes N.B.C. on Film in Berlin," *New York Times,* October 20, 1962, 2; "State Brands NBC 'Irresponsible,'" *Washington Post,* October 20, 1962, 13.
26. Robert E. Kintner, *Broadcasting and the News* (New York: Harper and Row, 1965), 37; Frank, *Out of Thin Air.*
27. "Statement of William R. McAndrew," Tunnel Details, n.d., Tunnel, Box 13107536 (RF-T); Kintner to Rusk, letter, 4; Frank, "Making of *The Tunnel*;" Frank, *Out of Thin Air.*
28. John F. Kennedy, Speech—"Cuban Missile Crisis Address to the Nation," October 22, 1962, *American Rhetoric:* Top 100 Speeches, http://www.americanrhetoric.com/speeches/jfkcubanmissilecrisis.html (accessed March 7, 2019); Richard F. Shepard, "N.B.C. Postpones Tunnel Telecast," *New York Times,* October 24, 1962, 62; "Clear and Present Danger," advertisement, *New York Times,* October 31, 1962, 55; Cecil Smith, "'Tunnel' Runs into Blind Wall," *Los Angeles Times,* October 31, 1962, C9.
29. Kintner to Rusk, letter, November 20, 1962, 1.
30. Kintner to Rusk, memorandum, November 20, 1962, 4.
31. Kintner to Rusk, memorandum, November 20, 1962, 5; Kintner to Rusk, letter, November 20, 1962, 4.
32. Kintner to Rusk, letter, November 20, 1962, 4; Robert Manning to The Secretary, "NBC Letter concerning the Berlin Tunnel," November 24, 1962, Tunnel, Box 13107536 (RF-T).
33. Dean Rusk to Robert Kintner, letter, November 28, 1962, Tunnel, Box 13107536 (RF-T); "Special NBC News Documentary on Building of Escape Route . . . ," NBC Press Release, December 3, 1962, Tunnel, Box 13107536 (RF-T).
34. Kintner to Rusk, letter, November 20, 1962, 4.
35. Robert J. Lamphere, *The FBI-KGB War: A Special Agent's Story* (New York: Random House, 1986); "The Man from Moscow," *Time,* February 17, 1947; Ira Henry Freeman, "A Communist's Career: The 'Story of Eisler,'" *New York Times,* May 22, 1949, E4; George Wheeler, "Freiheit für John und Sylvia Powell!," *Berliner Zeitung,* November 15, 1956, 6; Albert E. Kahn, "Die gelbe Presse," *Berliner Zeitung,* October 27, 1961, 7; "Die Gestapo des Pentagon," *Neues Deutschland,* July 17, 1955, 5.

36. Colin Good, *Zeitungssprache im geteilten Deutschland* (Munich: R. Oldenbourg, 1989). It should be noted that the first two titles remain in existence, albeit with new post-GDR orientations.
37. Peter Hoff and Wolfgang Mühl-Benninghaus, "Depictions of America in GDR Television Films and Plays, 1955–1965," *Historical Journal of Film, Radio and Television* 24, no. 3 (2004): 403; "Eine Westzeitschrift im Dienste des USA-Geheimdienstes," *Neues Deutschland*, December 7, 1949, 4.
38. "East Berlin Interview," *Broadcasting*, December 7, 1959, 92; "Gipfeltreffen müßte Friedensvertrag vorbereiten," *Berliner Zeitung*, November 25, 1959, 1, 3; Schorr, *Staying Tuned*.
39. Gerhard Kegel, "Was will eigentlich das USA-Außenamt?" *Neues Deutschland*, September 23, 1959, 2.
40. "Verhör im Feuilleton," *Der Spiegel*, July 4, 1962, 22–23. For this analysis, fully digitized versions of original GDR newspapers were accessed from the archives of the State Library of Berlin (*Staatsbibliothek zu Berlin/Preußischer Kulturbesitz*; http://zefys.staatsbibliothek-berlin.de/ddr-presse/?no_cache=1 (accessed March 7, 2019).
41. Heinz Stern, "Fünf Jahre danach," *Neues Deutschland*, August 11, 1966, 4.
42. "Mord—von langer Hand vorbereitet," *Neues Deutschland*, June 20, 1962, 2.
43. "'Stern' finanzierte die Mörder," *Neues Deutschland*, October 7, 1964, 9; "Tunnelflucht: Schüsse im Schacht," *Der Spiegel*, October 14, 1964, 37–39.
44. "Die Ultras planten Tote ein," *Neues Deutschland*, August 22, 1962, 2.
45. "Tote waren eingeplant," *Berliner Zeitung*, August 22, 1962, 1.
46. "Strafanträge gegen Spione," *Berliner Zeitung*, September 1, 1962, 2.
47. "Wachsende Erkenntnis," *Neue Zeit*, October 13, 1962, 2; "2500 Dollar pro Agent," *Neues Deutschland*, October 14, 1962, 8.
48. "Belemmerte Wühlmäuse," *Neues Deutschland*, October 18, 1962, 8.
49. "Tunnel 28—Film," *Der Spiegel*, October 31, 1962, 116; "Der Film, Tunnel," *Frankfurter Allgemeine Zeitung*, October 20, 1962, 4.
50. "USA-Monopolkreise organisierten Grenzdurchbruch," *Neues Deutschland*, October 20, 1962, 6.
51. "USA-Monopolkreise."
52. GDR to US government, "Unofficial Translation" of protest note, October 19, 1962, Tunnel, Box 13107536 (RF-T).
53. "Protest gegen Grenzanschlag der NBC; Note der DDR an die USA—Bestrafung der Schuldigen gefordert," *Neue Zeit*, October 21, 1962, 2.
54. "DDR stellt USA-Verantwortung fest," *Neues Deutschland*, October 21, 1962, 2.
55. "Film über Agentenstollen abgesetzt," *Neues Deutschland*, October 25, 1962, 6.
56. "The Reaction of West Berlin Authorities," *Pravda*, February 2, 1962, 4; "The Front-Line City Has No Future," *Pravda*, March 16, 1962, 5.
57. S. Lurie, "Provocation Manufacturers," *Pravda*, October 17, 1962, 6. The Hearst quote is one of American journalism's most enduring myths, but most likely it never happened. W. Joseph Campbell, *Getting It Wrong: Ten of the Greatest Misreported Stories in American Journalism* (Berkeley: University of California Press, 2010).

58. Kennedy, "The President and the Press."
59. Kintner to Rusk, letter, November 20, 1962, 4.
60. Morris to Secretary of State, memo, August 10, 1962, Eyes Only Telegrams 1963 + S/S—L.D., box 36 (FSP-DS).
61. John Kenneth White, "Seeing Red: The Cold War and American Public Opinion," *The Power of Free Inquiry and Cold War International History* conference, September 25–26, 1998, National Archives at College Park, MD, http://www.archives.gov/research/foreign-policy/cold-war/conference/white.html (accessed March 7, 2019).
62. "U.S. Criticizes N.B.C. on Film in Berlin," 2.
63. Schorr, *Staying Tuned*, 66.
64. "Unter dem Tage," *Der Spiegel*, June 19, 1963, 75.
65. Lawrence Freedman, *Kennedy's Wars: Berlin, Cuba, Laos, and Vietnam* (New York: Oxford University Press, 2000), 269.
66. "USIA Digs NBC's 'Tunnel;' Global Spread Likely," *Variety*, January 23, 1963, 1, 52; Frank, *Out of Thin Air*.

EPILOGUE

1. "Awards Search," *Television Academy* website, https://www.emmys.com (accessed March 7, 2019); Bill Leonard, *In the Storm of the Eye: A Lifetime at CBS* (New York: G. P. Putnam's Sons, 1987).
2. Reuven Frank, *Out of Thin Air: The Brief Wonderful Life of Network News* (New York: Simon and Schuster, 1991).
3. Paul Gardner, "Taking a 'Frank' Step Forward," *New York Times*, September 5, 1965, X11.
4. Spiro Agnew, "Television News Coverage" speech, November 13, 1969, http://www.americanrhetoric.com/speeches/spiroagnewtvnewscoverage.htm (accessed March 7, 2019).
5. Daniel C. Hallin, "The Passing of the 'High Modernism' of American Journalism," *Journal of Communication* 42, no. 3 (Summer 1992): 14–25; Herbert J. Gans, *Deciding What's News: A Study of CBS Evening News, NBC Nightly News, Newsweek & Time* (New York: Pantheon Books, 1979); Edward Jay Epstein, *News from Nowhere: Television and the News* (New York: Random House, 1973); Gaye Tuchman, *Making News: A Study in the Construction of Reality* (New York: Free Press, 1978).
6. Frank, *Out of Thin Air*, 253.
7. Michael J. Socolow, "Anchors Away: Huntley, Brinkley, and Cronkite and the 1967 AFTRA Strike," *Journalism History* 29, no. 2 (Summer 2003): 50–58; Frank, *Out of Thin Air*.
8. Don Hewitt, *Tell Me a Story: Fifty Years and 60 Minutes in Television* (New York: Public Affairs, 2001); Leonard, *In the Storm of the Eye*; Mike Wallace and Gary Paul Gates, *Close Encounters: Mike Wallace's Own Story* (New York: Berkley Books, 1984); Frank, *Out of Thin Air*.
9. Frank, *Out of Thin Air*, 314, 310.

10. "Weekend," 1975, *Peabody Awards* website, http://www.peabodyawards.com/award-profile/weekend (accessed March 7, 2019).
11. Charles Montgomery Hammond Jr., *The Image Decade: Television Documentary: 1965–1975* (New York: Hastings House, 1981); Frank, *Out of Thin Air*.
12. "A History of TV News Via a Man Who Invented It," *Variety*, June 4, 1986, 89, 105; Jeff Fager, *Fifty Years of 60 Minutes: The Inside Story of Television's Most Influential News Broadcast* (New York: Simon and Schuster, 2017).
13. Marvin Kitman, "Reuven Frank," *Washington Journalism Review*, July/August 1982, 41, Magazine Press Excess, '82–85, Box 13107538 (RFT); Reuven Frank to Larry Hatteberg, letter, April 21, 1981.
14. Linda Ellerbee, *"And So It Goes": Adventures in Television* (New York: G. P. Putnam's Sons, 1986).
15. Kevin Goldman, "NBC's Frank Backs His Troops, 'Camera' in Gotham Press Gabber," *Variety*, October 19, 1983, 40; Frank, *Out of Thin Air*.
16. Don Hewitt, interview with author (DH-OH2).
17. Reuven Frank, interview by author (RF-OH2).
18. Frank, *Out of Thin Air*, 310.
19. Bob Dotson, *". . . In Pursuit of the American Dream* (New York: Antheneum, 1985); Bob Dotson, *American Story: A Lifetime Search for Ordinary People Doing Extraordinary Things* (New York: Viking Press, 2013).
20. Bob Dotson, interview with author (BD-OH).
21. Robert MacNeil in *"The Huntley-Brinkley Report" and Remembering Reuven Frank*, DVD, directed by NBC News (New York: NBC, 2006).
22. John Hartley, *Uses of Television* (London: Routledge, 1999); Mike Conway, "The Ghost of Television News in Media History Scholarship," *American Journalism* 34, no. 2 (2017): 229–39.
23. Lisa Gitelman, *Always Already News: Media, History and the Data of Culture* (Cambridge, MA: MIT Press, 2006), 6.
24. Jacques Steinberg, "Reuven Frank, Producer Who Pioneered TV News Coverage at NBC, Is Dead at 85," *New York Times*, February 7, 2006, A18.
25. Tom Brokaw, in *"The Huntley-Brinkley Report,"* DVD.

Index

60 Minutes, 130, 155, 225–26, 229–30

Adatto, Kiku, 103–5
Agee, James, 132
Agnew, Spiro, 224
Albertz, Heinrich, 36
Alexandra Palace, 51
Allen, Spencer, 181
Alley, Paul, 56–57, 87
Amarillo (TX) News and Globe, 163
American Broadcasting Company (ABC), 61, 74–75
American Foreign Correspondents Association, 168
American Journalist surveys, 172
American Newspaper Publishers Association (ANPA), 163, 166, 197
Anderton, Piers, 13, 22, 30, 109–10, 112, 195, 202
Anhalt, Edward, 135
Army-McCarthy hearings, 61–64
Aronson, James, 64–65
Associated Press (AP), 164, 168
auteur theory, 154

Background (TV public affairs program), 68
Bannerman, R. LeRoy, 128
Barnhurst, Kevin, 130
Barnouw, Erik, 118–19

Battleship Potemkin (film), 125–26
Baughman, James, 182
Bay of Pigs invasion, 18, 197
Bazin, André, 138
Before and After Stalin (TV broadcast), 67
Bendick, Robert, 135, 138
Berlin: East Berlin images in *The Tunnel*, 110–11; East to West emigration, 12; East to West escapes, 24; postwar sectors, 14; World War II, 14
Berlin airlift, 15
Berlin Wall: building wall, 24; closing border, 13, 18–20; comes down, 229; deaths, 28–29; tank confrontation, 22–24; television coverage, 19–21
Berlin Wall tunnel popularity, 24–25
Berlin-Window on Fear (TV broadcast), 67
Bernauer Strasse, 19–20, 110–11
Bernstein, Lester, 208
Big Ear, The (TV documentary), 223
Billboard, The (trade publication), 187–88
Bleckman, Izzy, 116
Bliss, Edward, 129
Blue Book (FCC report), 76–77, 139–40
Bluem, A. William, 115, 134, 155
Bodroghkozy, Aniko, 74
boundary work, 6–8, 120–21, 127, 157–58, 166–67, 169–70, 174–75, 178–79, 190–93, 195–96

Bourke-White, Margaret, 130, 132
Brandt, Willy, 21, 29, 35
Bretz, Rudy, 88, 135–36
Brinkley, David, 144; in Berlin, 12–13, 69–72; as celebrity, 184–85; after Huntley, 225
British Broadcasting Company (BBC), 51, 163
Broadcasting (trade magazine), 181, 192
Brokaw, Tom, 234

Calmer, Ned, 188
Camel News Caravan, 57, 70, 91
Camel Newsreel Theatre, 56
Capra, Frank, 137–38
Caro, Robert, 39
Carter, Boake, 168
Castro, Fidel, 38
Cater, Douglass, 59
Cawston, Richard, 77
CBS Reports, 73–74, 145, 154
CBS Views the Press, 188–89
Chalmers, Thomas, 133
Chancellor, John, 72–73, 225
Checkpoint Charlie, 23–24, 31
Chomsky, Noam, 65
cinéma vérité, 146–49, 151–53
City, The (film), 135, 151
Clark, Blair, 202, 205
Clay, Lucius, 15, 21–24
Clear and Present Danger, A (NBC documentary), 39
Cohn, Roy, 61
Coit, Henry, 44
Cold War: beginning, 15–16; culture, 46–47; journalism and, 184, 197–200, 212, 218–22; media blacklist, 140
Collison, Robert, 152–53
Columbia Broadcasting System (CBS): critical of NBC project, 37; ratings dominance, 40
Columbia News Service, 165, 173
Columbia University Graduate School of Journalism, 44, 48, 64, 159, 173
Columbia Workshop (radio program), 128
Corwin, Norman, 128, 140–41
Crisis: Behind a Presidential Commitment (TV documentary), 152
critical juncture, 2–7, 42–43, 96, 119, 158, 190, 196–98, 211, 232–33
Cronkite, Walter: 1952 political convention anchor, 68; 1964 conventions, 223; *CBS Evening News*, 79–80; Korean War, 57; learning journalism, 174, 181; magazine coverage, 184–86; takes rating lead, 224; *You Are There*, 144
Crosby, John, 62, 176, 189–90
Crowther, Bosley, 139
Cuban Missile Crisis, 37–39, 209
Curtin, Michael, 154

Daily Mirror (tabloid), 129
Dallas (TX) News and Journal, 164
Daly, John Charles, 67, 147
Dealey, George, 164
Dehmel, Peter and Klaus, 13, 22, 28, 109, 195, 204
Denny, Charles, 50
de Rochemont, Louis, 133
Detroit News, 163
Dickson, William Kennedy-Laurie, 121–23
Dobyns, Lloyd, 227–28
documentary film: deception, 122–23; differing definitions of, 151–53; early television collaboration, 134–37; history of, 124–27, 136; Hollywood, 126; journalist vs. filmmaker, 118–19; postwar, 139; re-creations, 148–52; on television, 147–48; Workers Film and Photo League, 132; World War II films, 137–39
Doherty, Thomas, 65–66
Dotson, Bob, 116, 230–31
Douglas Edwards with the News (CBS newscast), 66–67, 74, 91
Dreiser, Theodore, 171–72
Drew, Robert, 146–47, 151–54
Drifters (film), 126
DuMont network, 61, 66, 74

Edgerton, Gary, 61
Edison, Thomas, 121–22
Editor & Publisher (trade publication), 162–63, 169, 178
Edwards, Douglas, 56, 66, 68–70, 79, 169
Ehrlich, Matthew, 140
Eighth Art, The (edited book), 175–76
Eisenhower, Dwight, 16, 17, 180
Eisenstadt, Alfred, 130
Eisenstein, Sergei, 125–26
Eisler, Gerhart, 211–12

INDEX

Elements of Journalism, The (Kovach and Rosenstiel), 171
Ellerbee, Linda, 99, 227–28
Emmy Awards, 41, 195–96, 223
Epstein, Edward Jay, 115, 145
Escape from East Berlin (film). *See* "Tunnel 28" movie
Evans, S. Howard, 166
Evans, Walker, 131–32

Fairbanks, Jerry, 142
Farm Security Administration (FSA), 131
Fechter, Peter, 31
Federal Communications Commission (FCC): commercial television, 52; Fairness Doctrine, 147; news and public affairs requirements, 55, 76–77, 139–40, 167; television license freeze, 74
Fielding, Raymond, 123
First Motion Picture Unit (FMPU), 138
First Tuesday (TV magazine), 225–26
Flaherty, Robert, 125, 137, 139
Frank, Reuven: Berlin and, 12, 32–34; career after *The Tunnel*, 223–53; *cinéma vérité* and, 147–48; defending *The Tunnel*, 39, 191–92, 207; documentary symposium speech, 118–19; early TV impressions, 48–49; early years, 47–48; interviews (soundbites), 103–5, 114–15; journalism and, 156; journalism exclusion, 169–70; Korean War coverage, 57–58; longer-form productions, 67–68; NBC News president, 224–25, 228; *Newark Evening News*, 44; news ratings success in 1960s, 80; pairing Huntley and Brinkley, 69–72; starting at NBC, 54–55; storytelling, 229–30; thirty-minute newscast, 105–7; "transmission of experience" memo, 81–84, 95, 97–107; tunnel payment, 26–28; visual maturation, 92–93; watching tunnel film, 11–12; writing and editing *The Tunnel*, 34–35
Franklin Dinners, 159
Friendly, Fred, 60, 130, 141–45, 149, 154, 174, 185, 225
Frontier Films, 132

Gans, Herbert, 64, 234
Germany, East, 17; Cold War journalism, 211–14; criticizes tunnel project, 36, 207; *The Tunnel* stories, 215–18
Germany, West, 17; Berlin Wall and, 21; government protest of *The Tunnel*, 207
Gibbons, Floyd, 168
Gieryn, Thomas, 7, 170
Girrmann Group, 24
Gitelman, Lisa, 10, 257
Gitlin, Irving, 144
Goring, Peter, 28
Gould, Jack, 37, 60, 157, 189–95
Green, Gerald, 48
Grierson, John, 126, 136–37, 154

Hagerty, James, 36, 79, 180
Halberstam, David, 59–60
Hallin, Daniel, 103–5, 147
Harper's Weekly (magazine), 129
Harris, Ed, 163–64
Hartman, Steve, 116
Harvest of Shame (TV documentary), 152
Hatteberg, Larry, 227
Hazam, Lou, 151–53
Hear It Now, 141–42
Hearst, William Randolph, 165, 171, 217
Heath, Harry, 88–90
Heller, Robert, 140–41
Henry, Bill, 69
Herman, Ed, 65
Herschel, Hasso, 30
Hewitt, Don, 130, 155, 169–70, 225–26, 229–30
Hildebrandt, Rainer, 201
Hollenbeck, Don, 188–89
Honecker, Erich, 19
hot news, 164
Howe, Gene, 163
How the Other Half Lives (Riis), 131
Huhn, Reinhold, 28–29, 213
Huntley, Chet, 13, 68–73; as celebrity, 184–85
Huntley-Brinkley Report, 13; end of, 225; fiftieth anniversary, 234; magazine coverage, 184–85; major awards, 78–79; show business criticism, 79, 96–97, 186–87; start of, 69–72; success of, 196, 223; Texaco sponsorship, 74
Hurwitz, Leo, 132–33, 135

International News Service, 168

266 INDEX

Jackaway, Gwenyth, 166–67
Jacobs, Lewis, 125
Johnson, Lyndon, 21
Joint Operating Agreements (JOA), 182
Jones, John Paul, 173
journalism: competition, 197–200, 204–10, 218–22; definition of, 170–72; excluding radio and television, 168–70; government cooperation, 197–200, 218–22; "high modernism" and, 147, 224; McCarthy and, 59–64; newsroom learning, 172–73; professionalism and, 159; television and, 176–81; who is a journalist, 174–75
Journalism & Mass Communication Quarterly (journal), 231

Kaltenborn, H. V., 168
Kefauver, Estes, 61–62
Kennedy, John F.: 1960 election, 18, 78–79; Berlin Wall and, 20–21, 221; Cold War journalism, 197–98; Cuban Missile Crisis and, 37–39, 209; Vienna summit, 18
Kennedy, Robert, 23–24, 38
Khrushchev, Nikita, 16, 213; Berlin and, 14, 17; Cuban Missile Crisis, 37–39, 209; Vienna summit, 18
kinescope, 50
King, Martin Luther, Jr., 72–73
kino pravda, 125, 137
Kintner, Robert, 74–75, 208–11, 224
Korean War, 57–58, 141
Kovach, Bill, 171
Kuralt, Charles, 116

Lange, Dorothea, 131–32
Leslie's Illustrated Weekly (magazine), 129
Let Us Now Praise Famous Men (Agee), 132
Life (magazine), 130, 179, 193
Lightner, Allan, 20, 22–24
literary thesis, 176
Lorentz, Pare, 132–33, 151, 154
Lowe, David, 73, 152–53
Luce, Henry, 130
Lumière, Auguste and Louis, 121–22

MacDonald, J. Fred, 65
MacNeil, Robert, 231
Mannes, Marya, 176
Manning, Robert J., 204–7

Man with a Movie Camera (film), 125–26
March of Time, 140, 152; film version, 133–34; radio version, 127–28
Markel, Lester, 183–84
Maysles, Albert and David, 146
McAndrew, William, 27, 67, 70, 95, 204, 206, 223–24
McCarthy, Joseph, 59–64, 143, 188
McGee, Frank, 72
Mickelson, Sig, 180–81
Milwaukee Journal, 163
Miner, Worthington "Tony," 135–36
Minow, Newton, 77
missile gap, 17
Montagu, Ashley, 175
Murrow, Edward R., 136, 149, 167, 173–74; excluded from journalism club, 168; *Hear It Now*, 140–42; leaves CBS, 145; *See It Now*, 60–63, 142–44, 188; on television, 177–79, 185–86

Nanook of the North (film), 125
National Academy of Television Arts and Sciences (NATAS), 151, 169. *See also* Emmy Awards
National Association of Broadcasters (NAB), 77, 140, 168
National Broadcasting Company (NBC), 161
National Geographic, 129
National Press Photographers Association (NPPA), 179, 227, 231; TV video workshop, 116, 230
NBC News Overnight (TV newscast), 228
NBC television news, 54; *Camel News Caravan*, 57; *Huntley-Brinkley Report*, 69–74; more resources, 75; newsreel influence, 84–88; ratings dominance 79–80
Nerone, John, 130
Newark Evening News, 44
new journalism (literary journalism), 81, 94
News of the Day (Hearst newsreel), 143
Newspaper Preservation Act of 1970, 182
newspapers: economics and, 159–61; media critics, 187–90; postwar economics, 181–83; response to radio, 161–67
newsreels: television and, 89; theater, 84–88, 124, 177
Newsweek (magazine), 79, 184–85
New York Daily News, 130

New Yorker (magazine), 185
New York Herald Tribune, 62, 94, 176, 189–90
New York Illustrated Daily News, 129
New York Sun, 126
New York Times, 35, 37, 171, 178, 183–84, 189–92
Nixon, Richard, 17, 78, 224

objectivity, 161; McCarthy and, 59
O'Brian, Jack, 189
Ochs, Adolph, 171
Omnibus (TV program), 146
One World Flight (radio program), 140
Outlook (NBC public affairs program), 68–69

Paley, William, 74
Parks, Rosa, 72
Pathé's Weekly, 124
Peabody Awards, 79, 159, 168
Pennebaker, D. A., 146
photography, 129–32, 178–79
Plow That Broke the Plains, The (documentary film), 132–33, 135, 154
Point of Order! (documentary film), 63
Polikoff, Gerald, 32–34, 110
political conventions: 1948, 49, 68; 1952, 68–69; 1956, 68–69
Pravda (Soviet newspaper), 217–18
Press-Radio Bureau, 165
press-radio war, 165–67
Primary (TV documentary), 146, 152
Project 20 (TV series), 144
public interest, convenience, and necessity, 167
Pulitzer, Joseph, 159, 171, 173
Pulitzer Prize, 159, 168

Quick and the Dead, The (radio program), 140, 149
Quill (trade publication), 181, 183
quiz show scandal, 75–76

radio, 127–29; news economics, 167–68; newspaper competition, 161–67; postwar radio documentaries, 139–42
Radio Act of 1927, 161, 163
Raphael, Chad, 155, 183

Resettlement Administration (RA), 131–32
Richmond (IN) Palladium, 163–64
Riefenstahl, Leni, 137–38
Riis, Jacob, 131
River, The (film), 133, 151
Road to Spandau (TV program), 67
Rosenstiel, Tom, 171
Rosten, Leo, 176
Rotha, Paul, 126, 139
Rusk, Dean, 20, 29, 155, 202–11

Safranski, Eddie, 35, 110
Salant, Richard, 36, 186, 206, 217
Salomon, Pete, 144
Sanger, Eliot, 178
Schechter, Abe, 165
Schine, G. David, 61
Schmidt, Peter, 109, 111, 150
Schorr, Daniel, 22; CBS tunnel, 30, 200–203, 220–21
Schroedter, Wolf, 26–28, 109, 200
Secondari, John, 151–53
See It Now (CBS program), 60–63, 76, 142–44, 146, 149, 154, 174
Seldes, Gilbert, 133–37, 175, 188
Sesta, Domenico, 26–28, 109, 111, 200
Sigma Delta Chi, 159
Siodmak, Robert, 26, 41, 200
Smith, Howard K., 73
Snyder, Tom, 227
Society of Professional Journalists (SPJ), formerly Sigma Delta Chi, 67, 159
Soviet Union (USSR): Berlin and, 14–15; Berlin airlift, 15; Berlin Wall tank confrontation, 22–24; Cuban Missile Crisis, 37–39; prewar television plans, 52; reporting on *The Tunnel*, 217–18
Spina, Luigi, 26–28, 109, 200
Springer, Axel, 213
Sputnik, 16
State Department, US, 36–37, 192, 202–8
Steiner, Ralph, 132–33, 151
Stindt, Gary, 13, 22, 67
St. Louis Globe Democrat, 171–72
Studio One (TV program), 135
Strand, Paul, 132–33, 135
Sulzberger, Arthur Hays, 178
Swayze, John Cameron, 56–57, 66, 68–70

Taishoff, Sol, 181
Taylor, Davidson, 50
Tegel Airfield, Berlin, 15
television, 44; 1947 World Series, 45; 1948 political conventions, 49; 1950s expansion, 55–56; 1960 US influence, 77–78; early documentary film influence, 134–37; negative views of, 175–76; pre-World War II, 49–52
television news: 1950s newscasts, 55–56, 66–67; 1960 election and debates, 78–79; authority and responsibility, 99–101; CBS 1940s innovation, 53; civil rights coverage, 72–74; Cold War, 58–66; documentary film definitions, 151–53; economics, 88–91; expansion of documentaries, 144–53; journalism exclusion, 169–70; lack of scholarship, 231–32; as show business, 177–78, 186–87; staff background, 91–92; thirty-minute expansion, 93–95, 105–7
Television Quarterly (journal), 42, 155, 169
Tews, Walter, 28
Thomas, Lowell, 52, 165, 168
Thomson, Virgil, 133
Three Men from Suribachi (TV program), 142
Time (magazine), 35, 128, 183, 191
"transmission of experience" memo, 81–84, 95, 97–107; on *cinéma vérité*, 147–48; enduring legacy, 115–18; promoting television news, 169–70
Triumph of the Will (film), 137–38
tunnel, CBS involvement, 30, 200–203, 210, 214–15
Tunnel, The (NBC documentary): boundary work and, 190–93; broadcast, 40; Cold War, 108–16; criticism, 35–37, 190–93; as a documentary film, 153–56; escape, 32–34; escape scenes, 113; finding tunnel, 25–26; Kintner negotiations, 209–11; NBC defense of, 205–9; payment, 27; postponing program, 39; recreations and staged scene, 148–50, 154; reviews and awards, 41, 193–95; secrecy, 200; "transmission of experience" and, 107–16

The Tunnel, escape project: change in plan, 31; diggers protest payments, 36, 207; escape, 32–34; East German and Soviet coverage, 215–18; origins, 26–28
"Tunnel 28" (*Escape from East Berlin*) movie, 26, 41, 200
Twentieth Century (TV series), 144, 152

Ulbricht, Walter, 17, 22, 212–13; closing Berlin border, 18–19
United Press, 165, 168, 173
University of Georgia, 168
USA Today, 181

Van Dyke, Willard, 132–33, 135–36, 151–54
Ventura (CA) Free Press, 166
Vertov, Dziga, 125–26, 137, 154
Victory at Sea (TV program), 144

W2XAB (CBS experimental TV station), 51
W2XBS (NBC experimental TV station), 48
War of the Worlds (radio broadcast), 128
Wasserman, Albert, 152–53
WCBW-TV (New York), 52, 136
Weaver, Sylvester "Pat," 69, 74
Weekend, 226–27, 230
Welch, Joseph, 62
Welles, Orson, 128
Weyrauch, Eberhard, 36, 215
White, Clarence, 131, 135
White, Lincoln, 36–37, 206–8
White, Paul, 173
White Paper (TV series), 144
Whiteside, Thomas, 185
Why We Fight (film series), 137–38
Wiseman, Frederick, 146
WLW (Cincinnati), 128
WMAR-TV (Baltimore), 142
WNBT-TV, 52
Wolfe, Tom, 81, 94
Workers Film and Photo League, 132
World's Fair, 1939 New York, 48, 52

Yanki No! (TV film), 147
You Are There (TV series), 144

www.ingramcontent.com/pod-product-compliance
Lightning Source LLC
Chambersburg PA
CBHW030528230426
43665CB00010B/806